ON ME ||
ON MUSIC

ON ME II
ON MUSIC

James A. Landry

On Me || On Music

This book is written to provide information and motivation to readers. Its purpose is not to render any type of psychological, legal, or professional advice of any kind. The content is the sole opinion and expression of the author, and not necessarily that of the publisher.

Copyright © 2020 by James A. Landry.

All rights reserved. No part of this book may be reproduced, transmitted, or distributed in any form by any means, including, but not limited to, recording, photocopying, or taking screenshots of parts of the book, without prior written permission from the author or the publisher. Brief quotations for noncommercial purposes, such as book reviews, permitted by Fair Use of the U.S. Copyright Law, are allowed without written permissions, as long as such quotations do not cause damage to the book's commercial value. For permissions, write to the publisher, whose address is stated below.

Printed in the United States of America.

ISBN 978-1-951913-66-3   (Paperback)
ISBN 978-1-951913-67-0   (Digital)

Lettra Press books may be ordered through booksellers or by contacting:

Lettra Press LLC
30 N Gould St. Suite 4753
Sheridan, WY 82801, USA
1 303-586-1431 | info@lettrapress.com
www.lettrapress.com

Dedicated with Love to

My Parents

And also, to

My Good friend

And

Bass guitar player extraordinaire

Mr. John Bartlett

PREFACE

Music comes in many forms. Whether it is Rock, pop, instrumental, indie, country, jazz, or another genre, everyone has a favorite. Music can be used to express oneself and bring enjoyment to life. Music can be live or recorded. Live and recorded music have many differences and similarities that can be noticed and loved depending on the listener. Live music can be expensive, but the experience is full of entertainment and emotion. Recorded music can be cheap, but vocals and sounds are edited in a studio. Despite these and many more differences, both types of music have similarities. Recorded and live music both bring enjoyment to listeners, connections among similar tastes, and can be found at parties, sporting events, and special occasions. Recorded and live music are unique in their own ways, but also similar in the way that they make a person feel.

One difference between live and recorded music has to do with the ease of enjoying the music. Time is a major factor that influences day to day life. Most individuals hear their favorite musicians for the first time through recordings. With the ease of technology and development, individuals can get ahold of music in seconds. This can be by traveling and buying CDs and records, or by an online music store or radio. Online music stores and free online radios allow individuals to search their favorite bands and musicians and to play them instantly at any time. Live music is quite different. Once an individual becomes familiar with a musician, the individual will usually try to find out the musician's tour schedule. An individual may have to wait days, months, or even years to hear their favorite musician perform live. In most cases, it is worth the wait.

-Plato

Music is a moral law. It gives soul to the universe, wings to the mind, flight to the imagination, charm to sadness, gaiety and life to everything. It is the essence to all that is good and just and beautiful.

PART ONE
THEORY, RUDIMENTS & HISTORY

First Set

Wooden Spoons, Corrugated Boxes

Pots and Pans

Rhythm and Beat

Delivery and Timing

CHAPTER 1

We sing the praises of the noteworthy performance, adhering to the original arrangement or popularized interpretation. Through a progression from tolerance, to acceptance, to exploitation, much like the trip Blues and Jazz made during previous decades, we have embraced improvisation to the point of Jam Band Marketability.

Regardless of direction, earning praise ultimately involves measuring audience sophistication and expectation. Recording lends itself to either approach, because those elusive pseudo-productive masterpieces at times happen with no premeditation. The magic written must still transfer from raw files to machine, and during that intervention, without warning, Semper Paratus mates, and the capture is paramount.

There are thousands of all-time great moments in Rock music. There are published lists, anthologies and almanacs that describe everything from a big bang birth in Memphis, to undeniably defining moments throughout time; events, life stories and mortality. Generations of celebration, atonement and narrative have been mightily served and magnetically preserved by artists lucky enough to capture their own.

Recording momentary details and the truth by the music using any mechanism, be it shutter, tape, or pencil in hand is key. To step through the door, one must turn-on or be turned on, because the machine rolling keeps the momentary experience from slipping away. Musical flashes run just like the nighttime ideas you neglect to jot down.

The argument is that pretentiousness as such compromises the academic aspect of the art and overcomplicates creation. The answer, flawlessly ringing as true as a perfect algorithm, is to try to habitually record everything played. Stated simply, if you record it, you've got it. No question, or it could be gone forever.

Rock was once virgin, as was technology. The magic released between 1964 and 1974 offered commercial crossover; groundbreaking successes, earthy and pure. Today, there is Hip Hop. Yesterday, there was Hip Pop. Note-for-note and lyric-for-lyric, in a never-ending daisy chain of influence, the nervous eaters and the eaten, share at any given time, both the top and bottom of the proverbial food chain.

Elvis eating Blues -- The Beatles eating Elvis -- Everyone eating The Beatles: All who rise to the surface prove innovation hasn't died, even though innovation remains as difficult an achievement today as it ever was. The industry is smothered in consumerism like never, operationally guided by whims of the finicky public, typically dollar volatile. Let us thank Kurt Cobain and Nirvana, Pearl Jam, Soundgarden, Alice in Chains, Stone Temple Pilots and all their followers, for at least trying to save us; Grunge...Alternative and that is good company.

Categorical subtitles assigned Rock music are meant to convey style. Once history, however, style degenerates in the name of progress. Modifiers and descriptors turn to time and place holders, and age renames the subgenre with a decade encompassing numeric label, representing simply the space in time; the sixties, the seventies, the eighties, the nineties, and beyond. The low-end decade we're just graduating from is going to be tough to name. We were in the zeros, man.

As each decade of Rock reflects the maturation by generation and internationality, they also note periods of regression and defeat. How did The Black Crows ever defeat the Southern Rock moniker syndrome? A strong continuum in Rock music is as much the celebration today as it ever was. But then again, some A/R representative hears a "Hit." There must be at least one hit on an album. And what the hit is, is chosen by the executives. Sometimes the choice matches the artist's, but not always.

Its rudimental development in the sixties and seventies offered a wealth of recorded goodness, stretching and pioneering. Today, astonishingly enough, we hear more of the same. Rock continues to soothe, heal and excite the young, and to just may defy, exploit, and shock the old, as well. It still moves, it still Rocks, and its Market remains open. The feedback factor is the secret. The Rock audience is as diverse and independent as the talent. And a lot of times, success blooms when they completely connect.

I love Rock music. Yes, Rock music eats other music, but it also coexists with, and compliments it all perfectly. It always has. Channels have expanded to a point where Rock has commercially proliferated into every media. True to core, with each transfer, tribute and sample, and even advertisements. Rock continues to pick fights with the tunnel-visional via lyric unorthodox, and foreign sound commercialized.

The Rock vibe is as strong and diverse as ever. No Hope – No Fear has adapted positively, and Pop has gotten downright nasty while remaining some lace and fluff, too. Rock can fuel a house party, and it can spawn or support internationally powerful socio-political activism. The genre is eventual, yet timeless, manifested by growth and limitlessness.

The reason is the inherent characteristic to remain open to redefinition, reuse and repetitive interpretation. Musicians have a better time adjusting the rules fitting better the time, than do Congress over our outdated Constitution.

Captured in a moment, up or down, in the raw, in bloom, even to imaged perfection, illustrated that records breaking rules are priceless.

CHAPTER 2

My father had shelves over shelves of music: Gospel and Blues; 78's & 33's; Early Blues and Jazz; Swing; Big Band, and some Contemporary and Progressive. Those were the first records I would hear, and they grabbed my complete attention in a short time. I had to then explore Rock music—"Rock & Roll," which was just coming on at the time. Blues, Country and Rock & Roll gets a start, or at least a nudge forward.

I remember some of the first commercial records I studied as a child, such as "Seven Little Girls Sitting in the Back Seat (Keep

Your Eyes on the Road and Your Hands on the Wheel)" that drove me further to Rock & Roll, along with these obscure hits: Queen of the Hop--Bobby Darin; C.C. Rider--Chuck Willis; Searching--The Coasters; Don't Make Me Over--Dionne Warwick; Do You Wanna Shuck--Bobby Freeman; Sh-Boom--The Chords; Let's Go–Routers; Fa-Fa-Fa-Fa-Fa (Sad Song)--Otis Redding; Mercy--Don Covay; Party Doll--Buddy Knox; Walk Right Back--Sonny Curtis & The Everly Brothers; Shimmy, Shimmy, Ko-Ko-Bop--Little Anthony & the Imperials; Shake, Rattle & Roll--Big Joe Turner and Mary Lou--Ronnie Hawkins. They shuttled along harder with the rhythm, straight ahead backbeat and dynamics.

Then, Rock took another leap that got me out of my seat. Johnny Get Angry--Joanie Sommers; Mr. Lee--The Bobbettes; Last Night--The Mar-Keys; Just One Look--Doris Troy; Easier Said Than Done--The Essex and Kansas

City ('59)-Wilbert Harrison. And, of course Elvis, Carl, Roy Orbison, Ray and Buddy Holly.

Rock music at that time finally settled itself in a pattern born of the blues from over a hundred years ago. It was the straight ahead back-beat, in 2/4 or 4/4 time, eight or twelve bar, 1-4-5 blues progressions. Electric guitars came up closer to the front in the mix. It invited lyrics or a lyrical dark hole that called out to listeners everywhere. It could be sad as a lost, broken heart, or as happy as a kid dipping his fries in his ice cream.

Limited as it appeared, it could be played a thousand different ways, by changing Time Signatures, rhythm styles, Tempo, movements and instrumental performance, such as key changes and septal timing. How many different things can we do with an eight-note scale? As it turns-out, plenty!

♪

Soon, I found myself pounding on different sized corrugated boxes and old pots and pans with wooden spoons in the basement along with all the songs I could--is all I wanted to. And my diligence, as it always has since, kept me there until I could make those steps, those leaps all the way into Rock music, and usher me up to the next level of pioneers.

Living in Cape May, NJ, the home of the US Coast Guard Academy, my father and I never missed the occasional USCG Marching Band performances or the USCG Drum & Bugle Corps work-outs and shows.

At one show, a man in the middle of the drum formation collapsed in the heat. He was immediately attended to and rolled away on a gurney.

And the band plays on... A low voice surfaced.

The First Chair snare drummer--the lead--lived across the street from us. Young me, I prayed all the time that he never fainted. I told my dad I wanted to meet the drummer. That was easily done, with just a walk across the street as the guy mowed his lawn. My dad had a word with him, no doubt letting him know he had a big fan in his son, who wanted to meet him.

When we met, he told me to call him Platt.

"I'm Jimmy," I said. "Why Platt?" I asked. "Is that your real name?"

"Because it's the sound a snare drum makes when you do a flam--rimshot. *Platt!*" He smiled down at me and chuckled.

"Well," I said. "What sound does a bass drum make?"

"Doom. With a swift hard-hit 'D' and a fainter and low-tone, yet edgy 'M', almost as though it ends with a 'P'. There is little to no resonation. It sounds like a glorified *THUD*."

Platt was also the local ice cream truck guy. He drove his little white cooler van all over the Cape May neighborhoods every evening, never they be dull. Kids running him down night after night.

One evening, he walked across the street to our house and was talking to my dad on the porch. He and my dad got along well, and dad said, "Hey Jimmy, come here. Platt has a question for you."

The ice cream man surprised me by inviting me to ride-along with him on his delivery route.

On the ride, besides taste-testing much of the fare, I took the time to ask him all about drumming; everything I could think of.

I started by asking him how old he was when he started playing.

"Whoa, Jimmy," Platt said. "You surprised me with that one." He laughed and asked if I was genuinely, seriously interested in playing the drums, or just happened to like them as a hobby, or was maybe imitating him.

I told him about the music I had been listening to and playing along with on my cardboard box-drums.

"Rock & Roll," I said. "But I have an affinity that reaches all the way back to the Blues, and before: An infinite attraction." I had rehearsed the reply to that question. Platt smiled: An affinity.

"Wow, that's decent, Jimmy. The good stuff."

"Rock & Roll is where it's at though, huh, Platt?"

"I couldn't agree more, but Fusion is cool, too."

We talked on and on about music and drumming throughout the entire trip through town.

"What else are you getting in to?" Platt asked me.

"I'm open to all of it. Buddy Holly and all his followers; The Doors; The Who; This Diamond Ring; Louie Louie; Hanky Panky; Wooly Bully and even gave the Monkees a chance, but they were bubble gum. British Rock impressed me beyond imagination. All the West Coast stuff, like the Grateful Dead, the Jefferson Airplane, and also Jimi Hendrix and Janis Joplin. L.A. Imports, Buffalo Springfield and CSN&Y, the Byrds. There's a new British band out; Led Zeppelin -- every player is a maestro of the art, especially the drummer, John Bonham.

"But, hands down, the absolute best; album for album, lyric for lyric," I stressed. "Is The Beatles."

"I love The Beatles!" Platt emphatically agrees.

"Doesn't everybody?" I factiously said.

Both of us shout "THE BEATLES" together and laugh our heads off. I did a drum roll on the dashboard.

Platt said, "Let me tell you just some of the firsts and other achievements George Martin and The Beatles contributed to the arts. George Martin was their long-time producer."

"Okay."

"George Martin is a musical and creative genius, but he didn't push it onto the band. He recognized and exploited the inherent genius of the band itself instead. He helped make the band's own visions a reality. When they 'heard something' songwriting, he figured out how to accomplish the sound if they hadn't already. He enhanced their music and arrangements with his own musicianship and shrewdness and practical understanding.

"Martin strongly encouraged the band to be who they were, and to sound like they did. For example, he didn't try to cover up John's nasally voice; rather he used it to its full potential and made it unmistakably John's, and in large part The Beatles' voice. George Martin encouraged diversification and musicianship, not only in songwriting, but in arrangements too. Arrangement makes a big difference and can be very telling of a producer and a Rock and Roll band. He suggested featuring strings and horns, which he knew how to arrange and write parts for.

"That band and George Martin continuously

redefined themselves with every record released. They grew as professionals, plus, they absorbed and delivered like prophets to generations of people.

"Together, George Martin and The Beatles were the first to introduce, or at least popularize and exploit many characteristics that are taken for granted today. Examples are techniques such as recording feedback, recording backwards, odd EQs, recording harmonics, playing guitar through a Leslie, putting chorus before verse in pop songs, building triads and choral harmonies from the top down - starting at the melody line, exploiting the use of horns and strings, as well as the old mellotron, early synthesizers, like the Moog and other unusual instruments, such as the Indian sitar. The list goes on and on, ad nauseam. All mono on a four-track tape recorder, mix-down after mix-down, until it was finally mastered. That alone was unbelievable and amazing. Musicians and producers have it made today with all electronic tools at their disposal.

"One important point is that their songs are so well done, so well-orchestrated and so well arranged, that better covers are considered quite rare. There may not be a Beatles song by anyone any better than the original interpretation. Even their own outtakes pale to the released gem.

"On the other hand, their songs are so friendly, that they beg for cover. For example, 'Yesterday' and 'Hey Jude' are statistically, by far the most covered Rock songs in history."

"Wow. Hey Platt, I know I can play, but I need some formal lessons to master the Twenty-Seven Rudiments and Syncopation, at least to start-with. I have a desire to learn drum theory, sight-reading and open style sticking, too. But maybe those can come later; I don't know."

"I'll tell you what," Platt said. "If we can get your dad's permission, I'll agree to give you three hour-long lessons a week--no charge."

"That would be so rich, Platt. Thanks." Cape May was a surf town and the language to match. Some words and phrases would not to be heard or used typically for years to come.

Platt gave me a stack of half a dozen educational drum guides, to help me learn, be it along with him, or by myself, such as the rudiments and the art of syncopation. He taught me how to pick-out sticks and heads and how to tune the drums.

Dad knew I'd need a snare drum, so he gave me a chrome Slingerland 14" x 6" chrome snare drum, a drummer's throne and a drum stand. He even got me a practice pad, so I could practice virtually anywhere. Of course, I picked-out a couple pair of sticks that felt good in my hands.

"Hey Chief," Platt called out to my dad. "You'll want to make sure he has a proper metronome, while we're at it." Platt chuckled. Many drummers shun the click-track, while others live by it.

"Well, now, this really is getting somewhere." Dad hollered back. "Will do."

The following Christmas, after noting how serious I was to learn, my father presented me with a blue sparkle, four-piece set of blue sparkle Gene Krupa Model Slingerland drums, including the 13" Hi-hat, and three cymbals. A 21" Ride cymbal, a 16" Crash and an 18" Crash.

They were, to me, the ultimate gift for a lifetime. In fact, although I had different drums through the years, my cymbal set-up remained the same, except that I added a 10" splash cymbal set directly in front of me. It was mounted on the front of the bass drum.

CHAPTER 3

Let's set aside euphony, or agreeable sound, not to intentionally disqualify it, but just to set it aside for the sake of this written artifact about me. The type of music referenced therein, for example, embody the phrase: "music to my ears." It might be the sound of silence, the cry or coo of a baby, the laugh of a child, wind chimes tinkling, ringing and clanging, the wind itself, the sigh or whisper of a lover, a feathered wing taking flight, or the voice of a loved one.

The second qualifier is that the writing is limited to that about music made by real musicians. That is, musicians who *make* music, they don't just play music. Naturally, the attributes of art in general carry over into the subsequent definition of music and will not be reiterated more than once.

Art is a tangible production that somehow expresses the artist's inner feeling, vision or emotion to those paying attention. Whether clear or abstract, it is the most intimate and completely honest communication the artist has with the audience. Finished works, such as sketches, paintings, musical compositions, written words, sculptures of clay, pottery and dance all represent the artist's soul, delivered and standing naked before the masses. All are forms of personal expression, or art; the human efforts to imitate, supplement, alter or counteract the work of nature.

The obvious makeup of music is a perfect

combination of science and art. It is a logical progression that always starts with Time and includes an ordering of tonal qualities or just sounds, in succession. These combinations form a sort of temporal relationship producing ultimately, a composition.

The composition is assumed to contain some form of unity or continuity. The sounds can be made instrumentally, vocally or mechanically and will also be constituted by tempo, rhythm, melody and perhaps harmony. I once saw Frank Zappa on the Mike Douglas Show playing a bicycle! Douglas also featured Edgar Winter, brother of blues great, Johnny Winter, the Texan albinos, where Edgar played solo with the house band an incredible take on the jazz song, "Misty." Given that we are left with an octave and our own decisions to make in the process; music is not so easy to do. Musicians may take license and admit a bad song when they wrote one, too, though some won't or can't. We must be shrewd and honest with ourselves when picking out the songs that would appear on our album.

Logical progression is an underestimated knowledge that is the very basis of music, *and*, to computer science. It lies at the core of modern technology. It can also be considered the basis of true understanding and problem solving, and decision-making. Spatial reasoning is not taught in kindergarten, aside from puzzle time, but it can be taught easily and naturally at a very young age, attained with a steady dose of musical training or lessons to some reasonable degree.

Instrumental performance or lessons, such as those formulated for the drums, guitar, piano, sax/clarinet and violin are the primary vehicles for nourishment in this context. Thus, a lifetime of musical traverses also represents a healthy diet of this ever-underestimated wonder.

Reasoning becomes important and presents itself very early in life. Abstract or spatial reasoning contribute greatly to musical composition, but it also applies to puzzle solving, how things logically fit together, relationships between entities, and to the theoretic, mathematics, geometry and to scientific angles within academia, as well as to life itself.

The magic here is that it does not matter how well or how quickly one picks up the theory or the instrument. The reasoning comes in an underlying way with one's progression through the lessons, or the instrumental performance at his or her own pace.

That is also an underlying pleasure of pleasures in the music world. There is always someone influential to look up to, but there is always a protégé looking up to someone else as well; maybe you!

Obviously, music is much more than that. Through the aural senses, the musician has the power to convey emotions and relay ideas and send messages, as well as evoke new emotions for the listener that were never intended when originally writing the piece. These conveyances, furthermore, can be implicit or explicit, but typically represent genius.

Music asks a question, and music provides an answer. Music is mood-altering, as well as mood-comforting. Unlike other forms of art, music heard often produces inner visions. In my experience, for example, a painting has rarely invoked an inner intonation.

Music is volatile, like dance, in that each instrumental performance is a risk. The risks are many, including but not limited to breaking a string or a stick, hitting a wrong note, or simply tripping over a cable which has been left out from under the carpet, or without the crucial duct tape covering holding it down. Let's not leave falling off the stage out, either.

Playing a concert in Albany, GA, someone threw from their table's centerpiece, a pineapple. It was a direct hit, right in the head. I was knocked off my throne, my riser, and then fell off the stage and rolled to the back wall. That started a riot, because it was an African-American kid that threw it. Crowds of blacks and whites hurried to the gate and formed battle lines between them. I need not go on. Let's just say that I wasn't the only one hurt.

Music is one of the only art forms that beg repetition. Unlike most other forms of art, the musical user may pleasure themselves and their listeners repeatedly with the same piece of music. After all, as Joni Mitchell once pointed-out, "Nobody ever asked of a painter: 'Hey. Could you paint that one for me again, just one more time?'"

Although some artists may. Is any art ever done or complete?

A large part of music seems all too intentional, or manufactured, and that's because it is, or may be. Particularly pop music is expressly produced with air wave exposure top in mind. The dots connecting professional influence, creativity, and hunger for a hit is a hard line to draw. There are many reasons for digging a little too deep for a hook, tease, or unique sound, but it's mostly about hype, marketing and sales.

Over-production, in general, tends to degrade the original music, but many struggling musicians and writers are so eager to sign the deal that in doing so they sign away all the production rights (as well as other benefits, such as publishing). Unfortunately, it is also a crutch for many talented artists. Many times, the song produced is nothing like the writer's original aural vision. That may be good or may be bad. That's why you here the number of takes recorded and which one was picked for the album.

Production can be a good thing. Over-production is not. The reason behind such extravagance is that the search for the magic note has simply encroached into that area where the foreign sound is as important as the pure musical note. We have all but outgrown the obsolescent boost of the Korg and Mellotron, brothers and sisters, but we continue to explore the essence in every other which way, perhaps and likely modernized.

Today, it takes a dozen producers and songwriters to put out one two-minute Pop song – pushing for a radio hit. In the pioneer days of the sixties and seventies, it was done with one producer and more likely than not, just one or two singers/songwriters, with a real band backing them up, and pitching-in their ideas, too.

We still use our acoustic guitars, and work to define, if not exploit ground-breaking auditory mechanisms. Pushing the envelope, or thinking outside the box, whatever we call it, is a true nature of our ongoing musical being. More and more, bands were writing their own songs. A giant leap.

We'd do well to keep doing it. I learned all that from Platt. The man was a force of nature with a head full of musical knowledge.

CHAPTER 4

By the time my family left Cape May, I was ten years old and had mastered the rudiments of drumming, syncopation, and how to play open grip, or open style. This also meant that I could play ambidextrously, in fact quadriaxial if we include my foot-work.

I continued lessons in Cleveland, Ohio. My father's career kept the family travelling, and the family, especially me, thrived on it. I looked at it as training for road trips and travel yet to come. Add a dose of simple wishful thinking; my dreams.

We found a middle-aged man who had two full

vintage trap sets in his finished basement. I would take his ninety minute lessons twice a week.

He found me quite ready to learn sight-reading. Written drum music can be made as difficult or simple, often depending on support for the necessary patterns of the relative piece in question. Practice drills are written in a mere one or two staffs, but on the other side of the same coin, may be presented in up to four or five staffs. Some drummers learn theory, but most Rock drummers play by ear: The drummer is the click track, they will boldly announce that to a producer insisting on using one.

Drum music is presented and represented as tonal qualities, symbolically noted, mnemonically or annotated, and establishes tempo and the all-important Time

Signature -- the only signature shared by all instrumental performance on staff paper.

And besides the Clef, the prompting Time Signature always comes first. Because without time, there is nothing -- no timing -- no music -- no initiator - no tempo without a count-off. Time comes first. If one thought and reality held close to my heart as a drummer, it is this: Without the establishment of time, no music can possibly even begin, let alone exist. Think about it.

Each line and space of the staff is assigned a different part or voice of the drum kit and these are often laid out at the beginning of a piece of music in what is known as a key, or legend, or occasionally may just simply be labeled on their initial appearance. The example below is a simple look at what a drum staff looks like.

Embedded in drum music include but are not limited to: Keys and Legends. Here is a sample master drum key (or legend):

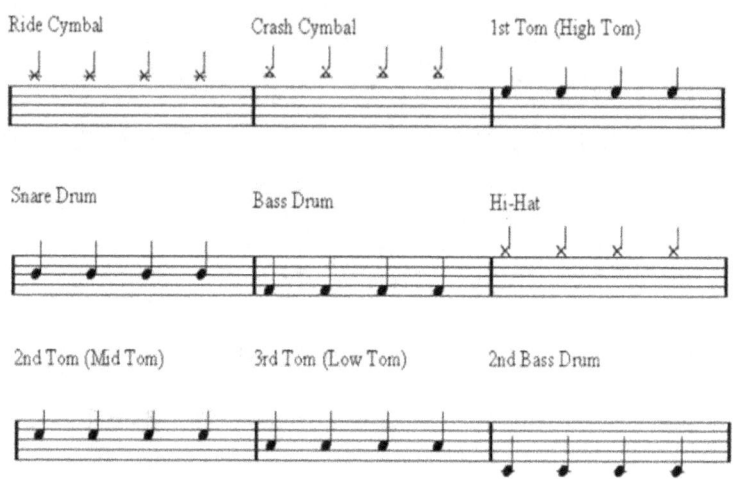

♪

My favorite lesson plans involved trading licks: My teacher would take a riff and pass it to me to copy-back. He often had me pass one of my own riffs to him, too. He had a way of splitting-up technique lessons that kept me happy, involved, intrigued, and always learning. On TV I once saw Buddy Rich trade licks with Ed Shaughnessy on The Johnny Carson Show. Man, I loved that shit.

I founded my first ensemble in Cleveland. There was an older teenage guy who lived up the street that had a basement full of equipment. He was the Mark Lindsay character of a Paul Revere and the Raiders tribute his band played. He showed us his wardrobe… boots and all. Cool. He also let us use his group's stuff to practice, and, taught my band members how to use it all. How to play. What a good guy. Musician to musician.

I named my group "A Living End" and everyone I told liked it, except my mother. She balked and said I should change the name to "The Jiminy Crickets" for at least one obvious reason.

I fought back on that tooth and nail, telling her, "We're not a bunch of babies, mom. And there was already a famous band called the "Crickets."

I got both my sisters' votes – they loved it -- as well as my dad's. Hmmm, did my mother, or any of the others really get the double entendre? I doubt it: I was the only family perv.

We played anywhere and everywhere we could; mostly parties. Mostly backyards. We played a Beatles and Stones set. We also played a commercial set that contained other popular music, but two sets are all we needed. At the time, that's all we had down tight. Of course, the more we played, the better we got. The longer our hair grew, the more popular we got.

Besides my private, formal lessons, my favorite way to practice was to play along with all my records. I would play an album at a time. Not only did I want to know the hit songs, I had to know *all* the songs…the deep tracks. I had been practicing that way since playing along with old records on those boxes and pots and pans. So, while the neighborhood kids still listened to too much commercial nonsense, I listened to The Beatles. While they listened to Dino, Desi and Billy, I was listening to The Rolling Stones. And while they zoned in on Frankie Valley and the Four Seasons, whom I did like, I was digging on The Rascals with their branded New York City soul.

My first concerts were there in Cleveland. They included The Lovin' Spoonful with The Blues MaGoos, and The Turtles. And I also got to see The Who and The Doors share the stage. Those shows began a long series of concerts I would attend over the years until I was playing too often myself to be able to take the time off to see anyone else perform in concert. The occasional show I was able to catch, you know I'd be there with a van-full of friends.

CHAPTER 5

Learning is a never-ending quest. Never consider yourself satisfied, because once you've done that, you've admitted that you've got nowhere else to go. You are declaring that you're all done...giving up.

Continued education should become embedded into your musical soul; your spirit, like practicing and exploring. Expect to leave your footprint, but never forget learning and learning *how* to learn - continuing educating one's self - is as important as what one learns in the process. Never lost are the process and product of education. After all, a lesson well learned, be it through error, uneventful fortune or by a well thought-out or formulated plan, constitutes experience that can never be taken away. Spread it around among your counterparts.

No artist or musician, including myself, has a bigger trombone to blow than the one you carry with you, day-to-day. That's merely part of the artists' nature. Passion carries heavy but hopefully keeps the EGO in check. We should have just enough EGO to feed us confidence in what is most important -- and that is the courage to put your music on record -- and share in many ways your spirit through live performance. That's all you need.

There are some fundamental elements of instrumental performance that are often overlooked, or worse yet, through limited experience or exposure, unfortunately, never learned. You may well have at least come across some of the following tidbits of information. If that be the case, or if you find yourself above the ideals herein, at least consider the message in the words, if nothing else, in the avenue of positive reinforcement, pass them on.

There are a few essentials that I learned early and kept practicing for the duration. The three biggest things to remember when performing in ensemble professionally, and the three biggest things to remember when learning to play. The example I use here is professional drums. You won't find these in a typical drill book.

Playing music and making music are often two different things.

Studio situations, though not without exception such as jazz, blues, progressive, lend themselves nicely to playing music – that is, what appears to be the ultimate solution is written, and then played for the record. The studio musicians most in demand, however, are the ones that can take a written piece and play it with the blaze and energy of a live performance. Truth.

With the above statement in mind, it has always been in some bands' best interest to capture the essence of their live performances on record. Rock bands sometimes play, and record live in the studio and then dub only what is necessary for the quality of the recording; not much track stacking.

These sessions can go long, no matter how well rehearsed the band is. Once a band is in the studio, and listening deeply, anything can happen. It is extremely personal to sit in the control room with everyone peeking into each of your musical soul, let alone critiquing you're playing. It's like they are looking into your most personal brainwaves, your personal soul. Your musical voice. Everyone muted except for you.

When something sounds wrong, the producer will usually offer insight, or when we hear something good – very good – it's a producer that will make the call: "That's the one!" or "This one is the take!"

Live playing situations, though not without exception such as orchestral, or classical, often offer or present the opportunity to make music – that is, to shine in your very own way, as you share the energy of the experience with your audience, and with the other musicians with whom you are playing. In the presentation of a tight show, one may have little room to stretch, but the smallest of creative windows can make a big difference to a being on stage, as well as to a song, and the experience itself, many times over during the concert.

No matter the instrument, focus and groove are paramount. The performer must be responsible for holding up his or her end of the tune. This sometimes means not playing -- consider taking a rest. Just as other arts feature spaces, punctuations, pauses, different colors, or no colors, and so forth; it behooves a musician to be mature and shrewd enough to know when not to play through, say, if for no other reason, the sake of musical dynamics and musical storytelling.

In drumming, the stick bounce of a stroke represents half of the note. The rests are strategic. Try to find the balance of creativity without overshadowing the others you share the stage and song. Similarly, stage mates stand up high, at stage-edge in their own moment if or when they happen, or simply when the time comes. There may or may not be a time and place, depending on the piece and the intention. Pay attention to what your producer or maestro might have said. An easy way to explain this, is, *look like what you are playing.* That's 90% of a cool performance. That is second nature to me and should be or become to be that for everyone. That is the foundation of stage choreography. If you hear the music, you should be able to move to it.

Listening to others (as well as ourselves) helps to form our own expression even stronger.

To enjoy truly the playing experience, and to be productive and conducive at the same time, you must hear and listen to what is going on around you. To execute in this way, playing your own instrument will become seamless; an expression of you.

This comes only with practice. And if you grew up like I did, along with a lot of practice, especially with others, this less tangible quality becomes acquired behavior. But required behavior. For life.

Rhythms, riffs, calls and responses, breaks, bridges and melodies and polyphonies spawn off each other during jam sessions. If possible, record every jam session you play. Listen and reflect upon what really worked well, and what did not. You may have discovered a hidden gem ready for a song to wrap around it.

Some of the biggest things to remember when learning to play professional drums is assuming, you'll at some point be sitting-in on some foreign drum sets, such as rentals. Make sure you are comfortable with any given configuration from behind which you sit.

Don't hesitate to adjust seat or drum

height, tilt, tension or tuning, muffling, or anything else that promotes your style of drumming, and the sound you want your drums to produce.

Do not be afraid to take the time to do so, and do not feel that it is not just as important as tuning a guitar or adjusting its strap or tuning the piano. You'll find that many studio situations, such as television, you'll sometimes have to play a rental or house set.

If the drums aren't fat, even when tightly tuned, or otherwise duly present in the mix, the band sounds slighted. Placing the drums properly in the mix is masterful. On playback, I placement-mix my set from the way they are set-up and the POV, where they face the listener, stage out: Bass – middle-vertical, snare slightly left and a little higher, toms slightly upper left or right each, cymbals and percussion, in whole are sweeteners could end up or appear all over the place in the stereophonic universe. Maybe the 16-inch crash high left and the 18-inch high on the right, the splash in the middle high for example.

Records with the best sounding drums typically have the superior sound quality. *I tend to nudge up the high-end some on every mic, just enough to capture the direct stick attack. I want my stick attack to cut like a mother.*

Anything beyond may be left for the producer and me to discuss, to decide upon, though not necessarily without the player's opinions. After all, you are the drum player. It is in one case or another, your song, at least your part--you own it. But it behooves the player to work together with the producers and engineers. Day one in the studio is dedicated to getting the basic drum sounds. The drums will be the first rhythm track to be laid. The musician, like the drummer has the power of veto.

Practice with a metronome as much as you do by playing along with others--recordings or live--it is necessary to do all this. Most decent drummers have a knack for delivering perfect track(s). And those drummers may not need the metronome or click track.

I once saw a documentary about synching Paul, George and Ringo to two lost John Lennon songs, meant to be early demos. They successfully produced two more number one songs. Along the way, producer Jeff Lynne asks to set-up a click-track. Ringo, very vocally, nearly shouts: "What click-track? I am the fucking click-track." Ringo had certainly learned and crafted to his bio-clock married to some intangible click-track. Just follow him! Count on him.

It is extremely important to be able to adhere to and enhance meters and time signatures smoothly and confidently.

It is equally important to be able to join in on collective improvisations and to support dynamics, accelerando, ritardando, crescendo and decrescendo structures, usually noted above or below the staff.

Whatever I practice, I do the exercise three times as much with my weaker side as I do my stronger. When I practice my rudiments and syncopation, I make up some one-handed and foot exercises as well and others including straight eighth, sixteenth, thirty-second notes, double strokes, triplets, and do them three times with my left hand or foot for every singular set done with my right hand or foot: I am right-handed.

I practiced and played open style as well as traditional, and with straight grip as well as the traditional, French grip. Open style practically requires an open grip but playing open not only makes logical sense; it is efficient, effective and functional. I practice it every day. Why cross-stick if you don't have to? For show? I don't think so. American drummer Joe English is a master of the art. Watch the DVD "Paul McCartney and Wings over America" and watch him. Listen to him. Joe is quite amazing. He's one of a kind.

I learned all I've written about thus far by the time I was a preteen. This should serve you well forever, as they did me. My hope is that they will serve any reader to any degree a view into the core, perhaps, for a non-artist (yet good listener). In time, for the learning musician, they shall become a familiar matter of course.

By the way, I am a mongrel, in that my musical parents and ancestry are made up of every artist I have ever been intelligent enough to let in to my head. I was always eager to let the lessons of others in. It doesn't matter what they play, it's that they *do* play, and want to. And I thought nothing of lifting a drum part off the groups I listened to. Everyone has their own influences. Shsh.

CHAPTER 6

Artists are thought of and sometimes portrayed as such troubled individuals, so temperamental and sensitive. Indeed, we may be, but we are so much more. Musicians are, without exaggeration, essentially brilliant, sometimes bordering genius. Yet, we are at the same time somewhat mad. Not angry – crazy.

The musician's world is simply-complex, an oxymoron often fitting. Young musicians and people in general seem curious about why artists, especially, or the successful behave the way they do, become addicts, grow angry, why they OD, why they are eccentric. Let's delve into a musician's world to examine these questions and more from my world.

I will not concentrate wholly on drug use inside of Rock music. That is a small part of a large culture going back decades. Without at least an inkling of why disasters occur with some of our most beloved and gifted musicians, however, the subject would not be complete, or the piece fairly written without mentioning it.

I will also not concentrate on the fact that some of the most influential and talented people in history experienced regular bouts with mental disparity to some degree. Volumes have already been written on artistically influential beings from our past, such as Beethoven, Schumann, Tolstoy, Keats, Williams, Van Gogh, Hemingway, Michelangelo and Dickens. Obviously, as we forge ahead the list grows: Syd Barrett, Jim Gordon, John Entwistle,

Butch Trucks, Tom Petty, Chris Cornell and Kurt Cobain. All passed way too young.

"Read no history: nothing but biography," Disraeli once wrote. "For that is life without theory."

Certainly, everyone has a story.

Disraeli's admonition may well be taken under this guise, because any given modern artist's story may well present a case study in the mysterious relationship between genius and madness, and a possible metaphor for a civilization of both the bohemian and futuristic: They have seen the miraculous achievements through the twentieth century, and creeping into the twenty-first, overshadowed, at times by the madness of crime, injustice, war and extreme activism. Inspiration comes from events of continuity of any kind, as well as one-time happenstance. And it's usually got some personal declarations in there, as well.

That paradoxical imbalance inspires many but kills others. Lives suffer by nature and adapt, too. So also, do artists.

In a profession that places a certain premium on eccentricity and outrageousness and in which a lack of social graces is considered part and parcel of being an unreal Rock and Roll star, some rockers are more outrageous, eccentric and lacking in social skills and emotional attachments than others. Look. We're all different. We're all human. We all evolve.

That can only be looked upon as either a maturation issue, where one essentially fails or chooses not to level, grow-up or rise, or, it could mean that the being is simply experiencing emotional or mental phenomena. No matter how outlandish or comical the behavior, under those circumstances only the lucky survive, or even excel, despite or because of the haughty, sometimes cruel treatment of self, loved ones and peers.

Some, perhaps more sophisticated, "dress for the occasion." I always prefer a quiet, dark room to return to during or following the after-party. I've met many super-stars, and I must tell you, some were perfect ladies and gentlemen, and some were royal asses, regardless of their mark in the musical world. That brings sorrow and misunderstanding to the peer and fan.

Contrary to the stereotype, musicians are more like geeks than they are freaks. They spend their days and nights completely wrapped up in their keen, sensual and complex world. They dedicate and devote all of who they are and what life has offered them to studying their craft, practicing to perfection. We try repeatedly to somehow recognize, apply and gain recognition in the meantime. Many forever purchase or remodel and maintain their instruments of choice.

The recognition for them is thought to be only through and for their music, however, and not necessarily for them – themselves, kind of a chore, but a good one. Ultimately, we are indeed faced with how others perceive us as people, and not just as stars, and that is where some of the pressure begins. Your family and true fans keep your feet grounded.

Musicians are also under great stress to produce. And that is often under microscopes that magnify the tears. Think about the lengthy history of music and then think about how easy it would be to come up with any new and attractive take on an eight-note scale. Oversimplification? Absolutely not. It is not coincidence that much of what you hear today sounds like something else, from somewhere else that you've heard before, even though the 90's introduced something very new and distinct, as I mentioned above. I'm still waiting what will follow creatively.

Stepping away from that curse is preeminent and the ultimate for any musician in more ways than one. This is wonderful in today's world, because it essentially forces the modern musicians to consider other avenues for that balance of diversity, commercialism, energy and noteworthiness. We are being more thoughtful about instrumentation, electronics and vocals now as intricately as the pioneers were when Rock was still very young, most notably, musicians introduced in the nineteen-sixties and seventies.

Back then, following The Beatles' example, every new album brought with it some uncharted movement of some kind, some sound conjured-up but now, only the truly unique, talented and special stand out. Soundgarden and Alice in Chains are perfect examples of those who cleanly crawled beneath the barbed wire. When "Stone Temple Pilots" broke out with the song, "Plush," Eddie Vedder, vocalist and songwriter for Pearl Jam asked, "Does that guy sound like me? Is he trying to?" Of course not. A totally new, never-before-heard vocal sound is hard to come by and difficult to make it different without effects. Maybe Eddie was simply the silent mentor to a new protégé. I wouldn't know.

Magnificence in unique progressions, time and lyrics came out the other end. Understand that Soundgarden's "Spoonman" was performed in drop D tuning; the main riff was written in septuple meter, in 7/4 time. The chorus is 4/4 time and a good part of the spoon solo is in 3/4 time. Guitarist Kim Thayil has said that oddly, Soundgarden, in this irregular instance, did not consider the multiple time signatures of the song until after the band had written the other elements were in it, and said that the use of odd meters was "a total accident." Fantastic! He had a job on his hands. That is one good, strong song with one fine drummer.

There is more than personal sacrifice in the life of a musician. The road to success is sometimes long and bumpy. What makes matters worse is that while some extremely talented and gifted musicians struggle for a lifetime, persevering, perhaps never to make it, success comes easy to others, whether it be through pure talent, luck, perhaps through a known associate, or by how much money they have behind them. I gasped. It could have been also a stroke of genius without even trying. I urge you to listen to "Spoonman" by "Soundgarden." Find the changes and understand them. You'll likely have to play it several times, but it's worth it, and cool because it is modern fare from a great band.

One thing we all must remember, musicianship aside, is that life holds no guarantees. The future is wide open. It is a much easier idiom to swallow, however, when one's life dream is not dependent upon it. That simple yet weighty certainty of uncertainty for musicians, however, is a key ingredient to fear of failing the otherwise inevitable developmental stage – their true milestone, and the provisional drive to exert, survive and succeed. Still for others, it is musical feed.

Predominantly even, the mere song sequence of an album, as Bob Seger sings on "Against the Wind." He shares, "I've got so much more *to think about, deadlines and commitments, what to leave in, what to leave out."*

One reason so many Rock musicians over the years turn to drug induced recreation, is maybe that sometimes at some subconscious level they feel they haven't lived nearly enough of the blues to justify their playing or implementing it. So, some create the blues through manifestations conjured-up by drugs, alcohol and other dangerous or whacky behavior. It may read distantly, but it is sometimes a simple truth.

Except for a few, most don't realize, or they realize far too late, something very, very simple: Life is full of the blues anyway - one must simply wait for it.

It'll come.

In other words, as miraculous as life is all by itself - it can also be a room full of blues - we must recognize it and swim through it. Just ask Eric Clapton.

Another reason for self-indulgence and abuse is plain and simple: Boredom.

Musicians, like most artists, are inside very complicated moments and brilliant people; some manic, like me. As well, sometimes being tagged plagiarists, as when The Chiffons sued George Harrison over the structures and melodies in his masterpiece, "My Sweet Lord."

They claimed that he lifted the melody and chorus off the song "He's So Fine."

The nerve of those parasites chewing on one of the best songs ever written, and one of the most talented musicians and songwriters in the world! Needless to say, he was a fucking Beatle, for god's sake. That made me sick. Artists are often misunderstood and taken advantage of. The Beatles could have probably sued a million musicians that followed them.

As down-to-earth as they are within their art, ultimately their chosen profession, they are forced further and further out of their league with each measure of commercial success experienced, and milestone reached.

Disillusionment runs rampant in the music business. Moreover, it's quite simply, a lonely, lonely life in the art and on the road. The nagging question is always there; who is real, and who just wants a piece of the talent? Sadly, it may not matter if whoever it is delivers the goods.

The last epexegesis I will offer here is probably the most widespread, and yet unbeknownst to most.

Certain temperaments are conducive to creative expression. Fiery fluctuations of mood often accompany people who are inclined to creative activity. Tempering or off-setting such movement is a challenge. If that challenge cannot be met through some other means, in another way, or if the individual is partial towards altered states by influential virtue or prior experience, then given the history, the atmosphere, and the accessibility, drug use sometimes becomes imminent in any Rock arena. I cannot recuse myself from this, but fortunately, I eventually grew-up and matured personally and musically, and I am lucky and happy to be alive today.

Sometimes it is a torn matter between humanitarian love and the love of the art, public acceptance, and commercial relevance. Songwriters often become torn between loyalty to the band they struggled and worked with to get somewhere, and the mainstream business with which they are becoming familiar, some feel forcibly.

Notice that some bands stick to the original plan, which might mean crediting the entire band with the song writing or perhaps the arrangements, or just keep them sticking around. Others may have a written or have an unwritten agreement that only the authors in the purest sense of the term will be credited and rewarded by publication. This is finally, slowly becoming the standard. Writing a contract is like writing a living will.

I was advised to copyright publication of every drum take I contributed and played, obviously recorded and released. I co-wrote many songs and was seldom offered anything for doing it. So, for songs I did co-write and all the songs recorded using my drum takes I got credit for.

Still there are others that customize their own agreement. Tokens such as royalties, publishing rights, credits, points and the nature of the business are not fully understood by most fledgling musicians. Those are all parts of the rules of containment. It would behoove a band to retain an entertainment attorney, as well as intelligent management. Agents and promoters fit into the plan, too.

That is where close management and legal representation come into play, but here again; we are far away from the mind set and interests of most young rogue musicians. Luckily, the modern-day Rock musician is better protected and educated than were the musicians of yesteryear, even as recently as a decade ago. As generations evolve, we learn more exponentially by the mistakes of our forefathers and we make ourselves.

Most Rock musicians can expect to earn most of their money, dollar for dollar, off live performances. There are exceptions, such as the multi-multi-platinum artists who may have been shrewd enough to have signed a fair contract. They play out whenever they wish. The fact of the matter is, even a seasoned pro is vulnerable to losing it all to another - a thief in the business, even a spouse. Just ask Billy Joel©.

On a more subconscious level, Rock musicians, being the humans that they are underneath all the showmanship, may worry they are not contributing all to society that they otherwise might or were taught. They tend to be admired by some and shunned by others. That may lead to their shunning society itself or ubiquitously shying away from people or reaching furtively for attention by all the wrong means. You may be surprised at the amount of contributions some successful artists offer multiple charities. Many successful musicians are quite the philanthropists.

Some superstars become desensitized by

the business, some, perhaps their promoters, who no doubt force the unwilling musician to participate in the typical meet and greet activities After-Show. That's tough on those occasions when the talent feels spent and tired for the night, or just aren't into it.

The expectation is that any musician would be glad to get together with any other musician, by some assumed camaraderie - honor among thieves. But sometimes that is just not the case. Couple that with the idea of their dealing with non-musicians, fans, the hangers-on, and the tension tends to build. But most players like to be liked.

Younger musicians are typically more outgoing and inviting, they are looking for more and more fans, but the well-versed pros or more mature and understanding musicians are likely not to want to talk to anyone if the mood is not just right. They've earned that reservation.

Some can afford not to be accessible, but not many. A peer or a fan deserves as much respect as the performer does for being the star off the fans' dime. Besides, the After-Show Passes are limited and hard to get. Money can buy privacy, but the stars eventually may live with their own loneliness through their popularity.

Acceptance.

Hardly anyone outside the business is seen Pre-Show: That is a given. Artists do then what they want, or what they think they need to warm-up for the show, be it juggling swords, harassing the caterers, meditating, praying, shooting up, rehearsing, stretching, and that is their thing – what they do to warm-up. If the show was somehow hitched,

After-Show is out, too. If the show went off well, the invitations and the Passes stand.

Sometimes, stars end up resenting all outsiders, fans included. The Green Room has been afforded "Affirmative Action" since the early 60's. It seemed to have started with providers sending cripples in to see The Beatles either pre-show or post-show, as though they could heal. And in some ways, to some people, I guess maybe they could, and possibly, somehow maybe even did. Who knows?

Kreskin?

In that way, The Beatles were happy in general and were entertaining and conversationalists with their visitors.

Now however, whenever you go to the green room, even if you're first in line, you're always a little bit behind the challenged, and way behind the youngest (female) ones.

Curiously perhaps, the temperament of the musician does not always hinge upon degree of success. Rate of neither success nor caliber; be super star, struggling veteran or merely frustrated, at any given time, doesn't make the difference in humility. The difference is made by the moment, just like with the rest of us. "Leaving your work at the office" would be the comperand. It's just that simple.

Successful musicians are simply professional humans. They are also complex human beings. Again; simply-complex. Like anyone else, they have their problems. Unlike everyone else, except for peer artists alike, they are honestly living their dream. And that, my friends, can be as lively as it sounds inviting. Also, it could become very scary and vulnerable to the artists at times.

CHAPTER 7

We transferred back to Portsmouth, NH. My bands and musicians all over the region, some travelling a long mile to get there, rehearsed and jammed at my house in a finished studio space. As it was, I lead jam sessions there for years, blessed be my mom. My dad died when I was twelve years old, but my mom knew how important it was to support me in all I wanted to do - especially with music.

She gave me 10:00 AM through 12:00 AM midnight every day in my play space, no matter the crowd or the volume. Man! She was so cool. I must have, in one way or another, hatched a half a dozen decent groups out of that basement room. I played Blues, Jazz, Rock, Three-Piece, Fusion, Progressive Rock--hell--all forms of Rock music.

Sometimes, it meant work and effort, and others, just for the pure joy of it; the jam.

So, I grew-up with a whole lot of musicians all around me coming into my basement room - fit with risers, a PA system and everything needed - to jam and rehearse. Literally every musician in the area visited at one time or another, most much more, but most were regulars from somewhere or another. Many of us, like John and me cut our teeth jamming down there every day noon to midnight. It was fabulous. It was nurturing. It was pure magic.

I also had a built-in swimming pool open to all. Gotta love that. It was a perfect girlfriend hangout.

I had a four-piece band together for a while that featured a quirky, little, temperamental guitarist from South Boston. He was to a tee, a Harpo Marx look-alike. We named him Beantown Bob. He usually played a Strat through a Fender Twin, but sometimes played a Les Paul.

And he played it. . . *Loud.* But he had a gigantic sound. You could pick him out of line-up based on sound and talent quite easily.

One day, we had a guest bassist named Tom Barnett come in, who played along or took turns with my regular bass player, John. They both doubled on six-string, too, if they didn't want to sit a few out.

Tom was talking up his new rig to Bob, saying no one could ever blow his stack of two cabinets with two 15" SRO speakers in each. Well, huh, old Bean Town Bobby immediately took that as a challenge, and he immediately asked, South Boston accent thick, "What da fuck you just say?"

He was quite a genius and very, very much a shredder on the guitar. I am talking approaching Hendrix-Good and beyond, and sometimes better. He was a Stan Web and Chicken Shack follower, who wrote "Poor Boy." He also liked the band "Crack the Sky." He also had a certain style, but he was off the charts after plugging into Tom's rig. Every one of us ran up and out the bulkhead and stood, waiting in my front yard. It was still way loud out there.

It took Bean Town Bobby all of four and a half minutes to completely blow all four SRO speakers in Tom's cabinets.

Sorry Tom.

PART TWO
INSTRUMENTAL PERFORMANCE ROCK SHOWS & STUDIOS

James A. Landry

Second Set

A New Life is Gonna be Mine

--Toy Caldwell

CHAPTER 8

The Teneriffe Mountain Band

The Teneriffe Mountain Band was one of the first true travelling Rock bands I played with to date. We did a circuit throughout New England and the Maritime Provinces, Canada. I met The Teneriffe Mountain Band at an afternoon soiree our bands played on the park amphitheater in Dover center. I received a tip from a mutual friend, Gene Sibley, another genius musician and a regular in my jamming room, that they were about to boot their drummer. He knew I wanted a band with a plan.

I was looking for a new gig, something more organized and professional, and busy. I introduced myself to Sonny on the lawn. His band had seen me perform with my two groups that afternoon. And I saw their show.

We arranged an audition. The band was led by a duo - a husband and wife lead singing team. He played acoustic guitar, open tuning. By default, they were generally regarded as the commandants of the group. I don't like top-down management, nor did I like military-style command. But I was interested in what lay ahead.

The keyboard player named Mike had an old Wurlitzer electric piano. A Wurlitzer of all things: Unbelievable. He had to retune it before every gig. The Wurlitzer used metal tabs for each key. Then, he had to either shave, file or replace it with a new tab and repeat.

The guitarist was a hippy freak just like me. Sonny had a gold top Les Paul and a couple of acoustic guitars. Finally, my unlikely counterpart, the bass player, was a big goofy guy who only had one foot into the endeavor. Everybody sang. Although Trisha struggled with pitch, Mac was happy to coach her. It was a vocal group with good instrumentalists.

I passed the audition, and in fact they adored me. At the audition, we discussed a New England - Canada tour and circuit that I had a line on. That represented a choice to all in attendance. We're all in and put ourselves out there - go for it, or not all-in period.

I was hired on the spot, but we gave everyone three days to think about the possibilities that could come from touring, and of course my playing behind the couple. We had nothing we were touring behind for yet, except a couple cover songs recorded at a radio station studio done just for this tour. Radio stations at each stop were given, in advance, a copy of the recording.

We had stayed booked six weeks in advance, and then a new tour manager took over that end of things. Our fearless duo decided to leave their day-jobs at GE for the experience of touring. Our keyboardist agreed to break from school to tour, but there was always something fishy about the guy, like he would suddenly wake up one day and fly back to college on a whim. Our guitarist was in, no doubt and with no hesitation. He was bringing his wife and young toddler with him on one run of the circuit, which was difficult at times, but usually fun and no one was hurt.

I was ready to go. Then, the bass player spoke up softly, deep in voice, and said, "Guys, I just can't do it. My wife completely rejects my going on the road. The kids . . . the chores. You know."

We tried to talk him into it, but there was no budging to be had. He felt bad enough over it, after all.

I said, "Look. I know a great bass player that I've been working with for years. You saw him with me in Dover that day. One-hundred to one, with my involvement, he'll take it."

Without getting too deep into it, I called him right away. He asked to jam with the band first, before deciding to go. Well, of course.

Two nights later, we were jamming at Sonny's farm on Teneriffe Mountain. The guitarist had sixty acres right atop the mountain in Milton, with several out-buildings. His family nurtured and harvested small bush blueberries. Some extra income around August harvest. By trade, Sonny was a cabinet maker.

We all blended well. John and I always locked-in. That was us. In the pocket. We had been playing side-by-side for a long time. We communicated expertly, without words.

After the third night, we sat for a beverage and a chat. John had nothing better coming at him, and he liked the band, so he signed-on to tour. The deed was done. Now, it was time for some heavy lifting rehearsals, especially for me and John having to learn their entire repertoire of seventy songs.

Our first gig together, we co-opened with "Wheat Straw," for Terry Stafford, of the original "Suspicion" fame. Hell! *Elvis* covered that one. Our take was an all-expense-paid two-day trip to Boston. We were given the top floor suites at the Hyatt, ate at the revolving roof restaurant and we took good and well advantage that we could have anything we wanted, including drinks and Room Service.

We handily had, anytime we needed, a stage at Luneau's showcase club.

Mike's parents owned it. It was an excellent filler gig and a regular stop on our New England leg of our circuit. It was a plush, great sounding room and we always drew a great crowd.

For John and me, up until now were dress-rehearsed. It came off with just one hitch. Mac and Trisha insisted we wear coordinated uniforms. Trisha dressed-up, much too formal, like she was going to a friggin' wedding. And Mac got to wear black jeans, a cream shirt and leather vest. He looked good. The rest of us old sods had to wear white denim jeans and gingham shirts, swapping blue and red back forth every other night. Mike could care less, but Sonny, John and I agreed by protest and swore we'd get ourselves out of the crazy outfits as soon as we could. We looked like farming musicians from "Hee-Haw." Mac and Trisha ate up the visual of the group in that the onlooker could tell at a glance who the "leaders of the band" were.

After the audition, and the Boston gig, John and I were officially in. Our first stop was Dartmouth at an intimate showcase venue, then we got on the road to Dalhousie, New Brunswick, Canada; a town at the very top of the province. This was a headline tour, so on some stops we had opening acts, but some we didn't. The couple singles were on rotation while we were up there. That was the routine: Two weeks ahead of time, our songs got airplay. At that time, this was the norm protocol wherever we were booked.

The showcase in Dalhousie provided a fair-sized house for us to stay in during our stay in town, but we had to agree to share it with the opener. After a bit of head-scratching, we didn't mind, seeing as how our opener was none other than Miss Nude Montreal, Bunny Stewart! She was a lot of fun, all the time goofing around with us, often working us into her act. She was gorgeous and fit. Miss Nude Montreal Bunny Stewart, as I take this breath, please, where are you today, Bunny honey?

Smile.

It weirded us all out that she travelled with this old decrepit man. He must have been pushing 80+ something. He never left their room. She shared the bedroom with him, like a Canadian version of Anna Nicole Smith. That brought the balloon down quick, I know I don't have to tell you. It was so quiet in their room, that we often wondered if the old fellow had survived Miss Bunny over any given night and with any sense to the thought.

Like, "what a way to go."

CHAPTER 9

Our band leaders were straighter than W.C. Field's pool cue. They warned all of us that any smoke brought over the border would be a deal-breaker. No questions asked. Well, I took this in word by word, verbatim, and in a completely technical sense.

I met a girl named Debbie at the venue on the first night, we liked each other right away, so we went out after the show. The cute French accent practically unbuckled my belt for me. She had long, strawberry blonde hair constantly flying all about her cute, slightly freckled face.

I asked her if she could get me some decent weed.

"Ah, ha, ha, ha," She chuckled. "You silly Southern man, you. Of course, I can."

Apparently, if you live anywhere south of Canada, you are considered southern.

"Oh, this is too good." I said. "I thought we'd be dry our whole stay here."

"No, you do not worry with me, dear."

"You're a little sweetie." I said

"OK. We are at my friend's home, but I will go in myself, at least just once for this time, right?" Debbie said.

"Right. You're the boss." I replied.

She came back and handed me a half an ounce of sticky green bud with purple hairs. Raising different strains was already commonplace in Canada. We cracked the windows then, we passed the pipe puff-puff-pass.

"Wow!" I marveled. "Debbie. This is some damn good smoke. Oh my god."

"I told you, no?"

"You did, yes, and now I am a believer." I chuckled.

That skunk is in my jacket for good. Even if not, this stuff can be sensed, the odor smelled through the two-plastic zip-locks it was in.

Our fearless leaders took off for the day. How we could be so stupid, I don't know, but almost like a transporter, we led each other down the stairs to a slightly mildewed basement room. I stuffed a pipe and we puff-puff-passed it around. I was right: This was some incredible dope. We were all stoned maximus super after just two hits.

We were upstairs in the living room listening to the Poco Cantamos album while Sonny's wife cooked-up some Cauliflower steaks and beef tips with gravy. She was an excellent chef: We never went hungry. We all helped do the grocery shopping together, and the dishes.

Mac and Trisha decided to turn back and return to the gig-house. They took one step in and our whole world exploded. We were busted. Of-course, they could smell it. They were both yelling and screaming together at the rest of us.

"One at a time, please." I scold them. "We're a patient bunch of lads, you know."

I told them it was not taken over the border; it was acquired here in town, but the duo would hear none of it.

Mac said, "We are packing all our stuff and leaving."

And unbelievably so, that's exactly what they did. They screeched and sped away in their little mid-size sedan, as I yelled, "Go back to GE you fucking posers." They left leaving us the Subaru and truck.

Meanwhile, the rest of us looked around for another place to smoke, just in case they came back. Oh, for the priorities. I called upon my girl, Debbie, and I asked her where we could hide outside to get high. I went and picked her up, and she had a perfect spot.

Directly across from our band house, surprising to us, there was a skinny path that could barely be seen that led us through brush and woods to a small river bed. That spot immediately became our smoke house. It was beautiful out there by the water, standing on the stream pebbles and small river rocks.

None of us used after 4:00 PM pre-show,

but we usually looked forward to it after-show, before bed and off-hours.

We spent the rest of the day wondering what we were going to do come show-time.

Smiling, I said, "I can do a three-hour drum solo."

The band laughed hard, considering the situation; 'the infamous drum solo.'

We could do songs without Mac and Trisha, and ask Bunny to perform an encore following us.

Around 7:00 PM, Mac and Trisha burst through the front door and he yells that there will be no more pot smoking in the house, period.

"I don't care where it comes from.

"You are lucky we returned with a second chance. God Damn lucky." Mac was playing big man.

"Well, we're glad you did, Mr. Mac." And

staring at him, I said, "Let's all try not to be dick-heads."

Mac said, "We'll meet you there at show time. Jimmy, you write the fucking set lists. And there will be no more fucking around."

Bunny could not have picked a better night to include me in her show, by prancing over to me with a lap dance, her fluffy bunny tail shaking across my lap as I was trying to write the set lists. The crowd cheered when she turned around to show them her bunny tail and then stuffed my face between those grand beaux seins and jiggled the package back and forth. BLBLBLBLBLBLBL. It sure cheered me up; ahem, in more ways than one. I could have sat there all night. The crowd was having a ball. The band, sans Trisha and Mac, was laughing hysterically as I got a good going-over.

During the middle of the second set, Trisha, as usual... no, as always, intermittingly turned around to face John with a killer scowl. We all knew what was coming:

"John! John! Turn it down! You're entirely too loud. Turn it down." She, at that point, was much louder than we needed, and a bit much for the audience to have to put-up with. If I were Mac, I would have spanked her.

By this time, however, John had enough. He jumped up and down; each jump delivering a loud "Fuck you, Trisha." So, the three jumps, on beat, came with a:

Jump.

"Fuck you, Trisha.

Jump.

"Fuck you, Trisha.

Jump.

"Fuck you, Trisha."

He was jumping straight up and down while cussing her out! The group was near hysteric.

Trisha was astounded. She whipped her head around and looked to her husband, who, very smartly, ignored the entire scene. Mike, the keyboardist, sat, and watched with a smile of laughter that he just could not hold back.

John just looked at me and said "Let's get on with it, Jimmy." I simply counted off the next one and sang through my laughing, our "Elvin Bishop" medley. Sonny practically had to hide behind his amp and speaker cabinet to let his laughs play out.

We spent a little longer than usual on the river bank that night. We all knew already how utterly uncool Trisha was, and Mac, too, for that matter. But he had a sense of humor and a bit more of a foot in Rock & Roll, or musical tour door. He had to teach her all her parts. She was a flesh and blood marionette.

♪

Following the drama, and the Dalhousie shows, we routed the quickest route to PEI. We set-out to Prince Edward Island, Quebec to get a Ferry to Les Îsles de la Magdleine. With few concessions to modern life, there's a land-that-time-forgot vibe to Quebec's Les Îsles de la Magdleine. On this archipelago in the middle of the massive Gulf of St. Lawrence, Magdelinots speak their own singsong version of Acadian French. The remote islands' geography defines them.

They're an open window to the Gulf of St. Lawrence, with many who work at La Meduse Glassware studio and shop. This was a destination year round, so there were many shops all around; plenty of work for the locals. The winds shape the inhabitants, landscape, and its culture. The sandstone cliffs jut out of the sea on the northern coasts of the nine main islands. Sand dunes creating lagoons, adjacent wetlands, and miles of windswept beaches link most islands.

While Les Isles locals' welcome travelers, it's fishing, lobster caging, Rock crab, scallops, mussels, and ground-fish—that sustain the 7,000 year-round residents. In summer, brightly painted red, blue, and white commercial fishing boats line the docks at Port du Milleara. And, when winter snow blankets the cliffs and dunes, tiny ice-fishing huts in a kaleidoscope of colors dot the frozen lagoons at sea. It was quite breathtaking.

It's a ninety-mile voyage to the islands, with ferries available. We travelled on one with all the equipment and vehicles with us. I fell asleep inside the coiled anchor line:

It was like being protected by a callused, long, fat boa snake. It was summer and it was beautiful, but it was still a little chilly over the ocean as is usual.

The venue gave us a gorgeous beach house and an in-town bunk-house to live in during our stay. Of course, the not-so-great couple got the house, by default.

Fuggers.

It was the best thing we could have done: It made sense to keep Trisha away from the band. Let the band leaders get the perk. The only time we saw either one of them was at show-time, that's it. It worked out best for all around. Of course, they thought the house was a prize for the president and first lady.

The rest of us went to the bunk house, deciding that staying away from the front couple is the way to go. It was fit with a kitchen and six bunk beds. I sincerely believe I was happier without Mac and Trisha around, anyway. The heater didn't work, but the woodstoves did, so we kept them fired-up. The club owners made sure there was always plenty of chopped wood for the fires. We chose our beds and went to check out the venue.

It looked small from the store-front but opened deep and wide inside. There were some old local, gruff-looking men at the bar. They ask if we'd like a hand, and, of course, they all clapped for us. We were playing moderately sized venues, perhaps enough for a crowd of three-to-five hundred, so we didn't have to carry an overly big PA system. We travelled as light as possible and we had our own lights, spot and speakers and that's all we needed.

We took care of our own stage gear, and

the set-up went nice and easy. We had no audio-tech this trip, so I taught Mac how to ring-out the room and fine tune equalization from there. I told him to wander around and get a steady, balanced sound out of the PA to cover the crowd. Mike handled the monitors and lights.

After the sound-check, we all went out to eat, and then home to nap. Fish Tacos. Nineteen-seventy-four - Fish Tacos! Although I was from a salty dog town known for the seafood, this was a first for me, and a love-at-first-bite. We'd meet at the venue at 9:00 PM for a two-hour 9:30 to 12:00 PM show. I broke it off the two sets equally paced and spaced.

CHAPTER 10

The audience wanted stuff louder and faster. Heck. We could do that. As the night unfolded, we could clearly see the rotation of patrons turn from older to young, except the older artists and hippies. There were a lot of those on the islands.

We weren't sure how much of our show the folks out there knew, but they were drunk and crazy high in a damn short time. Aftershow, we decided to follow a caravan of vehicles up the back-beach road. It took us to the island's northeastern end.

By the looks of things, it was a

park-where-you-will situation; with no white lines to coral. We got out of the van and stood there, peering around at everyone. We couldn't see an entrance, so we decided to follow a small group of teens; not too close.

"It's a fucking cave." I said.

It is a little off-white with streaks of cream and light gray and felt chalky. It opens to a quiet sitting-smoking cavern. It was both naturally and donated furnished for places to sit or recline. Hookahs were smoking Hash, Dabs, and some, opium.

Is this what "The Cavern" looked like?

The other end we could see a curving hallway and decided to explore. And it certainly was a cavern. Like the front room, except it was larger. And there was music. At one end of the room was a rectangular stoop with a Ukulele player jamming with a mandolin player.

We found a spot to settle-in, check things out and listen to the artists.

The following night at the club, was much the same, but this after party, we had Sonny bring in one of his acoustic guitars to the cavern. Walking through the front room, we noticed some murmuring. We looked around only to see everyone speaking low in each other's ears.

We walked on, and finally into the music room. Sonny naturally yet slowly approached the stage and took a seat in the corner beside his guitar. He is kind of shy and not a show-off, so I knew what was buzzing through his head right then; Nerves. He's just a humble guy.

There was a flutist playing up there who sounded good. So fine. She was rifling through a bunch of Jethro Tull songs. Yes! Tull!

"Bonsoir Monsieur," she said in a voice that sounded like it came from a nice warm teepee.

"Bonsoir Miss." Sonny replied, holding out his hand. He couldn't remember Mademoiselle, so Miss was fine.

"J'ai presque tout ce que je connais. Mais peut-être que nous pouvons faire un couple ensemble, oui?"

Sonny asked the girl sitting next to his guitar case what she said.

"She says she play most she knows, but maybe both of you can do a couple more together. I think she has a couple in mind."

"Ask her what two songs she would like to do. Maybe I know them."

The girl asks the flutist, who replied: "Je connais deux arrangements de flûte de Joni

Mitchell. Qu'en est-il de la Californie et des trois côtés maintenant?"

The translator tells Sonny, "Joni Mitchell's 'California' and 'Clouds'."

Sonny gave his newfound partner a big smile and says to her that he knows both those songs. They swapped the vocals.

Sonny suggests they do "California" first, and then do "Clouds." He suggested they stretch them out a bit by taking two long solos each, in both songs. They communicated by eye contact and nods, live, during the songs.

A couple of pros.

Some of the people in the room are singing softly along with the two musicians. When the duo ends, Sonny hugged her and said, "Merci." She echoes that and gives him a peck on the cheek.

As Sonny began placing his guitar in its case, he hears he's not off the hook just yet. The hippie cave people began to chant, "Neil Young! Neil Young! Neil Young!"

Like, "Freebird!"

Or like, "Whippin' Post!"

Or "Paint it Black…"

Sonny knew a lot of Neil Young songs and was happy to oblige. He also threw in some of his favorites, "Delbert McClinton" and "Jessie Colin Young."

CHAPTER 11

The clan threw a bon fire for us on our final night right there on The Magdeleine Islands beach-front at the Northeast end. Sonny didn't bring his guitar. He wanted some peace and freedom sitting fireside with the rest of us. He was surprised when his flutist friend pulled-up a beach chair next to him.

With her came her sister. Sonny asked if she spoke English. She replied that she was a lot better at it than her older flute-playing sister.

"What are your names?" Sonny asked. He was looking at both but listening to one.

"My name is Sonny," he said. "The band is from New Hampshire, New England, USA."

"Her name is Madison, and mine is Jenna."

"Both very nice…very kind. Very pretty." Sonny said.

He then introduced them to the rest of the band, and, of-course, his wife.

"Where is the front two persons, la femme et l'homme?"

"They enjoy relaxing by themselves after a show. They are at the beach house that the venue owner provided."

"Oh. D'Accord. Je vois."

♩

As the fire burned its crazy colors and crackling sounds, a drum circle slowly begins and continues to moderate as more and more people join. I ran back to the van and got my bongos and grabbed a couple 1966 Ludwig tambourines—one with a head and one without.

"These are the same tambos that Ringo used in the studio – Ludwig 1966." I said excitingly as I passed them out. "I'll play the bongos."

Someone began a drone with an Ashiko. We hear a Bougarabou adding accents. We can hear Cabasas, bells and tambourines in a meshed rhythm. Claves and other hand instruments fill-in the high-end, as well.

Uh...Yuh...Here it is: The Cowbell.

Someone has a Dunun, another with a Goblet Drum. There are a lot of Rattles, ratchets and rain sticks coming in. Numerous shakers and Shekere round off the mid to high-end. Finally, Sonny hears what he is listening for; a Tambora and a pair of Tablas that set-up a mid-bottom end melody line.

Now it's time for me to jump-in.

After a long take with what started us off, the movement and accentuations bring us to another place. Pretty soon, everybody's eyes are closing or squinting into the fire. The players are putting each other into a trance.

"We're getting high off the circle," Sonny says to his wife. "Look at everyone."

Once a drum circle is in full motion, it's impossible to break up. Some may come and some may go and some to return, but the majority is hooked by passing solos around to different instrumentalists or even a single piece. I was experiencing a flash-forward.

We decided after departing the SPI Ferry from the Magdeleine Islands that the truck would travel better following a route that would carry us south to a border entry there. Sonny and I drove the equipment van southerly on the Lansdown West Side, and the others drove the cars and van over the upper-most border at North Pass way. They drove north and took a left, and we went south and turned right.

The southern roads on the Lansdown side of the border were engineered for trucking. We planned to cross at Grand Pass Way. No one should have any trouble crossing the border. We detailed everything, especially the equipment van. And Sonny and I were cruising swimmingly along, very nicely in that big old truck. Then, we hit the Grand Pass Way Border Crossing.

Sonny was on the driver's side and I was on the other. He was not quite as smooth as I was, not persuasive either. His nerves shot out all around him like sparks. Like me, he's just a mellow bohemian. But we were clean. We knew we were clean. Sonny did alright when he explained our presence in Canada, our work, our travelling their roadways. But the unwritten rule to search any male crossing that had long hair applied: we qualified.

We were asked to stand back and take a seat on the outside bench up against the office. A guard on both sides of the cab searched like blood hounds. And Sonny shook like a frost-bitten Rock wall climber.

"Sir," the cop shouted at Sonny. "Can you tell me what this is?"

Please, Sonny, play it, man. Play it.

Sonny looked at it, as the other officer came over to see.

Sonny put on his best play-dumb and said, "Well, I can't say I know at all what that is."

I was hoping he would crush it between his

fingers, or drop it at his feet to grind it, but he didn't.

"It is a cannabis seed, sir. Do you know what cannabis is?"

"I'm not sure, but could it be some part of a marijuana plant, cannabis sativa?"

A chip off the outer shell of a seed is all it was. How they found it, I have no idea, and will never know.

I spoke-up. "We recently bought this truck explicitly for this road trip. That had to have already been there. I'm sure of it."

"I'm afraid we're going to have to search your payload." The senior official tried to make himself sound tough.

"Do I really have to remind you that we just made your province here a hell of a lot of money?" I asked.

"We have every sheet of paper-work completed in this folder. All we have is listed, along with everyone's signatures you need." I was irritated.

"That doesn't matter," he said to me.

"I'm afraid it does to me, sir." I said sharply.

"Okay, you two: Open up the rear gates of your truck."

"We will do nothing of the sort," I said.

"Well, somebody has to do it." The lead officer barks.

"And it's not going to be us. That's not going to happen."

The Border Agent went into the office and looked through a three-inch binder, I guessed was their rules, regulations, policies, procedures and protocols. One half an hour later, he came out and said, "OK boys. Give me your keys."

I said matter-of-factly, "Just remember, men, that anything missing, broken, moved or mishandled is on you. And make no mistake. We *will* press charges."

"We'll do it overnight. Have fun looking for a place to stay tonight." Agent Asshole laughs.

"Can I use your phone?" I asked.

"Nope. Sorry. We can't do that."

"Fine, ass-hat, another charge noted on my list. So, fuck you."

Sonny said, grabbing my arm, "Jimmy, let's just go somewhere to eat and sleep."

Sonny and I walked until we found a phone booth.

"Sonny," I began. "Bed and Breakfasts are huge in Canada. I'm going to find us one."

It took a while, but we found one a few blocks away. The middle-aged woman welcomed us in and asked if we were hungry. We both had other things on our minds.

"We were hoping to find a night spot where we could snack and enjoy a few adult cocktails. Might you know of any, close by?" I asked.

We walked for twenty minutes to a place that was hidden in the woods. In fact, the name of the place was "A Joint in the Woods."

Burgers, fries and Ale. The answer to our prayers. We noticed a breakaway room with a hookah on each table. We wandered in, and it hit us right away. They were smoking hash and opium in there. Sonny and I grabbed a seat.

♪

It took all of three minutes to sign our way through the border.

"Jimmy, look." Sonny said. "They didn't even open the gates. The trip-string we hooked up before leaving yesterday isn't even broken."

"Couple of pricks, eh Son?"

"Let's go. We are Limestone bound."

CHAPTER 12

Limestone is a small town in Aroostook County. The population was around 2,314.

The town is best known for being the home of the Limestone Commerce Centre, formerly an Air Force Base; also lying on its former territory is the Aroostook National Wildlife Refuge Center.

The population center of the town is in Limestone in the east-central part of the town. Limestone was incorporated as a town on March 17, 1869 and was named for regional Limestone deposits. Much of it coming over from Ireland.

General Mark Grafton is known as one of the founders of the town of Limestone. Grafton was born July 4, 1785, in York County, Maine. He was educated in public schools and became a leading citizen in Bangor, prominent in civil and military affairs.

When a young man, he was commissioned captain of cavalry and served in the War of 1812. He was afterward brigadier-general of the state militia. He was a land agent for the eastern and northern sections of Maine before the office was opened in Bangor.

The Vermont based band Phish raised the income every year they came to Limestone for a weekend festival!

The Teneriffe Mountain Band had a two-night show at an old Officer's club-turned-theater in Limestone. All our expenses were paid. They had a bar and grill. We arrived a night early and went to bed.

Friday early afternoon I saw a guy at a table re-stringing his acoustic guitar. He looked extremely familiar. I was there setting-up my drums, taking my time. But I couldn't stop looking at him.

"Hey, pardon me, man, but are you John Prine?" I asked.

"Yeah brother. Yes, I am." We shook hands.

"So, I guess we share the stage tonight, or this weekend?"

"That would be correct, Jimmy. But you have the power of the veto, if you so wish to use it." He smiles wide.

"Oh man, this is too cool. We're on a circuit that brought us around the Maritimes – including the Magdeleine Islands, and then back through New England."

"What brings you way the heck up here?" I asked.

"Just taking a short break. I just finished a new record. I'll be touring behind it in six weeks."

"So, you're winding-down – up - in Northern New England?" I chuckle.

"I happen to have a cabin in the woods not far from Limestone. I built it years ago, after my first record came out. Management here lets me come in and play whenever I want. Pretty decent, right?"

"Oh yeah - Cool for sure."

"Maybe we can do an afternoon out there one day or have an After-Party out there one night."

"We'll get something together. Let me leave you to your work, for now, while I finish-up my kit." I would eventually introduce him to the rest of the band, as they each shuffled in.

A dozen relatives from my mom's side of

the family in Eagle Lake took that long ride down to see me on Saturday. They occasionally drive all the way to Bangor, just too go to the mall, so this is nothing to worry about. Nearly all the cousin-kin show, but the older folks chose to stay home. I never expected the aunts and uncles; or any of the older crowd to travel so far.

I paid a lot of attention to my people, especially Linda. I've loved her since we were kids. We took some time to watch John, after all he was half the show. He was like a pioneering hero in my eyes.

Trisha had no idea who he was. She was a Dan Fogelberg fanatic. No one else mattered. My cousins had no idea whatsoever who the star was. They didn't care. They were there to see me.

We decided to trade sets: John, then us, back and forth all evening. This bill worked-out very well. Each of us took three sets, had long breaks and free bar food and drinks. I was able to extend those perks out to my family, too.

♪

Next, came leg two through the Maritime circuit, and so we did the whole trip all over again. Afterward, we went south for a start at Luneau's for a two-week engagement. We played The Sand Dollar in York, right on the beach for one, and we played Lad's, in Rye, NH for another. Not a bad time to be had. Those were our favorite venues to play that were local to us. Finally, before heading back North, we took our four planned weeks off.

We each accepted the invitation to add a few new songs to our repertoire during our time-off. I picked a Jackson Browne song, a

Stones song, two Allman Brothers songs, a Dead song and a Grinderswitch tune. Our current circuit, with some exception, expected cover tunes. We didn't mind, and we tried to be selective in picking out our cover songs. It was fun and we were very happy of what we'd agree to play. We would not play a bad song.

The band spent the second two-weeks learning our new songs. We walked-through them for a few evenings at Mac and Trisha's place. We then went full throttle up at Sonny's mountain top. All told, we came up with eighteen new ones all bright and shiny: That's near a full night's worth of work in some venues, especially on top of our already crowded repertoire. It was a good thing.

A lot of bands like to put their own stamp on covers they do, and that's alright if their arrangements are as good as, or better than the original. Otherwise, give it proper treatment with due respect to the original artist. I am a firm believer in that and believe every musician should be. And I would hope that most probably would anyway. Exceptions might be a progressive jazz arrangement. Jeff Beck is great with that: Fusion.

Of course, we must be directly honest with ourselves and each other when it comes to making a call on an augmented approach or arrangement. Sometimes, all we need do is stick to or with the original melody line to open a door or two to instrumental performance.

We played The Allman brothers' "Jessica" and Grinderswitch's "How the West was won." Those are two long songs with beautifully played guitar work: That put a lot of pressure on Sonny, not so much as the rest of us, but both songs took a lot of practice and

On Me // On Music

listening from all of us to play them right and proper.

Upon re-grouping, I put forth an amendment to our Charter: No More Uniforms. We dress in Rock and Roll moderate, if you will, but no more matching outfits. Our two leaders fiercely objected, declaring it would hurt our image.

I said that that was the point - to change our image. They can go all-out with Buck Owens outfitting, but the band need merely to dress with a little bit of Southern style. We can dress down and still look cool, look good. Everyone was taken by surprise by my strong suggestion, but in the end, they all agreed with me. Except Mac and Trisha. And so, it was done by a majority vote.

Bah Bah Bah BING!

I always make it to the top of the heap, given my experience and talent, and can be very persuasive when need be. It's not about age, in music, it's about mileage, so to speak. So, while typically one of the, or the youngest in a group, I always end-up the intra-band manager.

Teneriffe Mountain was a very good band, and had no trouble keeping busy. We wanted to break our own stuff into the scene, but in those days that proved difficult to do, and make money, and keep the money coming in while pushing through the exercise.

We had talked about it at length, and everyone was excited to try to break-in. That seemed to breathe new hope and happiness with us all. We could continue to work the smaller halls close by that wanted covers while, in practice, we build-out our own show, with our songs.

It was known that the least dedicated to the band was Mike. It's too bad because he had a lot of openings to shine, both playing and singing. He always had fun. He loved performing with the group. When we returned home after the Maritime gigs, and following the finish-up engagements, and song rehearsals, Michael dropped the smoke blast.

He said, "I'm leaving the group.

"Guys," he continued. "I'm so sorry, but my father is putting pressure on me."

"Oh, shit." I said.

"He says he's going to pull the plug on my college funds if I don't return to school next semester."

"Pick what you really want out of life right now, and possibilities in the future, and make the call, man. Maybe you can negotiate with your dad," I said.

"I've already done that, Jimmy. I have to go back to school."

"Well, at what point do we start cancelling gigs, Mike?" Mac asked.

"I'm leaving tonight." Easy as that for Michael.

"No notice? That's real good Mike. Thanks." Mac said.

"Yeah, Mike. For real." I said, with Sonny nodding his head.

"I hate long good-byes. Sorry, Jimmy. And you guys."

"Let's go to the living room and talk while Mike gets his shit out of here." I said.

"Well, guys, now what?" Mac asked the group.

"Replacement, which may include some sort of reformation." I said. "First of all, is there anyone else contemplating an exit? Seriously, now.

"Speak it now or never speak again." I scoffed.

"Well, we weren't sure when it might be teed off," Trisha speaks. "But Mac and I are thinking of going back to work at GE."

"Oh, is that right?" I deadpanned.

"Sonny?" I ask.

"I'm in as long as we can keep it or get it together. It sure doesn't look like we are, at this point, though."

John says, "I'm with you Jimmy."

"Sorry Sonny. I'm out." I said.

"Listen Jimmy, John," Sonny said. "'Stray Cats' are about to break-up, so there is a big chance we could all come together to make them a whole band again – all of us included."

"OK, so Mac and Trish, you're out. The rest of us three are going to test the waters on this 'Stray Cats' thing. I thought they were solid, but, uh, what do I know." I said.

"Let me go to the kitchen and make a phone call or two right now. Why wait? I'm going to call them." Sonny says.

"Well, folks, as it stands right now, all they need immediately is a drummer. Apparently, theirs is kind of a sloppy lush, and the Cats are not happy. They may have a need for keys next, maybe another guitar later, but they're not sure yet. They *are* sure they need a drummer."

"Hey Jimmy, you've got a gig, man -- Yay you!" John said, laughing.

"Right. We'll see.

"By the way," I said. "Our demo is drowning and unimpressive to the labels I've shopped.

"They all said the same thing:

"The world doesn't need another 'White Mountain National Blend.'"

The "Blend" was a New England-based one hit wonder, signed to a two-year contract. They came and went like a thief in the night. But "The Blend" became unblended.

"So, we've already been tagged. Sorry guys."

♪

Stray Cats called me up for initial talks. I was to meet at Thom's apartment in Portsmouth. It was great to see them all together off-stage. I knew all of them from over two years ago. Everyone grabs a beer and a seat in the spacious living room.

The bass player, Thom, said, "You've seen us play, probably more than once, haven't you, Jimmy?"

"Yeah," I said. "I've watched you several times. You're good and tight, on key and have a rich set-list."

I had to ask. "So, what is your policy on sobriety? I heard it was an issue with your drummer. What would it look like on a band Charter or contract?"

They said that they prohibit anyone from the stage who is not sober but allow a drink between sets: That's one beer, or whatever. No doping before or during a show.

They try to maintain a fair set of rules over each other. Like me, they are purists. Only those contributing to the music making can set foot on stage. No one else. No extras.

They are an AOR (Album Oriented Rock) cover band and are damn good. They strive, though, to work their way up to an original classically infused modern Rock group. Perhaps fusion. I was interested and wondered what was next at this gathering. They have plans to shop some demos they recorded. They gave me one.

Thom said, "We're going to do a compatibility test." Everybody cracks-up.

"Oh, like my girlfriend insisted we did?" I joked back. "And then comes 'chemistry'?

I had to be intimately familiar with a wide array of artists and songs. It started somewhere around, "Do you like The Beatles?" and "Do you like The Stones? How about "The Kinks," "Led Zeppelin," "Dylan?" And, they worked through every great Rock band and Artists right up to all, out by 1975.

Then they began playing songs on record albums through the stereo. After each one, someone would ask, "Do you like that song?" Or, "What do you think about that song?"

This went on late through the night. My finale was to name my favorite artists, and their songs.

"Come on, guys, I have a million of 'em. If they are on your list, they'll certainly be on mine. I'm sure. And I bet I've got some stuff you guys have never even heard of. Do you like 'Grinderswitch'?"

It appeared we were compatible, and we shared that energy, chemistry and sense of brotherhood, necessary to keep a band together. I had a few questions, but not many just yet. Who writes the set-lists? Who is the inside-band manager? Who handles the money? Who books them? Do they have representative management and legal resources? Are they incorporated?

We all want to do a live audition, and they gave me a list of a dozen songs to learn and be ready to play in two weeks.

I told them that as soon as Teneriffe came unglued, I had signed myself out as a sit-in for a couple groups in the area. So, there could be a couple potential hiccups along our way - me and the Cats.

CHAPTER 13

Through my personal agent, I was immediately paired-up with a guitarist from Dover, named Francis Kirk. I was able to bring John in with me. Adam was a guitarist extraordinaire and an excellent vocalist. He was being looked-at. Bean Town Bobby did not make the cut. Someday, he'll learn that he cannot play blaring loud and expect a good review, unless he's playing "Red Rocks."

We were able to bring-in Adam, one of James Taylor's sidemen guitarists, whenever JT wasn't touring. He lived in Dover, too, right up the street from Francis. He was as good as you could get. A virtuoso. But, like James, our guy Adam also had a bad smack habit. He never missed a show and was superbly talented on guitar and singing harmonies. But he did make us nervous carrying around that luggage.

We were an R&B band, without the horns. Rock we played was Fusion, like Tommy Bolin, Jeff Beck, Billy Cobham, and Blues, playing progressive arrangements from Johnny Winter, Eric Clapton, John Mayall, and others. Best of all, we were finally called-upon to play our original songs, which we had all been writing together to add to the sets Francis already had.

We played three nights a week with good pay. We all shared two assistants, who also served as an audio-tech and lighting guy. We were a light load, but we could fill and reach a room of up to three-hundred people using the band's own production.

I discovered in dream-mining a deep desire to relocate south. Some of my favorite musicians were born of the South, and I heard from the owner of "Daddy's Junky Music Store," in Portsmouth, that the young players down there were the best in the country. I had that on my mind, and it wouldn't let go.

The Allman Brothers;

The Marshall Tucker Band;

Lynyrd Skynyrd;

The Outlaws;

Elvin Bishop;

The Charlie Daniels Band;

Jimmy Hall.

Of course, there were many more from all

over the country, let alone the South. And I couldn't keep my mind off them.

So, I had Teneriffe, but now they're gone.

The Cats are on indefinite hold.

Francis Kirk is loosely active.

But the dream of shaking hands with Gregg Allman, Henry Paul and Ronnie Van Zant grew more real every day.

♪

Francis had a one-nighter at The Sheraton, in Portsmouth. We had an opener of young kids, doing young kids' music. They played from 7:00 PM until 8:00 PM. The Sheraton flushed the club of the kids and opened the front doors to the adults at 8:30 PM. No one was paying the kid-band any attention, anyways. So, I felt kind hurt for them, for that.

Francis said to me, "Isn't that a shame, Jimmy?" I said, "Yes Francis, but they're taking a lesson into playing the blues on this very night. We've all suffered through it before, on the way up."

And the band plays on.

We had one long seventy-five-minute set to play. We studied our set-list. We had a rotation of four or five sets we were expert with. This one started with "Join Together" and ended with "The End."

We were playing "Low Rider" and we had the audience in hand. Suddenly, near the end of the song, Francis turned away from his microphone, walked up to Adam and gentlemanly nodded, like he would tip a hat for a lady, or a Royal in the medieval times, or from a butler to his master. He came to me, in front of my drums and did the same thing, then blew me a kiss. Finally, he turned to John, smiled and said, "Bye Everyone."

Francis began to shake horribly and began yelling randomly. He held his guitar in front of his face, tipped upside down as though he was adjusting his pick-ups using his teeth. He had letter-taped the words, "I'm done - Fuck it all" on the back of the guitar so all on-lookers could read it when he flashed it.

He roughly unsnapped the body from the strap, swung the strap like a rodeo lasso, and then held out the guitar, straight-armed, guitar-face down, slammed it down across a raised knee and onto the stage deck. The neck broke from the body and then he threw it all, with all his might, to the stage. Some people thought it was part of the show.

He looked down at the gorgeous black and gold Gibson Les Paul Deluxe, and then looked up and around at us, crying. Those in attendance had no idea what just happened. Francis turned slowly and walked off, stage-left, head down; the nearest to a club artists' exit. He left it all there and followed the pathway out the back door loading dock.

The rest of us had no idea what was going on, but we played the song to the end. I had a brief meeting with the club owner, and we agreed to us playing just another 30 or 45-minutes.

And, the headline read, "Francis Kirk Melts Down at The Sheraton!"

He would resurface eighteen months later a Pastor -- Father Francis, at The Dover Friends Chapel and The Dover Christian Science Reading Room. I was long gone by then.

THIRD SET

You know I was Born to Travel

Can't be Sorry I'm Not Home

Rand McNally wrote my Bible

Willie Nelson Sings my Song

-- J.A. Landry

14

Biloxi on the Gulf

Earlier that year, Susie's family, save older brother Bear, returned to Mississippi. Biloxi, they said it was, on the Gulf of Mexico. I had been entertaining the thought of packing it up and heading south, because many of my musical heroes hailed from the south. I was thinking "Jacksonville." But I still wasn't exactly sure.

It was commonly known on the circuit that the young musicians down there were not only exceptionally versed in roots music, they are quality players. The music scene in its entirety thrived with young and elders alike, delving into the fusion mixing Rock and Roll with country, blues and jazz.

So, it was more than just a convenience for me, when on this night I took Susie up on her and her parents' proposition – a ride down for her and a temporary place to stay for me.

Taking up the invitation, I felt comfortable with the idea of staying with her and her family in Mississippi until I found a gig. I felt confident that all I really had to worry about was fitting her into the car with me and my drums. As we fell off to sleep that pivotal evening, after sealing an agreement with a drink, a toke and some fine autumnal love, we were already making up personal itineraries, agendas to follow up on the next day, rethinking the plans we together made the previous evening.

♪

Having been a traveling musician for years, trying my way with every jazz, blues, and Rock band in the area, it was time for a formative move. I bent my step throughout the New England and Canadian Maritime circuits, and even though I was a Yankee boy by birth, I carried the attitude and disposition stereotypically reserved for a long-haired country boy, mixed with some mellow hippy. Influenced in might by some of the greatest musicians of the time, I even sometimes felt like a lonely, displaced and hybrid form of southern Rocker.

Get rid of the 'southern' sobriquet. Even born and bred musicians raised there despise the label 'southern Rock' to their music.

True.

I remember seeing tee-shirts sold at the beach that read "Damn Yankees and Sand Spurs."

I couldn't wait to get down there and show those boys what a real sand spur in the rear-end felt like, and how high this snow bird can fly.

Less than one week later, with everything that ever really mattered to me, everything needed; my drums, stereo, records, some books and a couple of bags of clothes, there I was, tooling down Route 95 South.

Oh, yes, and of course my passenger, too.

So much time driving in a car was like we were in a high-speed mobile confessional. Unzipped our bags, and let the history fly.

No more secrets to share by the time we got there.

We stopped over in DC. Then, from our rest in Georgia visiting one of Susie's sisters, we drove into Biloxi Beach the next day. I just had to get out of the car, take off my shoes and walk on that amazing beach.

The sand was so fine and white that it looked like sugar and squeaked with each step. The water shown in perfect aqua green-blue. The Gulf water was so nice and warm. I'd not seen or felt any beach like this since my visit to St. John, USVI.

After settling-in, I napped, but the next day I went around town putting 8x10 posts that had some history, some looks ahead and my experience as a drummer and a manager – *and* I needed and wanted a professional Rock band with plans to tour and do session work.

They went up everywhere a travelling musician might go, such as laundromats, clothes stores, music stores and record shops.

In the meantime, I was right-away picked-up by a jazz band who had immediate and steady local work. I played every night, taking some lead and harmony vocals and the drums. These guys were not the answer to my dreams, but it kept me busy and my chops tight.

CHAPTER 14

The Foolstars

Sure enough, I received a call from a guitarist named Scott. He saw my ad at the Double Bubble Wash & Dry. He told me they were losing their drummer – and soon. He invited me to see their show that very night – Monday – opening night: I'd be on the Guest List. I told him I'm looking forward to seeing them.

I arrived at 8:45 PM, just 15 minutes to their first set. I took a seat right next to the audio tech. Caught up in the initial excitement, I really didn't have the wherewithal to be constructively critical in any way. I just wanted to listen and watch, catch the vibe, nothing more. Just hearing original tunes, especially in any non-showcase venue in those days was refreshing, rare, and bold when the group let them fly nonetheless. They wrapped up the set and the guitarist walked over to me. He introduced himself to me as Scott and I said I was Jimmy.

Scott and I spent two band break times talking together. Right from the start we got along surprisingly well. I was used to considering the temperament of most guitarists I'd met, Scott was not boisterous. But I am different, and so was he. He had a professional air - a bright aura and was easy to talk with.

We were both serious musicians and playful humans. We clicked. Scott had, as I, been a professional, traveling musician from a very early age. He had been traveling throughout the Deep South since his early teenage years fronting the commercial band "Missionary Ridge," and he was considered by many in the business to be somewhat of a prodigy: The definite star of the show.

Scott was heavily influenced by The Beatles, as well as other British Rock acts, and by traditional blues. He loved Springsteen and other American Rockers, like Bob Seger. The complimentary outpouring was a unique songwriting skill and presence that smacked not only of fresh Rock hooks and productive sound, but also of traditional progressions and thoughtful, meaningful and very clever lyrics. No overuse of cheap bad lyrics, such as yeah, yeah, baby, baby and love: The three words most ever tossed into a melody line. It was sometimes sickening. Just take a rest replacing the nonsense words and lyrics.

Scott's extraordinary guitar playing was easily apparent within moments of the first set, and Scott, also being the lead vocalist, impressed me to no end with his ability to maintain an extremely noteworthy style amidst what was extremely complicated guitar playing.

He had a fluent voice with a dynamic range. He had mastered his vibrato technique already, something many Rock vocalists never bother with. Scott was also clearly the leader of the band. An audition was scheduled for the following afternoon. It would be held there at the club. I promised I'd be there by 2:00 PM.

When I showed up at the hall the next day, the band's truck and trailer were backed up to the loading dock. When I walked in, I saw that all but the essential stage gear needed for the audition had been loaded out.

"What the fuck happened here?" I had to ask.

"Fired." Replied Scott.

"You are shittin' me." I was shocked, because frankly, they were one of the best acts I'd seen outside of concert halls or theaters in a long time.

"For what?"

"Didn't play enough Top 40," Scott said matter-of-factly.

So, I think, they had been fired over their repertoire. Could this be true? This, thereby being an answer to my prayers - that is - a band of musicians that refused to sell-out? I showed them a tattoo I have on my right shoulder. The banner across the top of the tattoo on my right arm. It's a picture of the American Flag and a Confederate Jack, both hanging on Civil War swords, crossed in union, with the words "Rock and Roll Forever" written in a banner across the bottom, and the words "Disco Sure as Hell Sucks" written in a banner across the top.

Any group can play any one of the popular songs of the day, and get plenty of work, but not every band would justify the affordability of just flat out refusing to do so, despite the money. I loved it and had to say so.

Neither Scott nor I were in it for the weekends. We wanted to do our own stuff and would do only covers selectively chosen by the group, not entirely by the resident radio-heads and disco-dudes. His band of mates apparently felt as strongly about that as did he and I.

The live audition went well. It's kind of like a 'Technical Interview.' The band and I rallied through a good number of tunes, some I knew well, some I had never played before, and probably at least one or two that I never even heard of. I even played through two of their originals.

Surprise!

The coolest realization came at the start because right away their bass player and I locked together and kept a good groove going. That groove never let up. Dee, the bassist, was very good at listening and following leads, as am I. We remained locked in the pocket. He was also animated while on stage. And, he sang, and could hit the high notes. It had always begged the question why is it that bass instrumentalists usually handle the high vocal note – soprano – even using falsetto, albeit a strong one?

The band pushed each other hard and well, playing off each other, considering they had never played with me. Moreover, we didn't *musically* know each other whatsoever. I had a great ear and I'm keen on playing off others. They liked that. I garnered this fun in feedback from not knowing someone to play along so well.

Oh yes, I did have to do the token drum solo. Everyone wanted a fucking drum solo in those days. I, of course, had a few and had one handy by just for the occasion, and I laid it on them smartly and properly, without word, question or hesitation. They liked that, too.

I never was a whiner.

After the audition they left me sitting up there on the riser while they went off to a table in the corner of the adjacent dining room to huddle up. Fifteen minutes go by before they return.

"We have an agreement." Gene said. "We don't bring girls on the road. That's a band rule. No girls. They are a distraction. Hometown gigs are okay, or the occasional visit anywhere were playing, but not on the road. Can you agree to that, Jimmy?"

"I couldn't care less, Mr. Gene."

Scott offered me the drum seat.

Okay, so Scott was the front end manger and his older brother Gene was the back-office manager.

"Do you want to take time to think about it? Well, we don't have a lot of time." He laughed.

And I thanked him and said I'd take it.

It sure is nice to be loved.

I officially joined the outfit known as The Foolstars on Tuesday, Election Day, 1976, one day after their being fired and the same day I auditioned. I was on my way to Panama

City, Florida, traveling with the band in a small caravan of vehicles. I left my car in D'Iborville for Susie to use while I was away. That's one town northwest of Biloxi. I said I'd be back within two months.

I learned from the very first day -- one of the rules of the road: never go anywhere without a couple coolers full of ice cold beer. Alcohol is not available in Mississippi on Election Day, which threw a spanner, threw it in the hole; we righted the situation as soon as we crossed the border into Alabama. I am never without weed, so between the spirits and smoke, the inquisitiveness pours from the group. Plans made over a warm buzz; the trip was fun, felt shorter than it was, and was conversationally conducive and productive.

David, the audio tech asked if he could see one of my drums. He wanted to see the symmetry, color, rims and so on. I pulled a rack tom out of its hard-shell case and his jaw dropped.

"Holy shit. What is it?" David asked.

"It is a satin 3-D finish. Put your finger on the shell like you want to poke it through. Go ahead."

"Jeez, Jimmy, that is amazing! It looked exactly like my finger was penetrating the shell. Wow."

"You should see them under the lights." More excitement. "They are made by Camco, from Oaklawn, Illinois. Since the original company was bought-out a couple years ago, Camco from Oaklawn are now considered collectors' items."

We pulled into Lynn Haven, a small town over from Panama City, in the middle of the evening, and Dee's parents were not around.

I would bounce between staying with Dee and with Scott, until they found a more opportune place for me to live whenever we came home from the road. The lusty trip over interstate 10 and Route 98 sends everyone to bed rather early, which was just as well, because the band planned to start rehearsals early the very next day. They had a band house that had just gone off lease, so, that was where I would end-up staying whenever back home to Lynn Haven.

Dee whispered. "Sleep well this first night into your new existence."

"Yes. Okay." I responded in his ear. I was on the couch in an alcove just off the kitchen, snuggled with a couple pillows, blankets and ready to go to sleep.

I woke up the next morning - felt early - with Dee's mother and father crouched down, staring into my face. I opened my eyes, to see their noses just inches from mine. They were studying me as though I were a frog from a high school biology and science class. In a way, I certainly was, with all that hair I had – top to waist. It took a moment for my eyes to comprehend, and brain to kick-in, but I was able to focus enough after a short moment to say to them a simple, "Hello?"

"Do you know the difference between a Yankee and a Damn Yankee?" Nell, Dee's mom asks loud and clear.

"Uh… no."

"The Damn Yankee never goes back!" She cackles with laughter, as Benny, her husband smiles wryly. It's was not as though they heard the joke told by someone else, on The Tonight Show, or something. It was Nell's. Just the sound of her voice as she answered, in her deep southern accent, was enough to cause me to laugh. She is a parody of herself, but she was real. The funny scene had me laughing too.

Big smiles.

I liked them both right from the start. I would learn that the band and crew families backed their boys 110%. Very cool.

Three days of rehearsals supported my first gig with the band. We practiced in Dee's house from around ten until six. Dee's daddy was remodeling the large living area, which made a great practice area - there were no walls, yet, which offered more space. There were only studs on two outside perimeters. Both Dee's parents worked during the day, so the band had several hours to work with on Wednesday, Thursday and Friday. I learned forty-two songs, out from their full 200 song repertoire. My first gig with them was Saturday at The Beach Shack, and we must be prepared.

The Beach Shack is on the west-end middle beach road in Panama City Beach. With a full bar and game room, it's atypical with a lofty, open barn-like atmosphere. It attracts the locals, so crowds are a given whether managers Fred and Mitch offered entertainment, or not. The huge open room, with a bar and seating on one side and a poolroom on the other, offered no space for a stage, but our gear fit nicely at the end of the long wall, seating side, facing diagonally outward.

The Foolstars worked as hard as I did over the past three days, rehearsing song after song, and they professionally and easily survived that first night. I wrote the drum parts on drum staffs with tabs and legend-notes, which they'd never seen before. So, yes, I had learned forty-two songs in three days, out of two hundred they had in total. They will come. I learned them well.

The Foolstars hit the road again and hit it hard. We were due in Albany, Georgia the coming week, and I never looked back from there. Talking one afternoon, we all agreed that rich, or not, we shall afford a look back on life someday that will never deliver regret. For it was verily becoming a whole different life for us.

Right away, we felt the group had what it took to make it in the business, not to mention a habit of self-sustenance. I felt that way, too. We came to own a fleet of cars, vans, a band new RV and a big moving truck for our gear.

Scott asked me how I felt about the group now that we'd done a few more shows.

"Are you sure you want to hear that, so soon?"

♪

To review, musicians hear more than just the beat and lyric listening to music. We eventually assess, dissect and analyze every note, nuance, rest, mistake, miscue and reparative noise. We can't help it. We inevitably, if not subconsciously, hear music as we played it, or heard it. It's like Dr. Spencer Reid reading a book.

It's in the blood. We are sensitive to it, and about it. Our temperament reflects it, and vice-versa. Nonetheless, we are reflective and thoughtful enough to recognize superlative moments in music, holding them irreplaceably close, constitution and validation.

Regardless of direction, earning praise ultimately involves measuring audience sophistication and expectation. Recording lends itself to either approach, because those elusive productive masterpieces sometimes happen with no premeditation.

The magic written must still transfer from mind, then paper, to machine, and during that intervention, without warning, Semper Paratus mates, and the capture is paramount. That is your job.

There are thousands of all-time great moments in Rock music. There are published lists, anthologies and almanacs that describe everything from a big bang birth in Memphis, in Swamp Duck, to undeniably defining moments throughout time: events, life stories and mortality. Generations of celebration, atonement and narrative have been mightily served and magnetically preserved by artists lucky enough to capture their own.

Recording thoughts and details and the truth by the music using any mechanism, be it shutter, tape, or pencil in hand is key. To step through the door, one must turn-on or be turned on, because the machine, with tape rolling, keeps the momentary experience from slipping away. The Foolstars carried a Teac 4 Track reel to reel recorder and set it up on the Audio Tech's works station. We recorded everything we did.

Brilliant!

Musical flashes run just like the nighttime ideas you neglect to jot down. The argument is that pretentiousness as such compromises the academic aspect of the art and overcomplicates creation. The answer, flawlessly ringing as true as a perfect algorithm, is to try to habitually record everything played. Stated simply, if you record it, you've got it: No question… or it's gone; likely forever.

Now, how am I going to fit all that into a critique on each band member? Having been a traveling musician for years, trying my way with every jazz, blues, fusion and Rock band in the area, it was time for a formative move. I felt like a lonely, displaced and hybrid form of Southern Rocker and a Fusion band man. Remember:

Get rid of the sobriquet. Even born and bred musicians raised there despise the label 'Southern Rocker.'

True.

I remember seeing souvenir tee-shirts sold at the beach that read 'Damn Yankees and Sand Spurs.' All in fun.

CHAPTER 15

Chuck Damberk

The local record store manager held a great interest in the band. Sound familiar? Yeah, it does. He was not particularly a man brimming with energy. He asked us to come to his house for a meeting. We attended only to find out he'd like a shot at managing the band.

No doubt, we needed management, but did we need him? We wouldn't know until we gave him a try, so, we did. I explained our expectations, such as uninterrupted booking the group in showcase venues, around studio session dates, and, general business management, promotion and legal issues.

He asked what we thought of recording sessions. I said, "It's a given, as I just mentioned." And I added, "You have to ask?"

"Well."

"I can give you the short-term expectations." I said. "We foresee recording an album, whether it is a few tracks at a time, or one long session to finish the record in the course of two months or less. We would retain Co-Producer roles and will perform our own compositions.

"Do you have what it will take to gel all that together - in a neat and polished way? With a professional air?

"I understand that you may need assistance for one thing or another but know this:

Anyone you have to call in to help you that wants upfront payments comes out of your purse, not ours. Of course, there may come exceptions to that arrangement. We shall see how things go onward from here. For now, let's just see if you can keep us booked. What do you think?"

I think I just blew Chuck away, and the group was staring at me, too, jaws dropped.

Chuck cleared his throat and said, "Let's start with booking. What is my start date?"

"First, understand your cut is twelve percent, probationary. If you fly with the group satisfactorily, you will earn 18%. We'll see. Fair?"

"Fair for now, Jimmy."

"Okay, get us out there within four weeks."

"You have work now?" Chuck asks.

"I'm handling things right now for the group. But I am building a little flexibility in the works now. That said, your communication with me is paramount. Got that, sir?"

"I'm into it. Shake on it, guys?"

We shook hands on it.

"I am trusting we don't need a formal contract right away. Let's see how the probationary run goes."

"Okay Jimmy, that's fine. And thank you."

♪

We set out on the road to hit the places I had already booked. I told the other band members that I didn't trust Chuck and foresaw letting him go at some point soon.

"How about you guys? Any initial thoughts?"

One by one the group speaks up. Each of

them has at least one entity or element in Chuck that turned them off.

"He wanted to talk more about his music than about ours." Scott said.

"I noted that too," I said. "He doesn't look you in the eyes while you're speaking to him but glares directly into yours when he is speaking to you. And, he laughs far too much. Those are dead ringers for identifying a liar."

Scott says, "Let's just see if he can at least book us."

"Good idea, Scott." I tell them all. "But prepare a cross-stich pattern on our calendar. Mark my words."

I had us booked for one month, with an option at the end of the string. We played "Dusty's," in Gadsden, Alabama, then traveled east to Albany, Georgia. Then north to Atlanta,

Georgia for two dates. One in Underground Atlanta, the other in C.W. Shaw's. We went from there southeast to Dothan, Alabama.

We followed Lynyrd Skynyrd in C.W. Shaw's, where they had high-jacked the club while they held rehearsals for an upcoming tour. I was thrilled meeting them. Bob Burns was cooked my ear off. He really liked us and asked if we covered any Skynyrd tunes.

"Hell yeah, Bob. Of course we do!"

He asks, "Jimmy, would you see if your band will let me sit-in on a set of Skynyrd stuff?"

"Yeah, I can do that."

He went on next set, the last for the evening, and the band had Bob on stage for six or eight Skynyrd songs, closing with "Freebird." That boy had a smile on his face from start to finish.

I spoke with each venue's management about possibly speaking to an agent named Chuck Damberk, in my absence. I stressed to them that it was a chance, perhaps temporary, but not certain. They understood that we were shopping for a touring agent to take the tedious task out of our hands, so we could concentrate on the music.

It was not a sure thing, but just a possibility. I intended to set out to put us on a sensible circuit; a kind of loop starting at home, then up and west, to north, to east, to south east, then back home. Not unlike the leg we just completed. All the venues were interested in return dates. We played every beach town and other towns, such as Orlando and Tampa repeatedly. What fun! My circuit served the band well.

The group was happy with my work. What a weight off my shoulders. Come month-end, when we returned home, I had a meeting with Chuck. I shared the venues and their respective management contact. I asked him what he set-up next for us.

He took a turn south to start with. We traveled from Panama City Beach to Orlando, Florida, then to Daytona Beach. From there, oddly enough, he put us back up north. We drove all the way to Wise, West Virginia, then all the way back down to St. Pete, Florida, then back northbound to Raleigh, North Carolina.

We were already becoming frustrated at his approach. How could I work out a smart road trip, itinerary and he not? We made it clear to him that we did not want to be run crazily up and down and east to west all over the place. His fabric was plaid!

"Chuck," I said. "You do realize that you just ran the hell out the group. What did you use for tour maps, work out sensible sequential steps and contacts?"

Chuck stuttered and cleared his throat. There was an uncomfortable silence.

"Well?"

"I've been partnering up with other agencies, two men, from Atlanta, one from Orlando, and another from Birmingham."

"So, you're sub-contracting."

"Um, yes Jimmy, I have to."

"I would only hope that won't happen again."

"Well, after another leg, I have a surprise."

"Okay. Second leg: Go." I said.

"We begin in Tampa and stay in the Gulf Coast beach area for three stops; St. Pete, Clearwater and inward to Bradenton, Sarasota and finally finish in Orlando."

I didn't need an atlas to see already an improvement over his first try. I asked him, "Did you hire the fellows from Atlanta?"

"Yes, I did."

"I'll table that just for now. Tell me about the surprise."

"I know you have a long list of songs – your own songs – and that you'd like to do some session work regularly as part of 'The Foolstars project.'"

"So, yes, what do you have?"

"There is a small, rather unknown studio just north on Route 201, called 'Candle Light Studio.' I took the liberty to go ahead and book a two-day session there."

"That's good, Chuck, really good."

"Which of your songs would you like to produce and press?" Chuck asked.

"We'll do 'Lay Down Your Love' for Side 1 or A, and do the song 'Dying' for Side 2 or B." Scott replied.

"When can we get in?" I asked.

"That is essentially up to you. We have time now – five or six days to choose from. Bring this to the group and get back to me – the sooner, the better."

I said, "I'll do that, Chuck."

We didn't know Chuck that well and were already leery of him after he booked that nonsense tour. There was talk of studio costs and there were other unknowns, we'd have to know, too.

We decided we'd like to go in as soon as we can.

"We're already ready for this." Dee said. "Solid."

"I'm planning 'Lay down' for first song side A and 'Dying,' the closer on side B." Scott announces.

"Agreed, Scott." I said. The rest of the group stared at me, surprisingly.

I told Chuck to get us in as soon as he can. We got a call back from him within a half an hour. He said we'd do our songs, plus one of his, called "Honky Tonkin". That threw us for a loop. There was not any discussion of this between us. He told me that if we wanted a record to release, we would have to record his song, too.

"Surprise, band!" I begin with a loud voice. "He said we could only use the studio if we agree to record one of his songs, too."

"Well, that sneaky little bastard." Scott said. "So, what do y'all want to do? Jimmy, you first."

"I say we just do it for our benefit and suffer through his song. We heard it when we last visited him. It's called 'Honky Tonkin.' Do you remember it?"

"Oh Jesus, yes." Dee sighs. As luck would have it, Dee would sing lead on Chuck's song.

"Well, the bright side is we get what we came for. Period. I'll tell him to leave any and all credentials of ours off his take, except perhaps the band name."

♩

It's studio day one at Candle Light. As we set-up for the session in the playroom, Chuck continued to rush us, telling us to hurry, and let's go, guys.

I simply told him to, "Shut Up. This is how its's done, Chuck, come-on man."

The band looked at me like I was an alien.

I said, "What. We're not just fuckin' around here. This stuff needs to get done before anything can happen in the Control Room."

As we would experience, we were rushed all day long, and the following day, too. I was suspicious of Chuck already, and his behavior toward us in the studio was anti-productive. So, I said to those in the control room, "We will tell *you* when we're ready for sound checks and subsequent takes. The Foolstars will act as Co-produces with the engineer."

We gather in the control room, and I start things off.

"Based on my experience, we'll play live, with everyone except me playing over full band saved as ghost tracks. Once I get a good take, we'll track stack bass guitar, then rhythm guitar, then keyboards, lead guitar, and finish up with vocals and percussion. Each time we play after a good take, we'll record the next subsequent track. By the end of today, we'll have a full take for 'Lay down.'

"We will mix it down and master it to complete today's activities. Let's get comfortable and head into the playroom."

I got a decent drum sound with our engineer. It wasn't the best, but we were under a time constraint.

I told the engineer we were ready to go for the drum tracks. That went down in two takes. Not bad. I was done until Side B, and then percussion and the mix-downs.

It was Dee's turn. He got it in three takes. His bass sounded great, if not a tad mushy.

Gene strummed his way through his guitar part. He got it in one take.

Allen got the rhythm track right away, and we decided to have him do his solo next. That took a while, but we lost no time, because everything was moving nicely along so far.

Scott had two rhythm tracks to do – acoustic guitar and electric. He nailed them first take, each. He also had some fills to do lead guitar to dance with Allen's solo. Those would be placed just beneath the keyboard in the mix.

"I'd say we're ready for vocals, then percussion, and this one is in the bag." I announced. "Is everybody happy with their takes?"

They were, and so the engineer and I sat side by side for the mix-downs and mastering for the song.

♪

Chuck tossed out an insinuation that we worked too slow. That sent me on what could have become a tandem, but I held chill and merely replied, "Chuck, I can plainly tell that you have very little session experience. I will be producing our songs, with the band and the engineer. You just worry about your shit that you conned us into doing for you. Okay? Don't get me wrong. This is good. It really is. So, why don't you act like it is? Simmer down, my man."

That was more an imperative than a request. He remained quiet the rest of the ride home. I guess I hurt his feelings.

"We'll be by to get you at 8:45 tomorrow morning. Good night."

♪

The band was impressed by the way I handled things and kept the pace going. They knew it was good, too. They found my methodology exciting, sensible and fun. That was a good day for The Foolstars.

We had some friends in a band named "Doc Holiday" that we'd bump into on the road occasionally. I asked them, "How is your booking agent and management working out?"

"They go from teetering on the brink of a cliff, to the sporadically waddle-on." Eddie said. He is a co-leader of Doc Holiday.

"Do you mind if we call them?" I asked, out of courtesy, or band etiquette.

"Hell, no. Go ahead and call. They'll love you guys."

We booked and would play "The Attic" in Greenville, North Carolina and invited the agency, "JAM" to the show.

♪

Chuck climbed into the van we were driving. I said, "Good morning, Mr. Chuck. Are you ready for another great day?"

Silence.

"Well, today should go even quicker than yesterday. We're already set-up and sound checked."

We stacked the tracks for "Dying" just like yesterday with "Lay Down."

"How many days did you book in here?" I asked Chuck.

"Just two." Chuck sounded like he had just received a spanking.

"Listen, Chuck. If we get 'Dying' by early afternoon, we'll have plenty of time to get yours done, too. It's an easy one, that song. Okay buddy?"

"Yeah, we'll see." Chuck replied.

Scott told Chuck, "We all listened closely to your tune, and already know what parts we each have to play, and sing. It's a decent country song but an easy song, and I bet we get it done within two hours."

"Then on to mix-downs, and most importantly, producing the master." I added. "We'll get an acetate soon and then, if we're satisfied, we'll press 'em."

"We got this, Chuck. Calm down." Gene said optimistically. He's big but didn't usually speak up.

We were right on the money with "Dying." Chuck's country song was easy and a pretty offering and savings, perhaps, so that afternoon, stretching into evening, he'd have his product. He handled everything else having to do with his record.

♪

Even though you're not supposed to overplay the acetate with too many spins, we had a party that turned huge. Folks just kept playing it, turning it over, and play both sides again. My guess was, as I listened to it repeatedly, that we had a good master. I believe it was to take time out for a phone call.

I called Candle Lite and told them to go ahead and press a thousand of them, and ship them to Dee's house, unless they'd like us to just go by there and pick them up.

I said, "Okay, let us know when and we'll come for them."

Two days later we picked up the records. First stop? The Panama City Beach radio station WPFM. The program director immediately announced it with a little hoopla, that hometown heroes, The Foolstars, have a new record for everyone!

He played both sides the first time, then the phones went wild and he replayed "Lay down your Love" in rotation.

"The phones are flickering and lighting up at the station!" He said excitedly.

The song went to Regional Billboard Charts at number one within two weeks. It knocked off Andy Gibb's "How Deep is Your Love." It stayed at the number one position for three weeks, also staving off Michael Jackson. We held a position for six weeks remaining in the Top Ten, then Top Twenty for months afterward.

We sensed some resentment from Chuck. He was dead silent. We didn't need that. He finally asked us if we would include "Honky Tonkin" in our rotation or sets. We declined, but he reminded us that our success stands on our deal to record his song for him.

"That's hardly the truth, Chuck." I said

"We'll play it when we feel the time is right and audience is ripe for it." Scott said. "How does that sound to you?"

"Okay, that's fair, I guess." Chuck is so downtrodden, but I didn't know why.

Chuck had some booking to do, so I reminded him of that. We had to go out this coming weekend.

"You know, Chuck," I said. "Having this record out should make your job a *lot* easier.

"We're counting on it."

♪

A friend of ours, named Lamar Mitchell bought an old amusement park in Panama City Beach that had been shut down for decades. It was on Middle Beach Road in Panama City Beach. He got rid of the old, rusty rides, but kept the old west town that had all the old store fronts you'd expect to see in an old western movie. There was a bank, a sundries store, jail and the sheriff's office, a blacksmith shop, a telegraph office and best of all, a great big saloon. We called the town Tombstone Territory. But it took up the name simply, Tombstone.

We helped him fix up the old place, refurbished the stage where I imagined the old place featured can-can girls and other old west entertainment. It was an extra-large stage, just perfect for a band to take. There was an open area in front of the stage with tables and chairs behind that space. There were several old barber chairs bolted to the floor between two seating sections that people ran for. The bar was old fashioned and warm.

We made a deal with Lamar to have as a house band when we spent time at home. Our first run at that started the very next week. Our record was on the radio. The crowds, from locals to out-of-towners were permanent fixtures. Replacing and filling the out buildings, or downtown shops and such, now housed leather craftsmen, jewelry makers, woodworkers, a Tee Shirt shop, cast iron artists, and more. There were tethered hot air balloon rides. People could mock arrest there friends and send them to the jail house, Lamar produced mock duals and other Main Street happenings to keep the town busy and popular.

Playing there was one of the most formative things we had ever done. The crowds packed the place, as this was a theater sized concert hall that had a capacity for over three-hundred. The acoustics were spectacular. We practiced there every afternoon and played live Wednesdays through Saturday nights. And the venue, audience and activities, and we, were cookin' with electric heat. So much so for me, that I got a tattoo right there at Tombstone Tattoo that has "Tombstone Territory" featured in a banner across the top. People often undressed to some degree. You can just imagine.

♪

After our maiden voyage into Tombstone, Chuck sent us to Clearwater Beach, then to Raleigh, North Carolina, then back south again to Daytona Beach, which included Bike Week and then Spring Break. Northbound, we land in Atlanta, GA. Finally, we are booked at Atlantic Beach for a three-night stay. Chuck is still booking us all over the map - no rhyme or rhythm. No reasoning. No mercy!

He hadn't even made sure the radio stations at each stop had a copy of our record. If I were him, I'd use that record any way I could to move; Milk it like a dairy cow.

The Foolstars up another notch with airplay. I had to tell Chuck to do that. I also assumed he'd shop it around the big cities, in NY, LA, Nashville, TN and Austin, TX.

But he was not planning to do that, and as much as told us he didn't have the time.

I stood up and looked down going nose to nose. I said, "Chuck, we know you are still having to sub-contract, which we also know comes out of your purse. So, why did you approach us for this job in the first place, anyway?

"We thought that finally, we had someone to help us get there, and you know what I mean. But it's no wonder you are behind sitting at home with forking over half your commission. And we assume your wife doesn't want you flying around the country for your silly Rock and Roll band. Ever think about just calling it a day?"

Scott adds, "Besides all that, you are

into Country Music. Not that there's anything wrong with that, but it's obvious you do not know the Rock and Roll sounds, labels, business, standards or players, like the all-important A/R representatives. Why else would the record not be properly distributed?"

Back at home I told the group I knew who Chuck was contracting for himself. There is the pair from Atlanta called "High End" that had openings and venues all over the southeast, higher and wider. Lloyd Hart in Orlando, FL, Earl Tennent from Atlanta, but also a successful company of two men, Rhet Matthews and Phil Caine, in Raleigh, called "JAM Mgt."

I began booking and managing the band again. Chuck's contacts we knew and gave each an equal share. What I am good at is a lively music business, inside and out.

CHAPTER 16

JAM

We played "The Attic" in Greenville, North Carolina and invited JAM to the show. Rhet Mathews and Phil Cain owned and ran the company. Happily, they came to see us personally. We opened for "Nantucket," another one of their acts. Their top act. They recently released their first album.

Incidentally, Gene brought his girlfriend, but nobody asked him about "The Rule."

Within a month, Dee brought his girl on the road.

And then, so did Scott.

There's something' funny goin' on here.

JAM had heard of us before, but we'd all been too busy to move on it. Now is the time. We spotted them second level first row center. We reserved those seats for them – best seats in the house. They heard a lot of originals and a few covers.

Scott topped himself by extending the already lengthy, dynamic solo in Neil Young's "Like a Hurricane" walking all over the SRO floor among the audience. He let folks' strum and pick at his guitar and touch him. It excited everybody. And eventually, he was face to face with Rhet and Phil in the upper mezzanine, who were equally impressed, laughing, smiling and reaching out to touch the guitar and the guitarist.

We all talked briefly after the show and

were invited to Phil's place for a brunch the next day; a Bloody Mary brunch and a grilled dinner. They explained their methodology in getting bands up where they belong. Their top act was "Nantucket" and "Doc Holiday" their number two. So, we would begin with them in the third slot.

Doc and we had been doing the same kind of gigs for years that had us cross-pollinating originals and selective covers all over the south. They did tell us that JAM was their best experience yet, namely booking-wise. JAM was a hybrid agency, and were record promoters, marketers, merchandisers and distributers. So, Raleigh, NC was our new home base while we were under Rhet and Phil.

We were excited because we knew that JAM got Nantucket a record deal with a major label. It was a shame when the label chose "It's a Long Way the Top (If You Wanna

Rock & Roll)" to release as their debut single, because AC/DC released the same song, although five years earlier, it was not to be forgotten. Guess who won. Yeah.

So, Nantucket was downhearted and frustrated because they weren't getting any airplay, and their concert ticket sales waned away. Under the contract, they had two more albums to make -- owed to the record company. They both sounded like Nantucket, alright. They did have their own sound, or "voice," if you will. I liked them fine except I was also sorry that they were behind the ball with that first single. I noticed after that happened, their bubble sank and so they turned mean, rude and so did their crew.

In Atlantic Beach, they were reluctant to share the dressing room, and got mean about it, a roadie marching in and yelling,

"OKAAAY – Everybody out. The Nan's here! The Nan is here!"

I said, "We aren't quite done in here yet, but will be in fifteen minutes."

"But the Nan is here now." Their crew man had never been challenged and didn't know what to do or say.

"Then we share as necessary. Is that alright with you and the Nan?" I asked.

"I guess it is going to have to be. Ugh shit."

We opened many shows for Nantucket, but I told JAM no more shows with them, unless they treat us with some respect or dignity, relaying a few stories we had, so JAM knew why we were reluctant.

I officiated that from then on, "Unless 'Nantucket' changed their ways, and showed some respect, we either went solo or headliner. We'll open for them – which has been successful - when they apologized and promised to treat us kindly. We're a family...a JAM family!"

Rhet and Phil understood, but had all their eggs in the Nan-Basket.

JAM outdid themselves when they instructed us to keep a wardrobe of "Florida Clothes" or "Beach Wear; OB and the like." What's more is that we were to carry crates of Florida oranges, so we could hand them out to the audience in the venue or toss them from the stage out to the audience. Why? So they can have orange fights and throw some back at the band? Again, we had to listen to this bullshit but we didn't have to do it.

We posed for a picture with the damn clothes on but drew the line on the oranges idea. And they thought themselves clever, even though I had to tell them we'd heard it all before. We rejected the kookiness then and still did.

The circuit around the Raleigh-Tri-City was tight; no overabundance of places to play, but enough to float us for a while. We played every venue once a month. But JAM tried to spread us around Atlantic Shore, and other nearby venues, which would be new for The Foolstars. However, they never talked studio sessions. We left them after nine months. I took over management and booking the group… again.

CHAPTER 17

Big Daddy's

There was a string of clubs we did a lot of work for in the early days called "Big Daddy's." He soon sold-out. The buyer renamed them all "Level III." They were all three floors: The first floor had a bar and housed the Disco Bar Room. The second tier had two bars and was the Rock Show Room, and the upper third tier was for second tier overflow, or just a quieter place to convene.

From our first experience at Big Daddy's and then the Level III in Orlando, we were in for the entire slew of them. We were getting a lot of hold-overs and return bookings. We had a quick and dirty demo we did in Orlando, plus charted songs beyond those in the hopper. We shouldn't be hard to not only book, but shop, as well.

One night, Otis Blackwell came to see us. Otis Blackwell was one of the greatest R&B songwriters of all time. He said he dug the band – our sound and songs, but he had no time at present that could give us what we needed and obviously deserved. He said that. So, we were honored just the same. He said he'd keep our contact info. We also gave him a Media Kit with a demo tape.

We bounced from one studio to another, as time allowed. We recorded a new song called "Room 28" at "Axis Studio" in Atlanta and it was the latest presented along with the others on our demo tapes. It would be soon when we put together a Media Kit that included our Singles, LP album and EP Demo. We wanted to chisel it down to just an album in the kits.

♪

It wasn't long ago that we were on the road practically following Molly Hatchet around, venue to venue. We pulled double-duty After Parties, but also talked often around the pool in the late afternoon. They told us that until they hit-it, they were on a "PBC Diet." That would be peanut butter and crackers. They poured every dime they made into the band investments funds and paid each other only $35.00 a week albeit all expenses paid.

That's how they paid for their nicer vehicles, any additional or replacement needed or necessary and, obviously, keep their weight down. We thought about that. Should we do it? Try it? Hell, can we do it?

We decided we would give it a go but give the crew members $10.00 extra. It was our tradition to always pay the crew at least what the players made, but whenever we could, a little more. Anyone who has ever enjoyed white-glove engagements, know that only a personal assistant and excellent production crew can deliver it to you; and ours did. Always – all ways.

It took a while getting used to it, and we sometimes substituted the mean ingredients, we kept our costs down and our treasure trove till filling up quickly. Within a year, we had a new equipment truck, an RV for the band and a Suburban for wardrobe, luggage and at least four seats for the crew. We would also keep the Subaru we had as different cars and vans came and went throughout our years on the road.

We also upgraded our production goods, buying three Crown Amplifier Heads to power a tri-way system of Klipsch Bottom ends, Ampeg mid-range and JBL horns. We also bought our audio tech a new state of the art mixing console and I bought, with some of the money I had cached, some new outboard gear, like reverb, echo, phaser, ring modulator and an Aphex vocal enhancer. We did the same for our lighting and riggers, with all the truss rods they asked for, dozens of Fresnel flood and pin spots, boxes of gels and more. And, finally got a couple new spot lights with extra bulbs.

♫

We were in South Miami, playing a Big Daddy's in Homestead, Florida. The one and only one-floor Big Daddy's in existence. One that hadn't been up for sale. Although it was originally a week-long booking, at the end of that week, the audience nor management would or wanted to let us go. It was a biker's club, and they made it clear to all who mattered that we were there to stay, and, that we were theirs.

The bikers yanked the cable and plug wires from the truck, so it could not be backed-up to the door for the load-out. The manager of the club, a retired Super-Bowl-ring-wearing Pittsburgh Steeler gave me a $1,400 bonus, which I tucked in to my pocket. He was on a conference call with Big Daddy, Lloyd, and the house-band's agent. Once the receipts were given to Big Daddy, he told us to stay. He and I arranged a $3,000 sign-on bonus, and a $1,500 a show raise to keep us. Lloyd was afraid of that. For his sanity, we gave him twelve-percent. We were put-up in an old two-story house a couple miles south from the club.

♪

"Hi! I'm Benny Benito."

"Nice to meet you Benny."

We shook hands.

"Call me Jimmy."

This kid had it made. Maybe he is a good-willing Trust Fund young man. That little guy was a millionaire. Hell, I didn't know what he did. Could have been dealing coke. Jesus, everybody else down there seemed to be.

Benny offered to let us stay in one of his several homes, all brand new in Cutler Ridge, free of charge. It would be much nicer than the old band house we were in.

He knew we were searching for a recording studio we could take control of for a couple months, but we were short-handed. He introduced us to a young lady, named Sally who also fell in love with the whole group of us! She was going through a divorce and moved-in to the Dominican Drive house that Benny gave to us in Cutler Ridge.

He totally fell in love with the band and crew and continued to take good care of us. We kept an eight-ounce ball of coke on a grinder, on his bureau open to us anytime we wanted some, a bowl of Quaaludes, like after dinner mints at a restaurant, and of course we always had weed.

Sally and her ex were into dealing and horses, and they were both quite wealthy. It wasn't long before he began to harass us. We were all tightly wound on snorting cocaine, but I had discovered free-basing, which soon became a nasty habit. It is such a high that scared the death out of everybody else.

We had to move, and we found a studio with the open time for us. Sally asked us how much money we needed straight-away, and we told her $65,000 initially, with a term of three months. The next day, she brought two old, beaten-up size ten shoe boxes and opened them up on the coffee table.

They were old, tattered and side-stacked Tens, Twenties, Fifties and One-Hundreds. What a sight to behold. Out of all that cash, our bank notified us of one, just one, counterfeit $20.00 bill. I wrote a letter and had TL deliver it. No problem. TL was our lead assistant and audio tech. And I am very persuasive.

They wanted to know where we got the money, and we said we've been playing the horses for a long time, it finally paid off, and we were saving it up to reinvest into our business. Surprisingly enough, that was all they needed, which is great because it's what I had to give them. I had to show them my credentials as the Corporation's owner.

♪

With that money we were able to book the studio for ninety days, 24/7 exclusively, and move closer by. And what could have been better than where we landed? One Biscayne Boulevard, Key Biscayne; right on Biscayne Bay. The Bee Gees Family lived four miles down the Key, and just six miles down the road, The Eagles were; in town working on a new album. Their Producer, Bill Szymczyk Production and his recording studio were right there in Coconut Grove.

I stayed a few days and nights with a couple special friends who lived in Coconut Grove. They were partial to roller skating every day for their exercise. I played a lot of hockey as a kid, but I couldn't roller-skate for shit! I joined them, and I fell a lot, which kept them in stitches laughing a lot at me!

I had a couple copies of our Media Kit that contained an EP demo, and with one of them, I knocked on Mister Szymczyk's front office door unannounced and after my apology, was welcomed in by a very kind receptionist. She said Bill was busy, so I asked her if she would please see to it that Mr. Szymczyk received our Media Kit and demo.

You just don't show-up unannounced at an internationally famous record producer's residence or office. I'll never know whether he ever listened to our stuff, or not. I was a little over jubilant at being so close to him, and jumped the gun.

Our place on Biscayne Bay was the first mansion on the left just over the bridge from the mall off Ocean Boulevard. It was a large one-story spread, too luxurious to call a "ranch" style home; laid spanned over two acres. The woman who owned it and leased it to us was a famous, globe-hopping Acupuncturist who was never there and always in demand. Besides that, her husband left her a bundle when he passed away a few years prior.

It was an easy commute to Studio Center and back from there, just up Ocean Beach Boulevard six or seven miles and around two left turn corners. It was just a couple blocks from Criteria Studios. Folks from Criteria visited often to see what they were missing from Studio Center.

We housed a few extra folks on the Bay, and good times were many, but we kept a tidy Studio Control Room. Except for people in the business, entry was by pass or invitation only. Only players and their special guests, assistants, producers and engineers were allowed in the studio play room.

The crew were first inside to perform their load-in. All there was to that the studio didn't already own were my drums, a Leslie, the strings and keys stage gear. The studio had a grand piano and Hammond B3, so we just needed the Leslie. The guitarists used their Fender Twin Reverbs and the bassist his big Ampeg. Finally, an assemblage of guitars was brought in and stood-up on the rack where the guitarists would set-up and play. Stump, our stage manager built the custom rack for us.

With the help of the engineer and his apprentice, and a studio intern, we got everything placed perfectly, based on their experiences there, and me in other studios. Being the drummer, I would be first-up to lay down the basic tracks.

CHAPTER 18

Everyone has their own ideas, likes and dislikes of Rap Music. In those early days, with RUN DMC, Dr. Dre, 50 Cent, all through the ranks to Jay Z, Kanye West, Beastie Boys and Snoop, P Diddy and Nicki Manaj.

And those were the latest pioneering experts and are truly inspirational and fun for a lot of people. These people are selling tracks and playing to good crowds.

Put a stake in the ground there, and then go back. Further. Further. The very first generation of Rappers were the trail-blazers. Besides the historian Rap buffs, most are unknown, uncommercial, yet still heroes for jump-starting the style from right there on the streets.

Art is a tangible production that somehow expresses the artist's inner feeling, vision or emotion to those paying attention. Whether clear or abstract, it is the most intimate and completely honest communication the artist has with its listeners, dancers and audience.

Finished works, such as sketches, paintings, musical compositions, written words, sculptures of clay, pottery and dance all represent the artists' soul, delivered and as written before, standing naked before the masses.

All are forms of personal expression, or art; the human effort to imitate, supplement, alter, or counteract the work of nature, and society. Rap runs deep and has breadth, the word (truths) flows or staccatos straight out of the Rapper's soul.

The various flavors of rap do indeed constitute an exclusive medium under the guise of art at the very least, if not a format that is, in fact art. Visually, think Mapplethorpe. The parts that tend to make up the sum of this medium, however, sound over intentional, pretentious, and reflect on-going misleading and misguided exercises in wallowing.

The view for many is that of a non-movement of the loud, foul mouthed and self-righteous, floundering in their own bed of wrath. Nonetheless, it is that expression, through that form, that makes it art forever and ties it in closer to, and then maturated Rap music.

Music is an art form. Rap is an art form, but you may ask, is rap music? I once threw an acronym out there that I thought described rap, the music: N.U.B. I did believe that the art form could be argued a classification of New Urban Blues. I wanted to see it, watch it grow.

After close observation, however, some now see this as a gross misuse of the "Blues" moniker. But also put a big dent in it. Rap is maturing and getting the success it deserves, like it, or not. Before there was ever any chance of opportunity, blues was about ultimate hope; singing and thinking about the solution. The blues was never about blame but some of self-pity. It was written from the souls working as slaves, and hard times.

Rap rejoices, almost celebrates and exploits the problem with rarely a note toward a solution. But lately it is moving that way. Rappers maintain that the intention is to raise the level of awareness, but it wasn't working. But *I* say it will. The groove had been reduced to a chronic and obscene complaint. Enter "Hip Hop."

Awareness need not be raised, brothers and sisters, *corruption needs to be erased*. We know what we face; now how can we fix it together? I see it, feel it coming on even larger with every generation. Hip-Hop is fun! And it is, no question, music.

Rappers may exploit the misfortunes and injustices that grow like mold in this world for their own good, much like the fat white capitalists that irk all of us so. This ever-growing phenomenon has now reached the point of internal familial corruption, including murder.

Changes in the urban community take place because good people rise and get involved with those who write and challenge the laws;

legislatures and culture, then tackle the issues to get to the real source of the problems. Can you imagine erasing our legacies? I wish that looking back and keeping at the surface, slavery. That would be a giant step toward righteousness. They are still really mad at us. And white pigs still look down on them.

Look at what is going on inside Rap's business empire lately and you will see the same underhandedness that is characteristic of white-collar crime or any Mafioso related crime. Many of those who have managed to climb out of the rubble have gone relatively nowhere and done little for their fellow man in the meantime. But most continue to try.

What's great about rap is the door it opened to the style. Much like the heal-less sneakers -- originating from the prison population, now sold anywhere -- it gave those without the implements or the occasion to excel the means and chance to do so. And it does that with expression and voice to which peers easily relate eras, heritage and soul.

Now that the style has proliferated into the mainstream, virtually anyone can make it, if they practice what they learned in grade school, playing cut-down, calling names and competing for attention. How detrimental that is to the roots of the genre and medium I am not qualified to say. They could be sparks.

Are we striving for the purist? No, it's all game. It's all acceptable. And nothing is sacred in the name of progressive culture. Many beg the question: where is the music, the musicianship in rap? Some may never find what they are looking for, but many more others already have. They have because they have opened their minds to the concept and possibility of receiving the message in a popular packet, easy to understand and one with which anyone can easily embrace and mimic and dance to. Lyrics are back.

People ask, is it here to stay? If we are marketing it, and it is selling, it will stay. I wonder if any young band would bother with acoustic music if the kewlness, had it not been marketed by MTV's "Unplugged."

To state simply a cure to the dismay of many a Rock and Roller, true belief in the spirit of Rock, means acceptance in the spirit of rap, too. Beyond influence -- everyone rips-off someone -- rap interpretation of recycled licks, melodies and progressions no matter blatant the samples, necessarily skip right over the cosmetic white wash. Do you remember the mark Steven Tyler made with Run DMC playing "Walk his Way?"

Rap gave birth to Hip Hop, which was an

ingenious way to get the latest and greatest young urban artists out there. The birth of Hip Hop, like Rap rose right out of the streets, and then grew there. The genre continues to grow and remains innovative.

We have watched the evolution of rap grow from the prisons, to the streets and up the ladder to success. And between rap and hip-hop, the curtain rose to show us a whole musical scene.

Now, I've just been offered a nice cup of shut the #@%$ up.

♪

Imperfect musical perfection is something nobody thinks about, outside the studio. Fans, most certainly not. As I grew more and more, and listened closely to more and more, I noticed brilliance through err or musical intellect. Here are a few.

Listen to "Derek & The Dominoes in Concert;" The ninth bar into Eric Clapton's solo in "Have You Ever Loved a Woman": I would venture to say that this squelch could not be repeated, even by EC himself!

You've got to hear the best kept cracked Vocal Track; "The Who; Quadrophenia," on pills and hysteria, "Dr Jimmy and Mister Jim;" The last half of the last verse:

"I'm feeling restless

"Bring another score around

"Maybe something stronger

"Could really *hold me down*".

Roger Daltry, of The Who, earns points for letting Pete Townsend talk him into keeping that vocal take in Dr. Jimmy on the "Quadrophenia" album. I understand why; it's a perfect part that couples with the song and its London punk character. Listen to

Roger sing the last half of the last verse. Another moment that I do not think even Roger could pull-off again.

Most Radical Lyric; "The Who;" "My Generation;" "Hope I die before I get old." This lyric screams, not just for their generation, but for all. Relatively speaking, it's not about the elder aged, it's about the attitude and hipness. The miles surrounding you. May we never grow "old."

Twentieth Century Blues; "The Kinks;"

"Muswell Hillbilly: Twentieth Century Man." The entire album is invaluable Davies satire, filled with insightful lyrics and instrumental arrangements and performances that stretch. The fearfulness of Twentieth Century Man is eloquently and fearlessly spoken and sung by Davies. Learn the lyrics to Twentieth Century Man. They work in the twenty-first century too.

"Twenty-first Century Man."

Influential Band of the Era; "The Beatles;" Perpetual motion and growth from beginning to end, record by record.

Far detached from the early stuff, are ya? No matter how good it was for the time? For me some of their best stuff came on the early albums too. But go ahead.

Think Rubber Soul.

Think Revolver.

Think Sgt. Pepper.

Think White Album, Abby Road, Let it be and Yellow Submarine, even if only for John's masterpieces, "I am the Walrus," "Strawberry Fields," "In My Life" and many more from him, from Paul and some from George, too. So very creative and productive genius and innovation by George Martin and The Beatles.

Dylan easily fits into that pseudo-vertical space. He stands the most creative lyricist and a fine maker of accompaniment in the world. He was so talented that Capital Records signed a lifelong contract with him.

Psychedelic Band of the Era; "The Dead;"

"There's nothing like a Dead Show."

Calculated risks hosting celebrations in music, culture and openness. There's no singular sound -- there's no set list -- drums and space are welcome.

Best Kept Guitar Slip; "Pink Floyd;"

"Shine on You Crazy Diamond."

On Gilmore's guitar intro, once the rhythm section begins, after the fade-in and guitar solo, third time through the chord progression, just before the vocal begins. He even tries to duplicate it on the next go 'round to cover it. And it worked. You can hear Roger chuckle in the background just as the first verse starts.

Noise Kept on a Track; "Badfinger;"

"No Matter What"

Someone taps their foot on the mic stand base right in the middle of the big break before the last verse and chorus. For a deaf guy, I even picked right up on that one.

Muddiest Lyric; The Kingsmen; "Louie Louie." No question – Controversy included.

Best Fit for a Quarter Note Triplet; Johnny Rivers; "I Fought the Law (and the Law Won)." The last verse. I can only hope it was the drummer, or rhythm section for this Rivers' session that thought to throw the six-gun triplets off the snare into that one.

Worse Stutter; "Bachman-Turner Overdrive;" "Ain't Seen Nothin' Yet." Very dorky.

On Me // On Music

Before and even some after Label Naughty Words Recorded Played on Radio; The Who; "Who Are You"; "Who the fuck are you?" Simply, no one knew – twice.

Runner Up; "The Stones;" "Fuck a Star," from the early days and "Start Me Up"; in the ending fade-out. "You make a dead man come." Mick and Keith are always playing on words, but that one was explicit, on the fade or not.

Why there can never be "Thomas Dolbys" or "Howard Joneses?" See the "Frank Zappa" Catalog.

Who kept us honest? "The Ramones;" "Soundgarden;"

"The Clash;" "U2;" "Nirvana;" "Stone Temple Pilots" "Alice in Chains."

Clearly, I have too much time on my hands.

Best long songs: "Freebird," "Les Brers

in A minor," "Mountain Jam," "In Memory of Elizabeth Reed," "Jessica," "Stairway to Heaven." Oh… There's so many more.

I could go on in this vein forever, but I know you have the idea.

Fuck lists.

See how I and we listen to our music as musicians? I told you.

As I wrote in Part One, musicians hear everything. We listen deeply into music.

Well, since this is non-fiction. Just thought I'd share that with you. Now you know a little more about me.

CHAPTER 19

The waxing gibbous moon was fat. Bulged and swelled in the midnight, hanging too low to the Southeast, like a bag of waters ready to break. There goes a meteor shower. It evoked anxiety, as I sat there inside my sister Jean's screened-in sun porch, letting the chill in the air on that Holiday evening cool my unease. Looking up at the moon, it felt like my own penumbra had gone a bit dim.

A lot can happen within the mind as one spends the time to recoup, recover and otherwise amp back up. To clean-up and get straight, as I tried that Christmastime wasn't easy either. In my case, this well-deserved time off, as have countless times before, hijacked the inviolable moment and forced me down. Down on a vivid excursion and another journey inward, to explore the lanes, ditches and gutters that run through the labyrinth of my memory: A life review.

Oh God, I'm on my way to a lesson.

There behind me, hidden so well that it was obvious, appears the headstrong trail that I alone blazed. I realized some of my aspirations and dreams had all fallen, thus far, sadly, short. Not all, just the past year or so. This trip never failed to take a turn, by offering a glimpse of what the future could bring.

It's a sometimes warm or sometimes terrifying, always powerful look into the shoulder blade of "The Illustrated Man:" I almost felt enchanted. I saw before me times that looked more like chores than a challenge. No longer could I view my life as I once did so confidently. The larger picture, once wholly constituted by all the smaller portions of my existence, was no longer sufficiently substantial. My colors, I felt, were running like blood off a flag in the hands of an enemy.

Some call it soul searching, others, confusion, or even mental illness. But, there's nothing mysterious about it, really. It's a life review. It boils down to what my conscience is asking the mind it oversees, and over which the soul passes small self-judgments, the classically philosophical and rudimentary questions: Who, what, where, when, how and why.

Yeah, how did it come to this?

I remembered… waking slowly. Sure, it's Big Daddy's annual Christmas party. The noise outside my hotel door, however, droned afternoon. How many afternoons following the party? I could not be sure. It's familiar territory.

I know I don't always wake up before the sunrise, which means I cannot be sure that sleep lasted the course of a single night.

Once again, compelled, like many similar vows before, I could change my ways. My innards hurt, as if I swallowed a sword. Moreover, the directives in my head were loud and clear.

A vow to me, yet again. I shall. I *shall* wake daily; before the sunrise. And, while the rest of my sick society slaves over a Gregorian watch, I will simply watch the sun and the moon, celebrate solstice and equinox. Always on time.

It sounds so heavenly, yes, but I easily

reasoned doing so reduced pure celestial events to mere timekeepers, nonetheless.

Hey, I am still a slave.

This has to be the worst hangover.

Never mind.

The auditory delay of the words formed by the girl's mouth wear off in a moment. I involuntarily jerked forward, realizing I was in the middle of a conversation, without knowing how or when it came from.

"He shut me off, so I told him off," I would tell the band and crew. I kept stretching and yawning. My bedmate looked and sounded quite spirited for day's first words. She was usually slow in the morning, though never nearly as inherently sluggish as me.

"Like some creepy redneck, you told Big Daddy he could just you-know-what your you-know-what." She sharply said.

She was clearly incensed but giggled at the very thought of having to utter the phrase, even in mere skewed repetition. She, at the same time, shot me an uncommon hairy eyeball to stress her relative disgust.

"You yelled at Big Daddy, you." She continued. "In front of his guests and best buddies, you really embarrassed him and pissed him off."

At least I didn't pee on him...

In my mind's eye, I could vaguely see my bad high self, standing up to the grand red man in the huge, green suit. Big Daddy's Irish and Latino entourage surround the group. It was later but not that late, and everyone else was still drinking as far as I could see. I too wanted another. My mind was spoon-feeding the information.

What else but a drink could have possibly mattered to a special guest at Big Daddy's

Christmas party? At the premier club in Miami- a town renowned for intemperance? I stumble through justice, my own.

"You were turned away by the bartender," She fills in the gaps. "Then you went right back to the bar, straight up to Big Daddy."

Echoes of laughter and the beautifully ugly faces bring with the rejection, belligerent intolerance. My hearty barter for an adult beverage turned into a trip over the edge of descent.

"I'm glad I wasn't there to witness it." My girl said. All glamorization of what a low-life situation was already dwindling away, as I imagine myself, eyes afloat, glazed and unfocused. My body sways rotationally, like Baum's Tin Man during the intoxicative middle break of his: "If I Only Had a Heart."

I am not standing in the middle of the

yellow brick road, though. Oh, no. I was standing in the middle of a human gauntlet of deep, dark Miami sludge, and my words sound more like I'm talking in tongues. Humorously, I hide my ride on the guilt donkey again.

"Someday," I began, "they'll say I am lucky to be alive."

"They already are, Jimmy."

No one was impressed with the branded humor. This incident could have easily turned worse. I rationalized using two favorite factoids: Things can most times be better, but things can *always* be worse. Of course, there is also hope eternal.

"I have a headache, girl." I murmur. "I don't feel too awful bad; considering." I reach for my girl's rear end to round out resolution.

"Jesus, you." She uncharacteristically

spits, "Go look in the effing mirror." She's crying now, into a flat, yellowing cheap hotel pillow. Nonetheless, the incident pumped me up, a short degree, and the more I took in of my wounds, the better I felt. Queued male ego, beast-like, await release. So unlike me.

Naw. That isn't me.

The boys in the crew were extremely impressed. Oh, but what about the boys in the band? They may be a little pissed. Our management team was appalled and embarrassed.

After all, it's not every day some displaced Yankee, a hot wire at that, walks up to and tells the original Southern Big Dawg, right up in his face, in the name of sheer defiance, to "just... SUCK MY D*CK!"

Uh huh. I did that.

"I accept that whole thing as pure comedy, not much more." I believed what I was saying.

"And, I expect the same reaction from the group. Fuck management, agencies, and let them sort it all out."

No real harm done, I streamlined, it was simply a hazard of the business; comes with the territory. Nothing more than an extra bit of good, free press for the band. Maybe not so undesirable press for the Big Daddy's chain, either. Media and ratings are hunger-driven, and people down Miami were hungry for trouble.

I shared an odd bit of humiliation, I justified, and then the press will have been all but dead within a week. Big Daddy was humiliated at having -- against his own better judgment -- invited a Rock band to his finest and favorite gala of the year in the first place. He was most embarrassed, however, for having to put-up with the cocky drummer's last-call nonsense in the second.

My humiliation shown plain on the ass I made of myself in over indulgence. Beginning by then to desensitize, notwithstanding Big Daddy's brand of punishment and discipline, that's what bothered me most. I was glad my girl was spared till the aftermath. Public humiliation, after all, made Big Daddy hurt even worse.

Always does, a Westie mobster ego.

I, however, was used to all that. Traveling with two personal assistants spoiled me somewhat, but I had eaten my share of knuckle sandwiches. The policy read, paraphrasing, the crew not step in, until or unless, the talent is hit, or hits the ground first. This was not a group favorite, but was agreed upon lawfully by all, as arising at all after hitting the ground can somehow build character. How long must talent lay still before the crew assumes there will be no ascension? The jury's still out.

I don't believe the oily, little grunt that slammed me in the face posed that much of a threat, but I was cut short the explanation.

"He hit you hard enough to send you backward eight feet," she interrupts, "over the brass fence rail."

All Big Daddy's clubs have those brass maze-like entries in the foyers that lead to the action. Stereotypically true to theme, getting into a Big Daddy's is reminiscent of a line for a Disney World attraction.

"Or, like a cow to slaughter," she said, "if you're a girl."

"Or, maybe a good milking," I forced a laugh.

She is still not laughing.

"Sawn," she put on her best Farmer Brown impersonation, "in the shape you were in, I do believe that a one-armed, rubber-breasted, Johnson City fem coulda done just as good a job, pinkie extended and all."

"I consider myself lucky that Big Daddy didn't haul off and hit me in his own defense." I replied. "Or offense, you know."

Still no smiles.

Big Daddy is an easy six foot three and two hundred-eighty pounds of solid, Irish bruiser. He was the larger threat; the body of the guarded, not the bodyguard. Known on the circuit as a hot little Yankee, I stand five-feet-nine in boots, maybe a few more with my hair blown Lyle Lovett high, but I didn't do that. A toned one-hundred-seventy-five pounds, born of northern Maine potato farmers, Blackfoot Indian and French-Irish boxers, I am full of Semtex and keg powder without an ounce of sissy. My ancestral clan coming in from Ireland settled in America with The Blackfoot. Mix all that up with a little alcohol and self-medication. Make that a lot of alcohol and medication. That's all I got, here.

"Early morning reports suggest you sailed backward, failed to regain your footing, and before you knew it, had a gut full of brass rail." She isn't finished. "You scored a ten from the crowd after doing a good-old-fashioned somersault over the damn thing."

With a crack and a splat, I hit those fucking Big-Daddy-green ceramic tiles, dead weight and face first. Mixing it up with kamikaze, pure white, and a head full of Ludes. The unfortunate norm; I was high, not hot. Higher than a Georgia Pine I was, until I hit the floor. From there, I was no higher than fresh cut timber; down, red sap running, ready to roll. I only need wait for the truck, like a log to mill.

I don't like conflict and fights. Confrontation is okay, with conversation built-into it. But not conflict.

Instead of unconditionally calling it a night, I numbly shook it off. I was blind to the splatters of blood on the walls surrounding me, as I shook my head for clarity, like a chair-bashed wrestler. His crowd had already written me off for the night and turned back toward the bar. While they were busy slapping each other on the back, I got up again.

There's no crew member in sight as I take a token look around for support, so I stalked on. I swaggered over to Big Daddy with nary a thought, grabbed a bulky, suited bicep, and with all my might spun the big man around. Bleeding all over his lapels, I forgave the thrashing, and then bartered on for the night cap.

I landed in the parking lot this time, not sure who knocked me senseless, and no longer cared. I felt the ache in the seat of my pants; the kick of a pointy leather tip on a Puerto Rican fence climber boot.

I manage one eye open just in time to see Droid pulling around with the RV. I fall up the step and collapsed on the deck with Hogweed cursing and grunting from behind. Scott was at the cabin table ingesting a late-night bump of the flake off the back of his '59 Telecaster. He was alert, alright, but doesn't bother looking up.

One wordless thought, in a moment, delivered me finally, from brownout to black.

♪

In that void, I recalled the night a

band I hatched from my basement room really discovered the Blues.

I am from Portsmouth, NH; a classic, coastal, Old Salty Dog town in earnest. I was hooked on music from a very young age, and it was mostly Blues, Jazz and Rock and Roll. Portsmouth is a partying town.

There was an old black man in town named Robert Johnson AKA Bob Johnson. He was a Blues Man who sang, played guitar, one finger style – open tuning, and harmonica. My blues line-up and I wasted no time hooking-up with Robert and began rehearsing. It wasn't long before we were known to set-up anywhere in town to be heard; parking lots, open-mic coffee houses, Prescott Park, and other places. One venue named The Koinonia Coffee House hired us to play a concert for a Friday and Saturday.

We arranged rehearsals for the gig two

weeks ahead of time. Surprisingly, everyone (namely, Robert) showed-up for every session. I noticed that Robert began showing up a little more intoxicated by the day. It became worse and worse. He was binge drinking.

I finally announced that I would not be participating in the concert, by an uneasy feeling about Bab's integrity in pulling-off a sober gig. I merely had a bad gut feeling, and typically I go with my gut first.

There is a stand-in drummer, named Jeff, sitting-in on our rehearsals who agreed to take over the drum seat in my absence. So, he did the last few rehearsals of the two-week stint, and planned on setting up his gear the following afternoon for the first of two nights at the Koinonia Coffee House.

Friday night rolled into sight, and all the musicians spent Friday afternoon setting-up, getting the stage arranged, laying down duct tape where needed – all the usual tasks involved with setting-up for an on-the-spot gig. Dress rehearsals and sound-checks began Friday early afternoon, but they went from beginning to end without Robert. He was missing in action: MIA, all the way. I went with the band to help with set-up, and when Robert did not show-up it gave me a bad, bad feeling. No surprises there. We drove around and about in-town Portsmouth looking for him.

Night time came, and show-time approached. Still, there was no Robert to be seen. Finally, forty-five minutes late, he shuffles vicariously in. The classic "Drift-In:" recently renamed "The Koinonia Coffee House." He was obviously very drunk. The band gets Robert to the stage and into his chair. The set began with a count from Jeff, and the band takes off in song. Whether or not the audience pick-up on it or not, we'll never know. I was seated in the back of the small hall, and I certainly did. Robert, I'm sure doing his best, was sounding his worse.

They broke into a favorite medley of three Blues tunes. Bob seemed to get a little more performance eroded, as each measure played by. They got through the medley, barely, and the band went nervously into Robert's signature song, "Sweet Little Angel (Love to See Her Spread Her Wings)."

The aged fellow was purely into the song as he always was. He was typically tuned into every song he played, no matter who he was with, even playing alone on the street. His singing went more and more off-key, his harp was way off key, and his one-finger style slide guitar performance fell way too short.

Finally, it happened; the worst. Old Robert fell off his chair, attempted to continue to sing and blow harp, but could barely grab the notes out of anywhere. Suddenly, he just stopped. Tension filled the air as the band continued. Then it happened.

Robert passed-out. Not only did he pass-out, he very noticeably peed in his pants, and it went on, torturing for the band to witness, for what seemed like forever. Robert had a very full bladder. The audience could see his trousers getting darker and wetter at the crotch and down his leg. Once done, he didn't get up. The band was hiding behind their amps, totally embarrassed, and not knowing what to do.

The barkeep and bouncer managed to get Robert up and carried him to one of the plastic-covered plush couches in the back room of the House. The band finished the song instrumentally, the best they could, given the conditions, and then snuck off to no one knew where.

Most people in the audience, admittedly myself included, could not help but laugh long. So, yes, I was laughing my ass off, too. But I felt it: The hurt; the pain; the sadness. The gig was over for the night. And *that*, my friends, was the night we (the band) truly discovered "The Blues."

♪

Life can be colorfully full of humiliation and flavored with darker embarrassment. Those disappointments can range from the mere petty, to the catastrophic. Two fundamental groups generally tend to represent most everyone dealing with bruised ego and wounded spirit. The first group takes all to heart, like a blow to an empire. The second group just wants to get on with their lives.

Some tend to dwell on, until their own self-critique drives them eventually to some degree of madness. A small blotch of blackness in a soul otherwise full of grace can feel punishment. Punishment causes anger, derangement can take hold, and there's no telling where that may lead. Watch out for those who keep it inside, where it grinds and twists, dissects itself, repeatedly, like a cell, taking on a life of its own.

In the brain, it squirms; until the day it bores itself insanely from within the mind back out. Regurgitated, unleashed, that humiliation having changed form, constituted by angry violence, sedates and massages the mind into clear, grievance akin to a sociopath.

Acting, no longer re-acting, the subject marches on to some self-justified vengeance. No more pleasant as time goes on, that humiliation having turned into sickening, vocal disorder that fills the mind with ammo, at which point we can only hope there will have been a witness.

Then, there is the second group. Embarrassed laughter at first may only serve as a lubricant, because then, before long, it was replaced by mutual, unabashed and guttural laughing. This group manages to shake the embarrassment and humiliation off, little by little, like shit off a sneaker with a stick, or a stubborn nose scab from a finger, standing on the corner.

We stand tall, hoping that no one saw that low place into which we inadvertently entrenched ourselves, or heard about what we'd done. Everyone has felt at the least that level of paranoia, of course, but if the mishap remains unmentioned, the cool fantasy lives. If the fantasy lives, the comfort level rises. If the comfort level rises, so does the confidence, forming a pivotal point in life where freedom actually rings.

Big Daddy had the best of all worlds. The man didn't even have to say a word. He didn't even have to nod. It was no more a cosmetic grimace, an abdominal knot of agita, only a flicker from his eye that told that little beaner of his to take the stance and floor the now unwanted guest. He was indeed a man empowered, filthy rich and all-powerful.

I didn't feel he should be looking over his shoulder over the incident. Why bother? Sure, Big Daddy keeps sloppy help, but I was the sloppiest of all in Miami Beach that night. To bleed all over that Big Daddy white, green and red Christmas suit is what drove me back up to Big Daddy in the first place. I wanted to make sure the man wore something, even superficially over the fine fabric, for all his efforts, and mine.

How well they really didn't know each other fed opposing views to both men. Outside a close-knit circle of acquaintances, no one really knows what capabilities Big Daddy resources own. Like Gotti, Daddy was Teflon. Big Daddy is aware of the power resident in entertainment but didn't know me at all. Big Daddy demanded background information on me, but little would he receive, because no one at all has anything to offer on me. Big Daddy rested assured, with no reason whatsoever to care.

I more typically leaned toward headier an approach, rather than physical altercation, yet I knew there was nothing like pain to stress a point unmistakably clear. Teach his lessons. Pass his judgments. Set his mind at ease.

Justice serves, be it from the church of the mind, temple of soul, or beating on the street with a wonder bar. Seeing both sides, coming from both sides, and understanding both sides make me, in the classic sense, a textbook diplomat *and* Libra.

Even when I was sober, and she was my girl.

That multi-faceted view sometimes crazes the Libran. Condition and action have always felt this way, I reflected. I have stepped between and neutralized heated debate, if not hostility, between friends, families, strangers, man and animal. I have put myself into, and then brought myself back out of countless situations, good, bad, indifferent and ugly. I was good. I knew I was good.

But I am sometimes bad.

From within that temple of mind, my church of soul, I tended also to try, decide, and sentence those who happened to get by on fate the first time around. I knew I could sometimes hurt people very badly those deserving, I maintained. Few, excluding even those closest to me, are aware of that third, darkest side. Others have certainly seen or felt the derivative, though the source of that force remains a mystery.

Oh no. Not Jimmy.

So, for as well-balanced and level-headed I thought I was, and as good a boy as I was known to have been as a younger lad, there was an outrageous, unconscionable brood inside. Through self-analysis and life reviews I have narrowed the actors down to a trinity. My normal operative disposition is entitled "The Correct and Tall"; my default mechanism of defense rightly named "The Catholicized Martyr"; and my non-compromising offensive, "The Fronted Schemer." The first two are usually essentially harmless, swinging from both sides of the pendulum - upswings and down – but the third may be, depending on the situation, considered dangerous. Deserving of a gun and a camera.

♪

One of the earliest recollections of my behavioral patterns is when I was six years old. Marie, my older sister by seven years, had lately been making it a practice to deliberately persecute, and pick at me until she had me in tears. Then, she would secretly tape record the little boy's sobbing, using her new cassette machine. I was never an easy crier, but, as little I saw it, Marie had a knack for driving everybody in the family nearly insane, anyhow. She constantly argues and fights with her older sister, Jean, manipulates and spins anguish into mother, and disappoints to no end, father.

Although I was in the usual correct and

tall posture, Marie had little trouble calling a storm of tears from my blue eyes sometimes. My strongest side falling to her worst.

One typical Saturday afternoon, I was there at home with several friends over to play. The group is engaged in a severe game of ARMY. That was the unofficial pastime of all-American boys, then. I brought onto the porch and tossed down into the yard nearly all my hundreds of miniature green and khaki army men.

Half of the boys choose the Americans and the other, well, the Japs, or maybe the Krauts. Essentially, whether it's ARMY or Cowboys and Indians, all they need for an afternoon of imaginative and excitement-filled fun were "The Good Guys" against "The Bad Guys," whomever they happen to be, or whatever the boys decide to name them. I was the only kid who happily volunteered to be a Bad Guy. It's not that I really liked to be them; I was the only kid not afraid of welcoming inevitable death.

Suddenly, mid-battle, we hear a loud, hysterical and babyish sobbing. It's coming from the front door. There is my sister.

...but the crying sounded distant. It sounded tinny and muffled.

...it wasn't live. It was... Memorex. Metallic and shrill.

She stood there, with her portable tape recorder held-out in her hands, smiling. I was already shattered but sensed there'd be more to come.

"You know who this is crying like a baby? It's him." She tells no one in particular. Nevertheless, she had every boy at full attention.

"It's little Jimmy," she laughs.

"Do you hear that? That's Jimmy, crying like the little baby he is."

I didn't blame my buddies for what happened next, but all the crying and calling for Mom was, suddenly, obliterated by a large disharmonious burst of laughter. It didn't come and go quickly, though. Uh-uh. It seemed to roll on, repeatedly. Sometimes, I still hear it.

Into the house and up to my room I ran and there I stayed until Dad came home from work that night. My friends rode home on their bicycles, laughing and giggling all the way, deep down individually thanking god they'd been blessed not having a curse of a big sister like Marie. She seemed like a cross between the Wicked Witch of the West – Margaret Hamilton and Sweet Baby Jane – Bette Davis. They had seen her in action before, but not anything quite as hateful as this.

I was still humiliated at midnight, but I wasn't up in my room pouting all night. I wasn't up there feeling sorry for myself. I realized that I would have to face the boys next school day, and face all told of the incident; everyone from Marie's upperclassmen to my peers. Yet, I wasn't up there wasting time. I knew that Marie had well planned her little coup against my realm, my empire, provoking, then secretly tape recording my bouts of tears.

I filled with anger and frustration, realizing the breadth of the carefully conjured-up plan. To play the tape, at just the right moment, in front of my friends, was unforgivable and punishable. I know in moments Marie wasn't going to get away with it. I'll plan one of my own, and until I decide to carry out the initiative, I pose as The Catholicized Martyr, and yet live as The Fronted Schemer.

Absorbing admonishment and strength from father, and sympathy from mother and oldest sister Jean, I, all the while weave a web-like tapestry, custom made special, just for Marie. Humiliation, this time, indeed turned into a sort of lunacy.

Yeah, therapeutically, I guess, it's good to identify them – the soul players. I just wished I had been born with the wisdom to understand their movements earlier in life.

♪

Whenever Marie had a phone call, she would come charging down the narrow south wing stairs, around the corner at the bottom, and jump over the last two steps, through the doorway into the kitchen to grab the phone off the wall, or out of the hand of whoever answered it. For this very reason, I knew the family always kept open the kitchen door at the bottom of the back flight of stairs.

Using that special number that causes your own phone to ring, I dialed. After one ring, I immediately pick-up. I don't even bother with an "*I've got it...*", although I did hear both sisters start to yell that same, ever so familiar phrase in almost perfect unison. And I'm sure they are both ready to fight for gain in the hallway, stairs and subsequently the receiver, but all I hear comes out before I pick up mid-ring was an, "I've got...."

I pause suitably, knowing there are two pair of ears throbbing with the anticipation of hearing their respective name next being called. After mouthing to myself what would have been the script if the call had come, and counting a one-Mississippi, I yelled up the stairs:

"Marie! Phone. It's Pat McGaye! Marie! Phone."

I heard, ever so faintly, a throaty gasp from both Jean and Marie. It's the kind of sound that all women make, by sharply and quickly inhaling through the mouth. The same sound mother used to make every time she thought toddler Jimmy was about to hurt himself, or whenever she was in the passenger seat of the car and father's trying to merge into traffic or take a left off a busy roadway. ...Like a backwards "huh." Or, a backwards gasp.

Then, here came Marie, barreling down that long flight of Victorian back-stairs. Just as she took that eighth double stride, with just one more to go before having to round the corner and jump through the threshold into the kitchen...

I <u>slammed</u> *that fucking door!*

CHAPTER 20

The Foolstars Forge Ahead

"Yeah. I'm sure. Go ahead." Back to Scott's eight month's old request for feedback on our band.

"Alright." I started. "As a working unit, this group is tighter than a grasshopper's asshole;" I eased the tension joking with him. Scott laughed so hard, beer came from his nose. "You feel that, don't you, huh?"

"I heard it the first night. You're good. Better than good. As a group, you guys gel.

"You were awesome." Addressing Scott. "And

they all backed you nicely; you do well as a high caliber band. Better than just well." I added. Then I said to Gene, Scott's older brother, "You've worked yourself into an unreal guitar sound. It, and you really stand out. Using Peavey, no less. And you have great vocals. What a range.

"Yeah, I noticed - but you hold a strong rhythm, some filler lead, again you have a wide vocal range. I'd like to get more out of you, enough to match your massive stage presence. You are well over six-feet tall. You look somewhat like Chris Squire of "Yes" - a big man stomping all around the stage. That's a move you could use. Finally, try to dig into my accents and breaks: You know. You create your own custom fills just by playing along with mine. I will certainly play off your riffs and accents, as well. That's just pure, natural arrangement! I'm sure you've noticed. You'll be surprised how cool it can get, really polishes the song-up; completes it and makes it whole. You'll be bringing a lot of that into the studio.

"Allen you're a well-equipped and keen sounding keyboardist. You're full of enthusiasm, especially in the Blues. I love that shit! But I'd like to hear you play more surrounding the progressions and melody lines. More targeted fills, more thrills, and use rests, even if it's a solo. Just for the sake of dynamics - take some rests, occasionally. You'll feel them. They'll come from the melody line and choruses you answer, the drums, bass and the rhythm, too. Pay attention to my accents and trills, as I do yours.

"Dee, it's an undeniable pleasure playing with a bassist with your talent and feel for the music. I think we match-up just right.

we have an auto-lock into the pocket. Plus, you are animated – very important.

"Finally, I agree with Scott that we were all relatively young, so we can only get better; projection is huge, right?"

"That's right!" Scott said loudly.

"That's right!" I repeated.

Everyone bursts with laughter, and yell, "That's right!"

No matter what lay ahead, this band finally found the all-devoted unit dedicated to making history with music. Our goal as individual musicians and as a band is a single, simple vision: Success by music. Success meant publishing our own compositions. Success meant records. I felt a full-length long play album represented a milestone to success. We were recording artists in a travelling Rock show. We wanted to tour. We wanted Hits, there is no denying. That's what A/R guys are looking for.

Like most rock bands, we played the bar scene on and off for a while, to pay the bills when I first joined. For every artist to whom we played tribute, we had two originals in store. Therefore, never a set went by where we didn't turn our audience on to a blast of our homegrown music, whether we announced it or not. People liked it.

The best part, aside from the fact that it felt great jamming our own music into the heads of those before us, is that everyone out there enjoyed it. Unheard of in a non-showcase situation back then, we consistently received more requests for our own music than we did for the covers. That made us feel so damn good.

I felt it became a priority to become and remain totally self-sufficient. I shared with them that I wanted the group to be a completely self-sustained unit. Do not let our livelihood dependent on anyone or anything outside of pure music and musicians -- nothing extraneous, accept a record label. We had already traded in the trailer for a larger Mayflower moving van. We hired a full-time road crew to help get us there, set us up and keep the group safe, and load us out. The band remained strictly devoted to the music (only). The crew was dedicated to the band (first).

"Our crew is a phenomenal team of individuals," I remind the group.

"They serve each as a personal assignment for every member of the band, and they share all the responsibilities of managing the transportation and production assets. Itinerary hauling management. The band members own our own stage gear, and we truck our own production: sound and lights with all the rigging and truss rods, and that monster PA system."

Over the years, we changed backdrops with every new tour or road trip. There was an artist we knew as Lee Bert, who was a fan from Orlando and volunteered to create and produce all our backdrops and other artifacts, such as shirts, emblems, buttons and other swag. She was great. Better than great. She was the best, and had a great sense of humor. If she was around, there was laughter.

I quickly became the manager of the group, so I formed for us an S-Corp Partnership, LLC. No one knew or cared what it was. It also implicitly put the burden of booking, merchandizing, marketing, distribution and promotion into my lap. Everyone thought Scott was the other half of the partnership, even if a token by name place only, but he wasn't. I was the sole proprietor of the brand.

There. And I owned the name.

So, I owned the group. We were legal and we paid our taxes. Make no mistake, we wrote-off everything. Even the pretzels and beer.

The band and crew picked up the used Mayflower to carry the equipment in. Economically, we spray-painted by hand, the old beast flat black. Stump, the resident stage manager, and artist of the group used silver paint to finish it off by adding images of corner guards, hinges and handles. It looked just like a gigantic rolling hard shell road case, or an old gigantic steam trunk rolling down the rails. Too cool.

The band and crew didn't do all that work themselves. When faced with a task, like painting a truck in this case, what we saw was a perfect opportunity for a party. Therefore, as always, party the crew did. Being in a Rock and Roll band is a lot like going to college – bon fires, frat parties, panty raids and all. And for this joyous occasion:

Topless.

'Higher Edge-ucation.'

Some contend to this day that all remain open to time spent on the road, the nursery of life; one could never have picked-up those lessons in a brick and mortar institute. The whole analogy is a bi-way avenue. It opens-up a completely new level of matter for discussion and debate.

The off-the-top argument from the right is that one *must* have a college degree to get a good job, period; assuming an opening door toward gaining experience, but not really collecting any. One cannot argue against such a stance.

However, from the left, experience -- in the field -- world renowned human experience and giving better behavior I introduced. In general, it offers opportunities one would be lucky, if not unlikely, to encounter within the confines of the typical campus or classroom or theater.

Whether or not an individual derives a career out of her college major or works in a position based on the degree in hand, or not, is dependent on many factors. The future is extremely volatile and never offers a guarantee. One must look beyond the education that simply gains entrance into a world based on material and money, and look toward education based on experiential recognition, analysis, reflection and realization – the human condition.

Jamming.

Every instance, word and glance may represent a different emotion, meaning or result. It is up to the individual to make or turn every event into experience by drawing upon it honestly and spiritually, by not dwelling upon it literally or within the confines of shallow selfishness, naivety or programmed stubbornness. Learning to ride sequential, logical progression makes a big difference.

Continuing education is a huge factor in the human experience equation. It may include a classroom setting, or it may not. One may fall in with an instructor who has done little more than base his own theories, evidence and presentation on someone else's experience and documented case studies. That's history. That instructor has merely memorized the textbooks. One should hope that the instructor will have had real world and modern-day experience, or better yet, be a current active practitioner in the field.

Continuing education can take on many meaningful façades. Regardless of the setting -- sitting on a Rock in a meadow or sitting at a desk in a classroom -- it is a matter of one being a listener and watcher. We should be conscientiously communicative, well-read, well-versed, open, and most of all, honest and sensitive to humility to sooth and serve the human condition. People learn from people. People learn from events. People learn from within themselves; unity and respect.

That, I believed -- and could explain it free form -- on or off a soapbox. It was as clear as that. I never forgot we can do both. I had an opportunity to go to Berklee School of Music, in Boston. And, I had other offers mostly having to do with playing in travelling road shows, concerts and making records. One could do both, but not concurrently. I was accepted twice, but again I was in the field.

The rest of the guys half get it. The only point I intended to stress was that education doesn't have to end when school does. To put a welcome end to this narrative, I offer this bottom line: While I could never discount a college education, I will also never discount an individual who happens not to have a degree. And in our cases, we got plenty of brain and body food out on the road and in the studio. Writing and performing songs – music, and building friendships.

We took full advantage of being a Rock and Roll band, of not having to follow the mainstream rules outside of music. Rock Music. We answered to anyone at any time and answered every excuse for doing what we wanted and how we wanted it. I taught them that. In our case, that meant doing what we needed, which was having that party to get the truck painted. Do not make the mistake of not knowing our southern girls like to show their tits. That's love, people.

With the wine, women, song and all, it was a regular barn-raising, again, not unlike a weekend at the old frat house, or a queer and odd Amish barn-raising. Every band does this from time to time. Ask any musician who's been on the road in their early days. Every occasion is a party and circular event of continuity in the making. It's all connected.

The group sponsored the truck painting party in our hometown, in the parking lot of JJ's. JJ's was a small venue, but a room the band loved to play. Being a comfortable room, JJ's offers a plush intimate setting within which to play for our hometown crowd. It was a great sounding room. I can compare it to "C.W. Shaw's" in Atlanta. In addition, the owner let us rehearse there in the daytime -- much to the chagrin of the noontime drunks at the bar. Eventually, we played every venue in Panama City and Panama City Beach, but besides Tombstone Territory, JJ's was no doubt qualified to call home. Lynn Haven.

'Berlin Haven'

There were two half kegs of beer at the painting ceremony, and enough people to finish them off in one long, sunny morning slowly turning to an autumnal evening. As if an even coat of flat black required the extra space, there was also, as always, plenty of stinky-sweet, green, seedless, stemless orbile. Sensimillian had just recently been introduced by a group of agricultural hippie students in Gainesville. That opened up the idea of custom strains in the first place.

It took almost all a gross of cases of paint to cover the monster Mayflower. That's one hundred forty-four cases of twelve cans of paint. Layered underneath, that yellow, orange, red and green colored Mayflower logo seemed to absorb the black. Even using the two power-sprayers took all day and into the night. The crew used the paint left over to cover their old Chevy Suburban. You know: So it would match.

The band caravan included numerous automobiles at any given time, depending on who happened to be traveling with us. Although the group once traveled using just one decrepit, old van and a home spun trailer, as we grew professionally, and with guidance from me, so did our fleet. Within fourteen months, we had the big truck for the equipment, the Suburban for the wardrobe and luggage, a new RV for the band, a Suburban for the crew, luggage and wardrobe, and a couple new vans for the guests, musicians and crew. Those are what got us there and back.

At least there.

Usually.

Among the menial tasks, such as driving the trucks and babysitting the band members when we got too high, the band relied heavily on their road crew to make sure the sound and look was as professional and polished as possible with us taking every stage. We had a white-glove gigging experience, thanks to our crew. As any musician who has played to live audiences knows, no matter who you are, the production crew will make you what you are or break you in the end. Boston's first time out failed in part because of faulty production, and so in part did George Harrison's first solo tour.

As hypocritical as it seems, while we

strived to be as self-sufficient as possible, we also felt a void. I had been the acting promoter, manager and booking agent of the group for the first two years, and then later, as well. It wasn't difficult keeping the group busy with roadwork, but it was difficult trying to manage the business of Rock and Roll music during creating the product itself, on top of the brokering. Something was missing. What did all the great bands have that we didn't have?

It was nothing material.

Nothing emotional.

It was more a connection.

"We need a manager. A real manager," I said, and continued with a vow to find one to take over with or for him and the group.

"Someone to go to bat for us;

"Somebody to strike that deal;

"Stroke the lion's belly;

"Kiss some ass;

"Lick some boot;

"Stick the neck out;

"Put his member out there on the block over us;

"Shop our tunes;

"Turn a trick;

"Yeah. That's it;

"An innovator;

"An idea man;

"A genius;

"A sneak;

"A crook;

"And most important of all," I finish. *"Someone who believes in us and our music."*

We had to face it. The Beatles had Epstein; Bruce had Landau; the Allmans had Walden; the Eagles had Sczymczk; Santana had Graham, and so on. Everybody had somebody.

Yes, we should be concentrating more on the product and the music, not where the next gig was going to come from, what the newest public relations game was, or who the hottest producer on the charts happened to be. That goes to the manager that our agent could help choose. Well, theoretically. As we held all final decisions.

I was eager to share or shed the load but was more eager to hire a real manager to take up the slack that had inadvertently let out. The local record store manager was a big fan. Chuck Damberk had, in the past, approached us on several occasions with desires to manage the band, but often burdened the group by expressing pipe dreams of his own. He was a radio personality, a frustrated musician, as most of those jocks are, you know, but he moonlighted at the store during his off-air time. He was also a songwriter. A bad songwriter.

Regardless of his background, early on, he seemed to have a sense of what the business was supposed to be all about, so I decided to talk to him. I got the feeling very early on that Chuck didn't have what it would take to work the group successfully into the charts. The first day I met him, he reminded me of a cross between Paul Williams and the Oscar Meyer Wiener kid. But hey, he needn't rely on impression, right? That would be us.

He was supposed to make us look good to the A/R guys, the professional agents and the label execs, too.

Unlike the hair bands of the day, we weren't hair sprayed, permed or spiked and we didn't dress outlandishly in spandex. That may be fine for others, but it was just not us. We welcomed suggestions, but the music and group as a whole, we believed, did the talking. It was Chuck's little, tiny, beady eyes that were too close together, along with that canned, butt-head laugh of his that made him a hard person for me to trust.

His eyes never met mine when I spoke to him, but they glared back into mine as he spoke to me. Additionally, he laughed far too often, at far too much.

All classic symptoms of the nervous and the unwritten confession of the guilty.

I'm not stupid. He being the unknown record store manager falling in with the regionally well-known Rock and Roll heroes sounds all too familiar doesn't it? Well, don't think the band didn't think about it either. We did, but rather than introducing rhetorical cynicism, it injected excitement into us. The "what goes around - comes around" mentality had me and Scott talking ourselves into the relationship before we ever talked deals with Chuck, or the rest of the band.

This band represented, we felt, what our country needed, like a new alternative to commercial radio, and disco. Manufactured music had saturated and dumbed down the public and setback the young and impressionable. It began to make weary the boomers that had pioneered Rock and Roll thus far, with a Rock and Roll listener's brand of disillusionment and discontent.

"Hey, why do you listen to all that older stuff, anyway?"

"Because classics are better music than most of what is coming out now." That is unless you are alienated into Pop.

That's why, with all our initiative, drive and intangible incentive behind us and the dreamy phraseology of "Hey, you never know." dangling in front of us, not unlike the proverbial carrot leading the horse. That, along with our outstretched hands, too eager to shake on a deal, we unanimously decide that 10% of our gross would be worth it. I decided that he will have a probationary period of six months at 10% to be increased to 12% if he cut it. This is only for booking for the time being.

If Chuck could score a record deal and help secure a producer for a world-class record, it would be worth it. Hell, I think if a record deal clause were written in as part of that initial contract, we would have paid him a bit more than the better than sub-standard twelve points. Regardless, I had a rider prepared for Chuck, much different than ours and it's an offer he shan't refuse.

Working with Chuck started out all right, lucrative. He managed to keep the band working live all over the south, be it in a somewhat haphazard circuit. The money was fair, $5000 to $7000 a show back then, but the miles rolled out before us week by week. To the very end, however, we noticed that's about all Chuck ever did, besides get on our nerves.

A typical road trip, mapped-out by Chuck, may have been Panama City down to Orlando; all the way up to Newport News, VA; back down to Daytona Beach, then way to hell back up to Johnson City, TN; and then down to a tiny little town of Thibodaux, LA. Many times, those dates came without a day between, so the group will have driven all night to get to the next venue, with barely the time to set up and play on schedule. Refer to your favorite atlas for details. It was nonsense: It was a burnout circuit to be certain.

Chuck's formula to make it in the music business was very different from ours. When the group found out all he was doing - which cost the band even more money in brokerage fees - was subcontracting other booking agents to keep us working, we flipped. We could have done that much on our own (and later we would go back to booking ourselves... again).

On top of that, Chuck had laid claim that there was little time for him to do much else. We knew in his heart he meant well, but he and we truly were in two different camps before long. Meaning well and doing well are two very different things.

♪

In the music business, one must have an ear. One must have some insight and have a sense of timing, cannot be afraid to take a few chances nor be intimidated by difference. Simply, one must learn of history, of course, but also have the stamina to withstand change, most importantly to take risks that *create change.* We knew we didn't sound like anybody. We had our own sound, style and voice. And, that's a *good* thing.

Beginning in approximately 1988 to 1990, Seattle hatched the most honest music again, since "Heart," this time labeled of course, the nineties, "Alternative Rock" and "Grunge." Excellence once again returned to rock music. We were the bridge to take rockers from pre-disco all the way to this real rock standard again. But the North westerners did so for over a decade, and beyond, thankfully nudging the old '80s L.A. hair-metal bands, most punk and teeny-bopper stuff into an "old" category. Very few survived. Metallica did.

At least our stuff was "Classic." You see,

only truly decent, good music is timeless, but not gimmick-Rock, easily labeled and way over-played. There we have a little give and take, mind you. Listen to "Soundgarden," "Nirvana," "Pearl Jam," "Alice in Chains," "Temple of the Dog," "Stone Temple Pilots" and more from that era. It is good Rock music, bordering on or fully into excellence maximus.

Chuck tried to make us as he saw others. Even worse, he tried to make us as he once saw himself. The one he let go of when he married his bride and began having babies. Every time we met with him to discuss our music, he would invariably introduce us to one or more of his own songs, or one of which he had co-written with some friend of his or another. He tried to convince us that it could be our one chance. He suggested that he held the vehicle upon which we had been waiting to take us to the big stage.

He probably still doesn't know how much that hurt. The worst part of it all was that he sincerely thought that what he brought to the table was superior to our stuff. The saddest note was that it wasn't. Truth. Just the facts. Anyone with half an ear would have agreed, all egos aside, this was enough for me to want to run away. I didn't want my band blatantly manipulated by a fledgling songwriter as a wing to the summit. You cannot be afraid to turn a song down.

Understand that I understood marketability, as well as timing and delivery. He tried to accept the idea that industry bigs sometimes wouldn't see or hear things the way we did. He and the group resigned that, fortunately, it would aesthetically be their loss, but, it's often the loss of the hungry musician, isn't it? But sometimes, by god, we win. He ignored the open door into the Indie market that erased the rules and pushed new talent and style from coast to coast.

We just wanted a chance to show off what we had, and what we could do; provide a good time for our audiences with music, and performance and that's all. Erase the room full of blues in every seat, the band sincerely urged those blues out and replaced it with music that made everyone happy and to forget everything for a couple hours. That's borrowed from our band Charter.

We were also quite up for co-production. Also, lyrics here and sweeteners there, and any collaboration that may enrich the effort and keep us gear, were always welcome. What made something special, however, was its natural charisma and freshness. Losing that is like squandering the gift itself. Don't strive to sound like someone else. Take who you are and make it bigger.

"This band is a devoted and dedicated group in need of a serious partner," I said, "And a serious break.

"We're a damn strong band."

We resented hiring a manager who dwelled more on image and standards set by someone else, and less on the art of building something original from the foundation laid by his new artists.

♪

The Foolstars produced an independent single, just to see where it would go in the Regional Billboard charts. We picked the song we thought had the best hooks and teasers fitting for the times, but a very good song, nonetheless.

It was Chuck's practice to make deals with the studio he would book, if he did, that invariably included the band having to back up some other artist. He made the group agree to that before he would agree to provide us the time and resources to record our own project. That was alright, as long as we got out of the endeavor what we showed-up for. The other artist would inevitably perform one of Chuck's compositions. Isn't that extortion? I pitied the other guy. Our name wasn't on it. That's for sure.

Side one of that first single, "Lay down your love," went to Regional Number One, made a big splash, and stayed there for three weeks, knocking out Andy Gibb's "How Deep is Your Love." Our song remained in the top ten for months. Side two was a Pink Floyd-sounding song. It was spacey. The group felt like they could have scored a springboard to a major or Indie label deal with our EP and that kind of ammo our hit single behind us. This also introduced the saddest part of our time with Chuck.

"He failed to capitalize on the success."

The music business was hard enough when you are single with no responsibilities, let alone when you have a wife and family to support, as Chuck had. So, when his crying for more no longer helped, and our group had resigned to the thought that our manager blew a significant opportunity, I told the group, we had to let him go.

I continued my search for truth, in the meantime booking the group while I legally breached the contract between The Foolstars and Chuck, who had breached it first. I hoped to find eventually that special party who might see the real potential in our band, crew and self-sufficiency; but most of all *our music*.

We eventually found ourselves talking with one of the fellows Chuck had been using to book them around Orlando. I booked a set of gigs down there where the band used the opportunity to set up an informal meeting with the subcontractor. It was a petting session, just to feel each other out a bit. The intention was to stress the importance behind getting along, attitude and disposition. Plans and dreams, and love and money were not supposed to enter the conversation, but somehow, it did.

That first meeting with Lloyd Hart was surely impressive. He lived in a gorgeous home; all pastels, palm trees and wicker furniture. He drove a nice, new Beamer, and wore island clothes. Dare I forget the cross thought that Lloyd also had a young goddess living there with him? She was a working, struggling model who nonetheless managed to stay busy in a business that was as crazy and lofty as the one within which the group had a foot.

There was little to no remorse or guilt felt by anyone as discussion ensued at Lloyd's house with talk of him replacing Chuck. Had it not been for Chuck, they probably would not have been there in the first place. So, acknowledgement that Chuck had indeed been merely a stepping-stone closed the conversation.

The combination of the surroundings, excitement, summer drinks, and, the prospect of forming what we were all hoping would be a fresh, lucrative and strategic alliance, obliterated any other feelings of guilt any one of us may have had to begin with. Lloyd, we discovered by his own admission, had always loved us. Lloyd had always wanted us. Then, he just might have us.

We were a band well known for being the best-sounding in the South. We were also one of the few unsigned bands from the south who had had records on the air. Our first single, which we wrote and produced, knocked the latest hit out of the Number One position on the Regional Billboard Charts.

Regional popularity had many of the up and coming local bands including our hit in their live sets. I thought that was so cool. Therein lay the main complaint with Chuck, after all. He was unable to capitalize on that unprecedented milestone. What other band could knock-off a Gibb and stave off an early aged Michael fucking Jackson for multiple weeks at Number 1, and remain in the Top Ten longer and still go unnoticed?

♪

Along with the club dates that we, coincidentally, no longer had any trouble booking ourselves, we also started doing a lot more concerts, often opening for the momentary top of the main. But, with the song on the radio, we also headlined some of our own shows.

One power that Scott had was what every songwriter in the world wishes he or she had; the uncanny ability to produce smart, intelligent pieces that are almost invariably, naturally hooked. Scott wrote from his heart, always, but you'd swear he was writing from his wallet. That, he did to the point where at times you would be justified in calling him a blues man.

It really was a phenomenon, a real balancing act, and his true blessing and calling. Musically and lyrically, his were some of the most comfortable and exciting songs that should be heard. They were some of the most pleasurable and rockin' I ever co-wrote or played. Sure, we did come out with bad songs, which we had no problem tossing away. Scott and I had passed that level of maturation and lesson plan.

Lloyd was aware of our talents as a group, and of Scott's advanced abilities as a songwriter. He made it clear that he was eager to join. Through long deliberations, the band and Lloyd decided that they needed to follow through with a plan to settle for a while in a town where they could procure plenty of live work. That need would become necessary, but moreover, I was eager to secure a recording studio where ever we landed to record.

"Play all day and Rock all night"

--Garcia-Hunter

We had already spent a significant amount of time and money feeling around different markets and studios in Orlando, Tampa, and Atlanta, but we were not satisfied with the facilities or the throughput of any of any of those. The takes sounded experimental. I blamed Chuck.

Axis Studio in Atlanta was the best thus far, and where we produced a superlative version of a song called "Room 28." All of us wanted to take it home; keep the master, except brothers Scott and Gene. Times like that are what had me shaking my head - Fucking band egos. They could not *hear it. The rest of us heard it.* The brothers never liked anything clever that they didn't make-up themselves and refused collaboration. They gave me agita. Axis producers and our engineer had given us the sounds we were missing on "Room 28." That was the point I first witnessed what I had heard about the brothers early on. I kept that behind mind, but a pinned memory, and I kept the master tape.

♪

We had yet to try North Miami.

North Miami was one of the busiest areas around for film, modeling as well as for music, yet Lloyd's fiancé wanted nothing to do with moving with us. She was very happy living up in Orlando and wanted to remain close to her parents. We already decided to set up shop in North Miami, with or without Lloyd. He, with dollar signs flashing before him, his eyes on the prize, disagreed.

Then, in a move that surprised and impressed both band and crew, he up and left her in Orlando and came with the group. He cashed in, bought himself a thirty-six-foot motor home and traveled with the group until we finalized arrangements and secured work and space for ourselves, and him comfortably present.

With that move alone, he proved to be someone willing to take a giant step on chance, a leap of faith, solely on the promise of, and talent behind the group; the product – music. Additionally, for the sake of the music itself, Lloyd, in the end, took quite a loss on chance. The goddess and he, as a couple, lasted for a short while longer, but as everyone knows who has ever been through it, long distance love, absence does not make the heart grow fonder.

Absence makes the mind go wander (and wonder).

Absence makes the eyes look yonder.

Absence makes the lonesome stronger.

Faced with an ultimatum, Lloyd chose to continue to pursue what he would declare his new career, his dream, without her. She would in turn continue with her own established career, without him.

The group was surprised to learn, when Lloyd

lost his love, that essentially everything; the car, the property, the house and everything in it was his girlfriend's. Everything was in her name. That woman was so substantially beautiful that one may feel slightly perverted and a little queer referring to her as merely "the old lady," she'd be more of a "my fine lady."

She had been carrying Lloyd from day to day, week to week, and eventually month to month. Who knows what might have been had he not gone on a Rock and Roll binge with us? I felt the break-up was understandable, yet a terribly sad thing. Now, well, they know she got what she deserved, for she sure deserved better than Lloyd. Me? I would have commuted.

That one monumental band meeting later was all it took. Our probationary offer to Lloyd was two points lower than we had been paying Chuck.

"When you ain't got nothin'

"You've got nothing to lose."

-- Dylan

Lloyd accepted the position, and the band elected me to call Chuck to officially break the news to him that the group would no longer be needing his services, thanks very much. I didn't mind doing it, for I had always been the unofficial manager, spokesperson, mediator and leading decision maker for the group anyway.

I am persuasive and a stand-up guy. The travelling clan loved seeing that and using it in me. I hadn't renewed our contract with Chuck, because he never signed one - beyond the original trial period, that ever guaranteed any revenue from the road shows. Mine was notarized. They were free gigs, from proxy agents. Of course, I continued to collect his hush hush top dollar-per-mile. An auto-draft directly into my own bank account. Still, much less than music agencies, promoters, legal representation and management. They were getting a good deal.

From the business point of view, Chuck had done next to nothing to further our collective career, and for me, it was simply time to move on. Everybody was getting kind of tired of waiting and felt like they outgrew the odd, slightly older fellow. Personally, all I had to do was think of just one of the many times Chuck had pissed me off - one of the many times he pissed off all of us.

So, the task of firing him took on an easier, almost appealing tone. The last I heard, he was doing commercial radio jingles and advertising somewhere near Tennessee. In fact, it was that asshat who was responsible for the Wuv's fast food chain using The Beatles' "All You Need is Love" as their anthem; sang, "All You Need is 'WUVs'." I still don't know how he got away with that. Can you believe he would do such a thing?"

"I can." I said.

"That's desecration."

After the storm settled, and Chuck found himself another means by which to pay the bills, he began phoning the group. He continued to call, from time to time, from different locations around the country, with always a different, often whimsical proposition. His ideas were each one cumulatively crazier than the one before.

The most amusing of which was the one he laid on us after tracking us down in Ormond Beach, Florida, north of Daytona beach, on New Year's Eve. He was calling from Nashville, promising instant success in the Country market if we would only change the name of the band to "Jack Rowbison".

And, record a catalog of songs that he had written, of course. Bah.

I am not averse to criticism, so I will say, "That's a bad song. We're not doing that one." When it needed to be said and heard. It's not hard to do but will break the newbie songwriter or the sponsor into pieces.

Aside from the song list and name change, looking back, that was probably the smartest idea he had ever contributed. The Country Music market within the next eighteen months boomed into an Eagles or Jackson Browne like manifestation that would last over a decade, seemingly forever in the music business. For a while there, country music was sounding much like the country rock genre of the seventies. We turned him down, just because it was him, but that would have been an easy market for us to fit into, even thrive. Our kaleidoscopic look, long hair, beards, etc., even became hot in country music. It sure would have been an easy market for Scott to write in.

Who knew?

Even after dumping Chuck, the circuit didn't change right away. It continued to bring the outfit up, down and across every highway, blue, green and red in the southeast. The road also brought us face to face with many other bands and artists traveling through that same breadth. We were in a land that was a virtual Mecca of hungry rebels looking for the party, as well as vacationers, who had left their scruples up north, along with their troubles.

I had to come up with a plan that was going to solve a few of our financial problems. In truth, we were alluded to one by our friends, Molly Hatchet. Molly was one of the road bands we had come to know and had been running with and running into quite often. We were friends and fellow musicians. They were just on the verge of striking the deal they eventually signed that would yield that first monumental Hatchet album: "Flirtin' with Disaster."

Molly had their own problems, though they did enjoy some success, and continued to tour every year until every original member had passed away or had quit. The extraordinary guitarist Dave Hlubek lasted the longest. But he is gone now, too. Bless you Mr. Dave.

Side Bar:

We were invited to one of Molly's shows in Daytona Beach. I notice Dave on stage trying to communicate something to the audio tech. It soon became obvious that Dave wanted his guitar louder, either through the room PA, or through his monitor. Dave was getting upset, and then finally dropped his guitar and *ran* to the audio tech, through the crowd, and dove right over the mixing board and took his roadie down. I thought he was going to kill him. Meantime, Danny Joe was puking out the back door. After the argument, Dave retuned to the stage. Whatever it was that had him in a fever pitch got fixed, as I could see from Dave's face. Normal again. It was kind of funny and kind of sad, but at least the problem was solved.

Those poor guys, back in the day, the critics all said of their debut album, that they were doing nothing more than capitalizing on the tragedy suffered by Lynyrd Skynyrd. The timeline barely fit, really. It wasn't Molly's fault that the release of their album was untimely, perhaps released much too soon. Sure, they were excited, maybe impatient.

The record company no doubt had the say in that matter and made a bad decision; a huge mistake. It's tough bearing a label of rip-off. Of all that we had ever been accused, never had we been labeled a rip. It's a mean, cruel business. Molly *did not* deserve that. Their sound was much more of a harder Rock vibe than Skynyrd.

Besides coming from the South and being redneck hippies, a yesteryears Blackberry Smoke, we already had quite a bit in common with Molly. While they were busy in Orlando working on "Flirtin'" we were in another studio right across the street, working on an EP. To save money and be ready at call, we slept at the end of a session right on the playroom floor.

In one instance, in the hotel we were sharing with Molly, in Vidalia, Georgia, desperate to get ourselves into a studio even if we had to buy our way in ourselves, we agreed to give it a go. Remember: Molly told us they went on a peanut butter and crackers diet. They paid out only $35 a show. That's how they got all their better equipment.

Our entire entourage agreed that the struggle might be worth it, personally each, if for the good of the band. That may have represented the beginning of the end for us as a group, for appreciative, mutual starvation does not nurture relationships, that is, unless you're a frustrated prisoner.

The PBC Budget did enable our group to put away a lot more money than ever before. It wasn't hard to figure out. At first, it looked very promising, as we thought to ourselves, "Shit, we'll just pay our own way into success." As facetious as the intent, that would not have been unlike what a few other musicians have done in the past - and continue to do. They must, for it's so often, so obviously, not the new talent or look. It just couldn't have been.

Little by little, we continued to put away our money, as we all continued to keep our weight down. Weight had never been an issue for me. Being a drummer, I would easily sweat-off anywhere from six to seven pounds a show.

There were at first many peanut butter cracker dinners, but the entourage eventually worked the whole idea down to a science. Each of us carried from place to place what was a small kitchenette in a steam trunk, and we always stayed in the least expensive hotels they could find.

There were many a night when Dee would plug in that second-hand hot plate and portable deep fryer, while his roommate, Allen, was busy blow-drying his hair, and – Ssssk, *Boom*.

"Power Down-Power down."

Every light in the hotel went out, the fuses blown, no doubt smoldering, or the breakers tripped. The rest of the group, along with any other guests that hadn't already been scared away, wandered around outside, murmuring, mumbling, grumbling and suggesting, until the power came back up.

We carried with us from town to town, hot plates, skillets, pots, pans, utensils, plates, crock-pots, bowls, mugs, coffee makers, cups, coolers and trunks that served as portable pantries full of non-perishables. It was quite the operation, really.

I ate a lot of spinach linguini with olive oil and Italian Three Cheese, rice and beans, American chop-suey, cucumber sandwiches, grilled cheese sandwiches, salads, and of course peanut butter and jelly, and banana and mayonnaise sandwiches. Yes. Really - Banana and mayo.

With salt and pepper.

Our business would inevitably pay the tabs to the fast food joints patronized while traveling over the road. Fortunately, in the evenings at the venue, as part of the rider, we got food and drinks free. The rider is always the best part of the contract, besides the money decided upon.

The discipline behind the PBC within a year we were able to afford the very best equipment we wanted or needed.

Our band had the finest Production in the land. A PA and light show that could handle a crowd of five-hundred or a bit more. Some disadvantages to scrimping cannot be justified by the business of the band mysteriously sounding and looking so damn good on the follow-up visits on the circuit. We stayed in the least expensive places in town, as opposed to the cheapest. The line is so thin between the two that it often goes undetected, until it's too late.

TL discovered scabies in Hollywood. He then discovered crab lice in Destin Beach, Florida. I was so paranoid, even undiscovered I had them at all, that after having self-administered two RID shampoos and combings, I shaved my entire genital area, from my fucking knees to my chest. After I shaved, I stayed in that shower with a third bottle of RID and a fucking copper pot scrubber, and I scoured until I fuckin' bled, I did.

Luckily, times like those were quite rare, and they more seldom occurred as we booked more hotels than motels. Eventually, all of us, band and crew, had come up against some of the other not-so-nice hazards of the road, as well. Those challenges had little to do with the place within which we were staying, and more to do with whose company we kept when we were a long, long way from home.

Humor just helped us get through it all, much the same as a team of homicide detectives can laugh aloud together, casebook in one hand, a ham sandwich or jelly donut in the other, while almost blindly looking down at the bloody corpse before them, which has just become the latest statistic.

No one knew what AIDS was back then. Oh, it was out there all right, but no one in the U.S. yet knew it. Our government made us believe that it was strictly contained to African homosexual men. We damn sure know the truth it is now, and the group all knew we are damned lucky not to have picked it up somewhere along the way.

I thank God twice every day for that small, yet significant favor.

I do.

We rented a house in Fort Walton Beach on one occasion. It was not far from the hall where we had secured a two-week long engagement. Many good things happened that first week. A friend of the band landed a spot on some soap opera, and they got to watch her everyday as she waited on the customers in "Kelly's Diner". She hardly had speaking parts, but like all those must when in the background shots for any restaurant scene, she and the guests mouthed the silence beautifully. Scott developed a crush on Demi Moore; her low-gravelly voice.

Bob Seger released a new album and did a great interview on Westward One Radio Network. Bob is a righteous mid-western gentleman -- he is genuinely cool in his ways and his writing.

He let our band and crew sit-in on his practice and sound check at a stop in Charleston, South Carolina, and would have had us as full access guests at the show, except that we had to play the University across town that same night. Heavy competition. His limos were all baby blue.

Lennono released Double Fantasy, and we sat around and listened to that one a couple hundred times. At least the John-songs.

♩

The fact that our band could on one night share a bill with Vassar Clemmons, and on the next with Rick Derringer, or one night with "Fog Hat" and the next with "Doc Holiday," for example, always seemed like an asset to me – we have no strings attached. We could play anything in any situation. We were not alienated. We had a repertoire of four-hundred good songs. It may have confused the executives, for they could not visualize us fitting into any or trendy mold. They were, in my eyes, either too blind to see, or they lacked vision. Can't you see? We could become the mold.

We could have been the mold. Yes! We could set neatly a new way. Still, we could have been anything. We were fresh. We were willing. We could give them anything they wanted and never heard before. The expectation in those days was that a band from the south played southern Rock; Point Blank. None of the labels wanted southern Rock: Catch-22. It was a very ignorant, closed-minded and bigoted marketing business. No lie: We did not shy away from our Rock with a little bit of southern style.

Our dream need not be a lofty one. But all the arts were lofty goals to begin with. It's a stupid business.

♪

The Foolstars were often the victims of circumstance. That is not to say that we didn't walk right into any given situation on the feet that carried us, but the occasional case of dislikable. We accepted all as part of growing-up, maturation and cutting teeth - still. Life in a Rock and Roll road show implied no apologies, no backing out and no quitting.

One of our young crew members hired on by TL, late, as we were already waiting in the vans to shuttle us to the gig, told us he was calling a sick-day. We told him we don't have sick days, unless it is a band member seriously ill; too ill to play. That had happened only twice. Once without Gene, in Johnson City, TN., and Dee with blood poisoning in Homestead. Both times, the band played on. He was told to get it together and get into the van waiting for him outside. He went to the gig, but shortly after that fateful night quit the group.

So, if nothing else, the years spent traveling and playing all over the south, conquering crowd upon crowd, in search of more success and the almighty record deal, led at some points by us by our heart-strings, were some of the group's most fun and formative years. We learned a lot about each other and see ourselves getting tougher and tougher with every town visited and venue performed. Experiences shared, and every hardship endured. We learned a lot about people in general, the attitudinal, and the condition humility.

Essentially, men are all pretty much the same. Cosmetically we may appear different, but we are all driven by sex, power, procreation, greed and fear of God. Yes, and for us, the music. Some believe that everything happens for a reason. Case in point:

Any time on the road that was any less severe than the time spent thus far, could never have readied our group for Homestead in South Miami.

CHAPTER 21

Big Daddy's Revisited

The Big Daddy's organization was an institution all around the south, headquartered in Hollywood, with an east coast home for itself in Miami. As unpopular as we were with the disco dance crowd, especially those who preferred a DJ to a band, our crowds did dance, kind of like the patrons of The Grateful Dead, with lilt and big moves. The Big Daddy's venues were known infamously to all rockers as nothing more than a collection of disco-lickin' joints one and all.

The unnatural irony, unreal as it seems, is that we had been doing a lot of work for them. We were selective about the places played, or more correctly, the music we were expected to play once there. The Big Daddy's were justifiably very selective when faced with where to put us once they had us. Truth be told, Big Daddy's and we made a lot of money together.

We were the shimmering black sheep of the showcase scene because of our show of talent, repertoire, demeanor, production and following. We played Rock and Roll, we looked like we played Rock and Roll. The Bohemian Brethren, listeners habitually and ecstatically blow their minds whenever they came to see my band play. Sometimes that in-turn would blow our minds. Perfect.

As a follow-up to our Number One record, we had been granted lots of air play on the couple Top Ten singles we released subsequently, "Lemme be your friend," "Turn it on - the Radio," and "Blood on the Tracks." Radio play helps tremendously in booking bargaining power. The "Dead Celeb" Circuit of the south - Big Daddy's, Level III, and the Crown Lounges are very much unlike the other smaller and intimate club situations our band usually welcomed.

We were more used to roadhouses and theaters, but we recognized that showcase clubs and after hour bars, our real homes were The Whippin' Post, in Augusta, GA, C. W. Shaw's, in Atlanta, The Attic in Greenville, NC, Atlantic Beach, and Dancing Bear, in Raleigh, and Chapel Hill, Raleigh. Anchor Point.

It was a wild ride. In Thibodaux, we started at 11:30 PM and played until 5:30 AM. Every break, the crowd exited to the lot to shoot off fireworks, drink beer and suck on crawfish. All were excellent venues into which to deliver our original music. The people were eager to hear a "real band," which puts us in that category.

Unfortunately, the musical temperament of the string clubs remained very unpredictable. The hired band is expected to make people dance. Like the fucking Indians make it rain. The band was expected to make the people drink. Like the fucking Indians share the pipe. But mostly to drink. And drink. And drink some more.

I love the beat – burp - *and it's easy to dance to.*

Commercial television shows like American Bandstand were great and all, but attendance, sales and high number receipts rise above in every instance, in every way, when playing a concert or showcase date. But we were guaranteed our take, no matter what. But you can't replace a good live Rock band with a fucking Juke Box or a DJ.

Keeping busy often had nothing to do with how well-rehearsed, creative or professional our band was. Sometimes it seemed like it was more about the brand of music my band played, compared to commercial Pop. Again, I was proud to retort, "We play Rock and Roll, and we may look like we may look the part, but it's just us. Who do you think we are? You tell us; you saw, you listened, and you always came back. So, who are we? What are we?"

So, not at all did we appeal to the typical suburbanite, tippy-toeing, polyester vacationers out, say, on Marco Island. They wanted disco.

Big Daddy's and Level III's are multi-level, with a disco on the bottom floor, a live Rock room, both, separated by floors: Disco downstairs and Rock & Roll upstairs. The upper third level was for overflow from the Rock room and an atmosphere that made it easier to congregate and converse.

CHAPTER 22

The group met some of our biggest, most devoted fans at clubs where we kinetically drew them out of the disco room and up into the Rock hall. Once watching, and hearing the group play most people stayed in the Rock hall to finish the night. Many became solid fans for the duration, like Leebert, Keelie and their wide circle of friends. I met a nice Indian girl named Cody who was a girlfriend for a while.

The unofficial home for many of the WWE wrestlers was, at that time, Tampa. They visited us often; Hulk Hogan and his younger brother, along with several others. Some of them knew a little music, for example, Hulk Hogan was a drummer before going into wrestling. I wonder what those drums look like now. Shrapnel? Others too liked to sit-in and most Spanish guys like to sing a song, with music or acapella. I met some of the best friends in Tampa at that Level III.

Daytona Beach was a favorite stop every time around. We played there at least three or four times a year. We always had a date at PJ's House of Rock over Bike Week and stayed over the following week for the collegiate swarm during Spring Break. We also played on DST fall back, having to perform the extra set at 2:00 AM as the clocks turned back. That was a tradition with the owner, who saw all the band house kitchen walls were covered with signatures for "The Foolstars New Confederate Army against Disco." The owner, for having to have painted the room, got us back by booking the DST, just to get that extra set come 2:00 AM. He'd lean on the corner next to our audio-tech, toothpick in his teeth and smile at us, nodding his head. So proud of himself. He didn't have a clue. I'll play a set anytime rather than painting anything.

Our audiences were broad. We had no demographic. Folks just liked us. Some of the covers are songs that they no doubt remember from their younger years, or their kids playing on their stereos. The Boomers. Traditional music, and Roots Rock were a big influence on us, and hence, our group to the audience. Much of the appeal was that we tried to have fun on stage - and it showed - and when it did, it was contagious. And the classics jolted the crowd, with positive energy and great memories. We still played selective covers, and more and more originals. A few tributes or medleys.

Be it the beaches of St. Pete, Clearwater, Tampa Beach, Deepwater Beach, Udall Beach, Miami, near Orlando, Panama City Beach, Souderton, Villa del Sol, Savannah, GA. Virtually everyone we played for who knew there was more to music than it being just crazy to dance to, although they did; the good listeners became instant fans, too. We were finally on our way, just what I planned, and the group needed and wanted. It was working because we were working.

You would never have found our group, say, at the Big Daddy's out on Marco Island, asking the middle-aged couples in their preppy outfits and Gucci sneakers "How They Were Doing Tonight?" and "Were They Ready to Party?"

Then, breaking into a polished rendition

of "Super Freak" or "Get the Funk Outa My Face" or friggin' "Celebrate."

UGH. It's their choice.

Never.

Not our thing.

CHAPTER 23

Though one would be hard pressed to get a thumb on us any given moment within the years of 1976 and 1986, for we were, for the most part, all over the territorial Rock music map. For a couple of those years in between, however, one could sure as hell find us at the Big Daddy's in Homestead, South Miami. That was the longest hold-over we'd had, besides Tombstone Saloon in Tombstone Territory in our home town. Homestead South Miami was the only single floor Big Daddy's. And everyone expected Rock music. Real Rock.

South Miami. South Miami, dear Homestead,

South Miami; besides Florida City, the farthest south you can travel by land before hitting the Keys. South Miami.

Little Havana.

Upper Columbia.

Outer Alcatraz.

L.A. - Lower Alabama.

Biker City.

Drug Haven.

And for a while there...

Home.

The inter-town within South Miami was Homestead. All it took was a one-week long engagement at the Big Daddy's South Miami to consummate the deal. It was sort of a live audition; or rather, a five day "try before you buy" kind of thing. We weren't sure whether that was where we wanted to be, but much more critical was that the organization wasn't sure we'd be accepted there.

Few bands were. Indicative rejection might have come to a group by any sort or means, from heckling, booing and verbal slaughter, to hurling trajectories, plug-pulling and riot. Just like those bar scenes in the movies, like "Road House" where there is a chain link fence protecting the band from the riotous crowd, beyond all other venues, was Homestead.

Homestead Big Daddy's was the only place we ever encountered the absolute premise that the customer is always right. The customers alone in Homestead call the shots. South Miami-Homestead is the only Big Daddy's that did not, and could not, enforce a dress code. The venue and the clientele both were Big Daddy exceptions. The reputation had been worn rough by the mistreatment of many, tarnished, and under the constant scrutiny of others that were leery and weary of the power that Big Daddy commanded.

It had to do with balance. South Miami Big Daddy's was the one club that honestly was always almost too crowded to clean; the sore thumb. The libertine, loose women, prodigals, fun folks and ruffian and wealthy; Daddy's black sheep remains in the end, all his and with us in there, the biggest money maker he ever had.

Bottom line: We made Homestead Big Daddy's their most lucrative money maker by far.

There, we played to the leathers, colors, silk suits, jeans and tee-shirts, as well as the naked and high. South Miami was all hair, tattoos and tits. When our first week in South Miami came finally to a close - the band and crew finishing-up an encore of Skynyrd tunes that included a sixteen-minute tribute finale to "Freebird" - with everyone in the place tripping on mescaline, some kind of a pseudo-psycho-cosmic bond had been forged, metaphysically joining band to audience.

Yes, damn it, we were trippin' too.

Forty-five minutes later, the crew went out to back the truck up for the load-out. They were stopped in their tracks about twenty feet or so from the back door, by Whale, who stood there with a handful of cables and ignition wires, wearing a sheepishly funny looking, shit eating grin on his face. His eyes were on fire and jumping all over his universe. He was apparently acting spokesman and assumed leader of the legion of some fifty or sixty other bikers and friends that gathered behind him.

The crew; TL, Hogweed, Droid and Stump bee-bopped elatedly out of the back door, the successful, wild, fun and tiring five-night blast behind them. Strolling along, they came soon to a sudden classic domino-stooges-stop, however, when confronted with the sizable crowd that assembled magically and appeared before them.

Whale said, without affectation, "We're not gonna let you go." As simple as it sounded, it was clear he was not kidding. None of them were kidding.

Meanwhile, another smaller yet powerful task force had the manager of the bar, a super bowl ring-bearing ex-Pittsburgh Steeler and me, cornered in his office. The assistant manager was frantically calling all over Florida trying to reach their booking agent, our broker, and their regional manager with the demands that had been placed before them this bizarre night.

Management didn't mind. Why should they? Good business is good business, and they had

had one hell of a week. That bar was packed Tuesday through Saturday, 8:30 PM till 2:30 AM every night. The manager snuck an award to me of $1,400 dollars. I pocketed it for the time being.

The wet tee shirt contests on Wednesday only added to the fun. Especially when we tossed Wilbur out there into the mix. Those girls would do anything for fun and money.

Who is Wilbur? He is just like Steely Dan, which is named after a dildo from the novel Naked Lunch. Ours had a suction base. Just for Homestead Big Daddy's.

To the band, once fired for not playing the right kind of music, it felt too good to be true. It was almost too peculiar to be true. The Homestead crowd, after just one week, seemed like family that the group knew they had, but had yet to meet until now. The crowd, the bikers, the dealers and the consumers were so happy that they finally had a no-nonsense Rock band in there that they, by god, were going to claim and protect their find. And their new friends.

The group was equally pleased to play for a no-nonsense crowd. We rocked that week in Homestead, and would every foreseeable week thereafter, playing every night like there would be no Rock tomorrow. And the crowds kept coming. What could have been a typical week-long engagement at just another club in the south, turned into a much longer and enduring relationship.

The fence came down over night on Sunday, which put us even closer to the fans.

Big Daddy gave the okay for an extension with only a verbal confirmation on the register tape totals, and the booking agent really didn't have a chance to decline so long as Big Daddy had already spoken. We went in there direct with Lloyd, who had previously established a working relationship of his own with Big Daddy.

The venue's booking agent is Big Daddy's exclusive, so he isn't overly thrilled with the idea of The Foolstars moving in, because he wouldn't collect any commission. He had plenty of other bands and plenty of other Big Daddy's to work with, so no one involved was very worried about him. We collected a sign-on bonus and a per-show bonus. And I was given a $1400 gift, which I pocketed for safe keeping.

The band that had been scheduled to restart the following week, who had essentially worked their way into what was a house band position there in Big Daddy's South Miami, weren't thrilled either. For them, it meant knowing that they would have to find work elsewhere.

Try the Rocking road shows, lads. It also meant replacement and rejection.

Been there.

The Foolstars, however, were damned happy.

CHAPTER 24

After years of being on the road, having traveled more than a quarter million miles, playing fifty weeks a year, we couldn't even comprehend the concept of not traveling. Right away, the idea sounded seductive and inviting. What it meant, as a band, is that we could concentrate more on recording than on chasing the next gig, which fell nicely in with our ulterior plans.

"Hey. How are you guys making out so far?" said Benny, one of those tee-shirts-and-jeans guys from the South Miami audience. We met Benny the opening week.

"We're okay. We love the crowd here, but lodging could be better." I replied and shook his hand. Benny Benito is a nineteen-year-old from Rhode Island. He introduced himself to me during the first week there.

"So, what's up, Benny?"

"You guys are fucking great!" Benny went on to compliment. "I can't stress that enough."

"Don't worry, you have, and we all appreciate it.

"Yes, well, thanks again, Benny," is all I can say. "I truly appreciate that and will again spread the kind words with the rest of the group."

"The crew, too," Benny insisted.

"Always."

Throughout the south, there were many, many people who believed in the band. They believed in the band, and they cheered for us. The most loyal of the fan base supported literally the band and the crew. They down right spoiled us rotten. Benny was one of those people. He did both.

He loved to watch us play, and he listened well to the songs. He went out of his way to get to know the entire band and crew individually. He understood the band's goals and measures. He knew we wanted to make money without selling our souls. He admired us for that.

He made it a point to try to understand all our strengths, and either accepted, made-well or medicated our weaknesses. Smart like that for his age. He asked for, and would accept nothing in return, except that the band just keep on Rocking. That is all he ever asked of us.

"Guys. Benny does more for the group than anyone, including Lloyd." I offered.

"It sure looks that way." Scott replied.

Benny had an unconditional commitment to teaching the group to stop occasionally and to simply enjoy life. He appreciated the amount of time, effort and money the group had invested, but saw clearly the sacrifices we made to do so. He reintroduced us to the concept of a happy life - a happy life, particularly off the road and the band stand.

Recreational travel, cocaine and Quaaludes.

Benny, at nineteen years old worked hard for himself. He was a set-in-his ways coke dealer. He had one steady customer. The fellow would fly into Miami three times a year and pick-up one hundred pure kilograms of 100% pure cocaine, and leaving Benny $13M. So, in a year's time, Benny would gross,

$39M tax-free dollars. He had it made. One connection. Three times a year. And the customer came to him.

The band signed the six months, with six month option with Homestead Big Daddy's. We first settled in to the house that Big Daddy furnished, and then we concentrated on setting Lloyd up with an office. After searching the Miami area for office space and studios, we found the needed vacant space at Studio Center in North Miami. It would be available in six months and was the most reasonably priced. Without much research or deliberation, we frugally went for it. The timing was perfect, so we put a deposit to reserve two months with in six months.

Studio Center was owned and run by a big Italian fellow named Montalvo. He was rich, and he was a true gentleman, and funny, too.

He is also the Governor's brother-in-law. We all got along, and Montalvo loved the group.

"This kind of relationship couldn't hurt." I remind the group.

The Center itself, and the key players within, are known more for accomplishments in television and advertising than for any significant contributions to Rock music. The neighboring Criteria Studios supported many great and classic Rock acts, including Crosby, Stills, Nash and Young, Eric Clapton, The Allman Brothers, The Eagles, The Bee Gees, AC/DC, Billy Joel, Bob Dylan, Bob Seger, Buddy Guy, Fleetwood Mac, Joe Cocker, Lynyrd Skynyrd, R.E.M., and so many more. You've got to get in line if you want to use Criteria.

Studio Center's fifteen minutes of musical fame came and went with the disco craze. They produced many of the various top money-making Miami-based pop stars of that thankfully short-lived era, including their big stars, K.C. & the Sunshine Band. Their gold records on the wall were impressive: Now let's see what they can do with us; with Rock music.

I was hoping to change all that and hoped the engineer would see it too. I kept a close eye on Lloyd. He had no studio session experience. And he pushed for many unacceptable changes to our vision of sound and songwriting regularly. He'd put on his deep radio voice, for instance, and introduce each song when he was sure we had a successful take. There was something really wrong with him.

"Uh, this is The Foolstars with 'Let me be your friend'."

I had to tell him: "Lloyd, this isn't radio, and your voice will not appear anywhere on our product. You got that, right?"

Gary Vandy, the legendary Studio Center engineer and producer was with me and the group all the way. He wanted to Rock. He was at that time playing rock guitar. And he could tell that Lloyd had no studio experience, let alone in a Producer role supporting a Rock band.

As is the case with most independent studios, day-by-day business at Studio Center survived contract to contract. A large part of the revenue came from various production deals, such as the one they had with Fayva Shoes. The studio handled virtually everything for Fayva: the ad campaigns, the commercial shoots, film and video footage, the models, talent casting, the sound tracks, the arts and graphics, and even play a part in associated promotional distribution.

The truly impressive asset, as far as the band was concerned, was the ever-present swarm of female models that hung-out there. Every visit to the studio was for the band like visiting the Playboy Mansion. Although we lived and played down in South Miami, and we commuted to Studio Center in North Miami, the recognized potential outweighed the distance. The group would soon be booking studio time, as they almost have what they need to fund the first engagement. They hoped that, by his settling-in there, Lloyd would inevitably form an alliance of sorts with Mr. Montalvo.

He didn't.

So, what.

Scott and I did.

Lloyd settled into his office and went about his dwindling business dealings for the band. He involved himself with, and recruited various local talent, and he called down a couple of old groups he had booked from Orlando. This helped put a few extra bucks in his pocket, not to mention a few more girls in his bunk.

He continued to live in the studio parking lot, plugging his RV right into the center for his power and water supplies. Whether this was for simple convenience-sake or shear shrewdness, we did not know or care.

"Certainly, he could have sold the motor home," the band agreed.

"It is like he is still on the road, but his wheels aren't turning," I answered.

We laughed.

FOURTH SET

"Cruising Through Life in Another High Speed Mobile Confessional."

--J.A. Landry

CHAPTER 25

Although I was always tied into music, I dealt a little dope in my hometown, but coke hadn't yet really caught-on. Oh, I was, on occasion, doing it with best friends, but not selling it. My generation of consumers were into Speed, Weed and LSD. Some people liked sedatives and other sopors. I had a good thing going, selling pot and acid part-time, dealing all through high school, right up until my tour with the Teneriffe Mountain Band. Then, I left New England for Biloxi Beach, and everything changed.

Outside of the time I spent touring, early

on, dealing was my only dependable source of income. I was moving anywhere from ten to twelve pounds of pot a week, along with eight or nine hundred sheets of blotter acid. It was enough to keep lots of cash in the pocket and stash for the head. Besides music, that's all I had going for me to pay the rent and spread the high.

♪

"Open the bulkhead!"

That was all Neil said before hanging up. If he was calling from home, it would take him eight to ten minutes to drive from his Grandmother's nursing home on Rye Beach over to my house at Home Port. I went downstairs, locking the door at the top of the well behind me. Only after I ran a quick pick-up around the room did, from within my own clean, stellar cellar, did I unlock the inner and outer bulkhead doors. There from within the thick expanse of Limbo I could only wait and wonder.

I didn't have to wait long; not even those ten minutes or so I thought it would take Neil to get there from Rye. In moments, Neil was through the doors. He had a brown paper bag from I.G.A. under one arm and unclearly motioned with the other for me to lock-up behind him. He managed to close the steel outer door behind himself in his own haste but did not slide the dead bolts into place. I went up the short flight of cement steps and bolted the outer bulkhead door. He then turned, went down the steps and through the interior door to the private sanctum, securing that passageway behind us.

Neil pulled out a six pack of Miller High Life and put it on the stage, where my drums were set up for practice, rehearsals and jamming. Without words, I instinctively grab a bottle and cranked it open, thanking Neil with a wink and a handshake for bringing the beverages. Neil grabbed another, twists it open and offers up a salute. We guzzled, we belched, and we smiled.

"So, what's happenin'?" I asked finally. "Why the urgency, man?"

Neil reached over and pulled another bottle out from the pack. It looked like a Miller, labeled, capped and clear. Clear. Miller is yellow like the pee it tastes like.

"Alright," I questioned with a tired sigh. "What is it?" I had waited long enough.

"Demerol," Neil leaned into me and said with a smile and quiet excitement. "Pure liquid Demerol."

I thought the brown bag was empty, but out next came what looked like a cigar humidor. It was a medium brown wooden box with a hinged lid and cedar-lined. Quite ingenious Neil's little travel pack, with the six-carton resting over and perfectly covering the thinner vessel at the bottom of the shopping bag. It looked like he had simply come from the I.G.A., where presumably he had just picked up a six to share with a friend.

I knew something was up the moment I saw the Miller come out of the bag. They never drank Miller. They drank worse than Miller, and better as well, but never Miller High Life. Maybe for them, the name brand was a bit too ambiguous. Neil bought the Miller for the clear bottles. How meticulously detailed, if not thoughtful, he had been. Very carefully was he having glued the bottle cap on the top of the cork, steaming the label off the bottle of beer and wrapping it round the twelve-ounce bottle of the opiate.

The fact that the liquid itself was near clear; a pale yellow, possibly the biggest bottle-job giveaway of all, did not seem to enter. Neither of them mentions it. I bet the arresting officer would have mentioned it, but not on that day, for Neil was home free at Home Port, free in the little underground music room, beneath the cares and worries of all that moved out in the world above them.

They didn't play with the stainless and tube works, because Neil's blessed box also contained a bag of thirty-six disposable insulin syringes. It was all too easy, and it was done in moments; and a few moments after that, done again, and again.

Neil, for his stay with his Grandmother at her nursing home on Rye Beach, did the work that she and the other old people there, could not. Lifting people back into, or maybe out of bed constituted most his responsibilities. It wasn't long before he discovered the existential in-house pharmacy, but it was just recently that he had decided to move in on it.

The Demerol is old. It had been there for a few years, untouched and unnoticed. The two older medicine cabinets that Neil had realized hadn't been in use lay just across the hall from his bedroom in a closed-off wing on the third floor of the old beach home.

Prior to that day, we shot-up only crystal meth and coke, but we had lately become interested in the smack experience that everyone else had been talking about. Yesterday's opioids. No one in the clan had ever diligently gone about buying any heroin, but now, Neil and I had the Demerol, which was close enough; up there with Morphine. The drug culture was a chaotic mess within which the boomers happily participate.

Those in their immediate clan were from time to time shooting dope, but no one ever formed a habit. Habits did form influentially by Neil and me when he took that bottle of liquid Demerol from his unknowing grandmother's. It was scary.

He and I hid in my basement for the better part of two weeks lining Demerol, and when we finally climbed out, we were hooked. We spent the next two weeks weaning ourselves off the Demerol by doing sub Oxone and Methadone. Self-medicating mad men; we meant no harm. We were just stupid. So long ago, getting high was built-in to our culture.

♪

Now, everybody knows that when you wake up every day to two or three grams of coke and ingest five to six more throughout the course of the day and night, you don't go to bed without a little more medicinal attention. I chewed up seven or eight Quaaludes a night just to wind down enough to get to sleep. Benny was no exception, and neither were any one of us, once settled in under his wing, and somewhat under the influence.

Regardless of the ensuing fuzzy head, Benny has a way to keep it all together. He maintains all the way around. He invests well; owns property and dwellings all over South Miami and has a small fleet of vehicles from which he could choose to drive on any given occasion.

He stays happy. He, like me, never let any drug steal our faces. We stayed, always, entirely cool. That was a welcome trait to me. All the abuse when I was a teenager helped me keep control. If I was going to get high, I'd better at least handle it: I better enjoy it.

Benny loved Rock and Roll, he stayed ultra-cool in utterly torrid situations, and he retained an excellent sense of humor. All of those are essential qualities if you are into what he is into, and, if you hang with a band we were reputed to be. Those were the traits of survival if you intended to remain balanced and sane at the end of not-so-typical days.

The group enjoyed the big, old, cheap house that Big Daddy supplied in South Miami for the first month, but when Benny invited us to stay in one of his massive homes there in a well-to-do subdivision in Cutler Ridge, we took him up on it.

The most hilarious night we had in the old house was the night I introduced Gene to acid: LSD. He could not get out of his own way. He was glued to a dining room chair at the table, refusing to move, watching his hands and fingers move. He couldn't move beyond that and he understood nothing, but he was trippin' and hallucinating. He was chuckling. Telling everyone, "Look! Did you see that?"

Then he started crying for his girlfriend. I was near hysteria. So that's when I stepped in. I spent my all-night trip on talking him down.

Benny alternated living between the house he essentially gave to the band on Dominican Drive, and another home he owned just a couple of miles west. There, in that plush, exclusive, stone faced home on Dominican Drive, we planned to live, and live high for the rest of our stay in South Miami.

♪

Word travels fast. Vaughn had done it again. He raped a fourteen-year-old girl from

Portsmouth South End. Her mother was afraid to press charges for fear the publicity would pain further the young girl and her family. The little girl was the younger sister of a friend of mine, and no one could stand the pain she and her mother were going through. The young girl's older brother alone could have killed Vaughn easily, for he was a stout little Yankee, built like a tank, Hulk or muscle machine.

He was the one and only kid that had to shave as early as seventh grade.

"Sadly, he was on probation, his hands are tied," I said. "Besides, his mother pleaded with him not to get involved."

Yes, he heeded, but oh, how he wanted Vaughn gone. Eventually, he would have had him regardless, if Neil, and our trio hadn't gotten to Vaughn first. We told him we'd get rid of him. Vague but promising.

They have charges of their own they are ready to press. Had I been home, it would have been all mine, but in my absence, the old posse followed through on a plan we had laid out a year earlier out on Witchatrot road. A one-way trip to Jamaica was on. Neil reviewed the plan, but then, upon checking flights, found the best they could do in a pinch was Miami. That was especially with the made-up Vaughn.

Altogether, that made better sense anyhow. It just seemed Miami Beach, Florida was the picture-perfect destination for a blue-haired old bag. The pieces fell into place just as they had planned before, back when I was still home. They loosened Vaughn up, they dosed him down with morphine, and they heavily anesthetized him. Once he was under, they made him up really good too, and got him down to Logan and on a plane, fast, wheel chair service and all.

You're right - money does swear, Mr. Zimmerman.

Without Neil, the stunt could have never worked. Not only did he provide the implements and credentials, but also with a fresh haircut and an inherently sly way about him, Neil did all the smoothing at the airport. He was very persuasive and non-obtrusive, and matter-of-factly all about business.

The dope, the clothes, the make-up, the wig and the wheel chair all came from Neil's Grandmother's nursing home. So authentic was the old woman Vaughn.

The instructions given Belle Airways called for an attendant to wheel her to baggage claim, retrieve her bag and then leave her for a personal escort that would plan on being there at arrival time. As requested, the attendant placed a placard across the old woman's lap that read, "Bent."

Thoughtfully, the three comrades packed Vaughn a bag full of old lady's underwear, some outerwear and some make-up. Vaughn woke briefly once, but he was unable for the next thirty-six hours to move or speak at all. All he could do at that point was look around him a second at a time - few and far-between - to sights quite a blur, then, he's out again. It would be another day and a half before he would regain at least some of his composure, if you call Vaughn's behavior at all composed to begin with.

He didn't know where he was and barely knew who he was. He couldn't keep his eyes open for more than a half a second at a time, with hours between blinks. He knew he was comfortable but had no idea he was in a wheelchair. He had no idea he was in drag. People walking by tried unsuccessfully to pass without staring, most looking sadly at the haggard looking, old woman in common sympathetic disgust.

"Bent."

By the time airport personnel had arranged to bring Vaughn to the nearest shelter for the homeless, he still wasn't conscious enough to respond, let alone object. Once there, he slept through the entire night. Vaughn slept soundly until at 10:10 in the morning, a beautiful Cuban volunteer from the shelter approached the feeble looking old person.

She knew the old woman was not dead, because of the tremendous snoring evoking from the openings to the cranial cavities of the elderly being. The young, dark woman tried gently to wake her, but was unsuccessful. She held the strange looking hand in hers and repeated just above a whisper: "Ma'am, Ma'am, time to wake up dear."

CHAPTER 26

Floyd

The group had just pulled the RV in to the field for Rob and Deb's wedding, and Gene was parking it. Before we had even a chance to jump out and stretch, to join the goings on, Floyd came climbing aboard, commanding two of his mechanics to keep post at the RV door.

When I saw Floyd, I involuntarily stopped right away, as did the band and crew. We were still. This was the first time the group ever actually met Floyd in person. Oh sure, everyone had heard of him, seen him from a distance at Big Daddy's Homestead. He sat up in the back-room table to the right side of The Columbian. Yes, "The Man."

We had all heard of his infamous and otherwise dubious acts, and his enforcement of the law -- his own. He also had his own corner booth in the back room at the Homestead Big Daddy's. I never comment about any of those stories, rumors or whatever, but what I did know immediately was that every word ever uttered intended to describe Floyd physically, as unbelievable as those accounts sounded at the time, were undeniably true. Floyd is an easy seven-foot-one, and at least three and a half feet wide at the shoulders.

What Floyd carried with him also proved to live up to the legend. He had four fingers (that would be two of Floyd's) of white in a baggy, and to serve it up, a standard issue seven and a half-inch buck knife, always held personally by him. Floyd with a knife to your face, even if it is loaded with coke, is a scary place to be.

After a one-sided introduction, big Floyd brought out the bag of white, and served it up over the tip of that buck knife of his, around, around and then around again. I could see the boys were lit after the first round.

This shit is pure.

The court acquitted Floyd on three counts of murder. He was up for two more soon. He was deep and connected. It didn't look good. He told me that I was a damn good drummer, that the band sounds good, and to keep on Rocking. By the time I got out of the RV, with what felt like my scalp peeling back off my head, all that my mind could pull forward was the thought,

"Wow, that Floyd. Huh? He's a pretty nice guy."

"It is well beyond me," I joked after Floyd and his small army left. "Whatever made anyone trust that man to hold his weapon right under each of our noses time after time?"

There is a commotion out in the pasture. Completely hilarious, there are five or six dudes chasing a good-sized goat all over the field. It strikes me comically that it took so much effort from those iron horsemen to catch an adult sized domestic farm-Billy. I explained it was all in fun; using any kind of firearm on that fucking goat just seemed too easy, you know?

The good old standard issue buck that all seemed to have hanging off their belts handled the culinary rudiments nicely. I still have mine. Our master game hunters bled and cleaned the animal right there where it had been tackled, then they carried it over to the pit, skinned it, and reamed that poor dead carcass primed for the spitting. With a makeshift rotisserie, they proceeded to roast a feast over which the Frugal Gourmet may well have been proud, given the implements missing at the BBQ.

The near-burnt beast didn't taste bad, though it was slightly tough, but the skin crunchy. Nobody did give a shit anyway, because all anybody ever really wanted was just another hit, another toke, another beer and another pull off the Bourbon: Tequila for the ladies and it is pants down. You ever notice that?

The festivities throughout the day could not have been better. There was target shooting, drag racing, wrestling and don't forget goat chasing. Target shooting meant behind the back shots and over the shoulder shots, some using nothing more than their old lady's make-up mirror. There were no fancy targets either. Men were shooting beer cans out of their partner's hand and shooting cigarettes out of mouths and from between fingers.

We'd all seen it done in the movies, or on Loony Tunes, but this was live, crazy and dangerous. We had to call it fun. The bikers used a nearby clear straightaway adjacent to the party park for drag racing. It remained, un-traveled almost all day. There were stationed a couple of finish line lookers, as well as a friendly traffic cop.

This family remained closer than blood in vein. There were a few friendly interventions from the real officers of the law, but there were no arrests. There were no injuries. It was fun. It was funny. It was loud. It was fast. It was crazy. It was a party like no other.

On Me // On Music

One thing that has always irked me was prejudice toward bikers. It does not begin and end particularly toward the men either. They share commode seats, after all. Someone inevitably must have something negative to say about the women, as well.

Guarded are the feelings of the righteous society, that men and women are merely, and secretly envious. Go down to Short Hills Mall and spy the nice-looking women with their silver and onyx slave bracelets, the denim skirts, the work shirt with metal buttons; said shirt opened to show off those lovely breasts, but oh, sorry, just enough of those things that they want to be seen, and no more. They have their riding boots, the expensive tightly-undone look on their heads, and the newest rage in make-up: the no make-up look.

What's the difference? The jewelry's

polished. The skirt is pressed. The shirt is crisp. The tits don't sag. (Enter Playtex - it's the wonder-bra, boy...or implants.) The boots, my friends, have never ridden on the backs of anything accept up and down their husbands' sorry asses. Ring up fifty dollars on that perfect upstairs bed head look; add more for the makeover at the local Bloomingdales.

Those are the differences and are the only differences. Please forgive me, but whether scooter trash, executive, professional, homemaker or minister's wife, they all like to f*ck. They like it and want it bad and good, and hard, and fast, and slow. And, oh gwad Madge -- what a gash: the magic button and that spot. Multiples!

Man! I miss my girl.

The difference is, that the free spirits, the scooter trash, none of them, bother bullshitting anyone about it. And don't count out the college crowds: If they want to show you their tits on Daytona Beach, for example, you are going to see their tits. In most cases, if you want to get a gander at those things, all you need do is ask, or hold up a placard. "Show me your tits!"

Nothing like Bike Week in Daytona Beach, Florida.

Like any band on the sacred mission, we were constantly on the lookout for a way to score a recording contract. We were generally aiming high but shooting low. We recognized and agreed we didn't necessarily need a major label deal, as an Indie would be great too. Indie markets were just coming-up on their own, and that was a good thing. It would be nice just to be able to finance a little studio time.

South Miami had, by then, become a second

home for The Foolstars. The group realized a tremendous and devoted following there. As a result, they were receiving many offers. Good friend Benny was always on the lookout for the band's welfare and development, and schemes right along with us when we sat around brainstorming our way to the top.

Even though many of the storms in our brains at the time were indirect results of the brain food ingested, we were driving forward even if with only one eye open. Traveled as we were, we manage at least to keep the fog lamps burning all the time. It's not entirely unhealthy.

Sure.

My typical days, following the After Parties, which usually lasted until 6:00 AM, I'd sleep until noon, exercise until 2:30 PM, then band practice until we'd decided we'd had enough for the day, then rest, have supper and clean-up for the show.

The band did well, with an EP and three singles getting airplay. I sometimes must remind myself, if ever down, is that I played fifty weeks out of the year, covered so many miles, cities and towns, and states. Add that to the work I did with Teneriffe in New England and Canada, and I can add three territories and provinces, many more miles and more cities and towns. That usually gave me my disposition high back.

CHAPTER 27

Sally

On one of those occasions off, Benny brought up an acquaintance of his, named Sally Clarke, he said might be interested in, and could afford, investing in the group. She was a close friend who was also the wife of an ex-partner of Benny's, but still reports to Floyd. Sally, he said, was into many interesting investment schemes already, such as horse breeding and racing, boxing, and other assorted money-making endeavors. She might be interested. She's rich. She was a one-of-a-kind lady, and very fun loving.

Without thought about implications, that's all we needed to hear. We decided that Sally could be a perfect candidate to approach. She just might want to join us on our mission, and thus, want to throw some dollars into the hat, especially with Benny accompanying us already.

We looked upon it as investment; risky, yes, but hoped she would too. Yes, an investment, that is, if they made any money off the initial funding she would provide. An investment, that is, if she decided to give it to them in the first place.

If -- If.

"'If' is the middle word in life."

--Colonel Kurtz.

Benny brought Sally to the club to see us perform, and back again later to meet the band and crew, to talk. There eventually came several get-togethers with her, and it didn't take long for The Foolstars with her to come up with a possible plan-of-action and hatch a musical love affair.

It was a simple POA. She would advance the group (the partnership I owned) sixty-five-thousand dollars, initially, and we would make her the Executive Producer of the album. Points and lump sum came with the title, of course.

The band would use the money to produce as many finished recordings as we possibly could, assemble an album's worth, and then use that recording as a demo worth shopping. It may turn out so good as to be the actual release. Using advance money, we would contractually plan to pay Sally her money back with interest, on top of her points on the deal and her Executive Producer role. If it didn't happen first try, we'd somehow pay her back subsequently, like trying it again, or something else. And she was fine.

No one talked of the possibility that there may not ever be a deal. That was understood and assumed. And, we did not jinx. Sally liked the idea as much as anyone involved did. She was as excited to be a part of it, like, 'With the Band,' makin' the music.

The Foolstars, but not so much, Lloyd, immediately drew up the plans that would get the group off the platform for seven weeks to record then two more weeks to mix-down and master. Securing some solid time in Studio Center; just what the doctor ordered.

"Here's your money," Sally says to me happily. "Honey."

She delivered the money within a week. It was not in the form of a money order for sixty-five thousand. Nor was it a cashier's check for sixty-five thousand. It was not an electronic deposit advice for sixty-five thousand, and it was not a personal check for sixty-five thousand.

She handed me two size ten shoe boxes a bit frayed and tattered at the edges. She hand delivered to us exactly two size-ten shoeboxes packed tight full of cash. Dirty cash. She handed it to me, two fucking shoeboxes full of tens, twenties, fifties and hundreds snugly in a stack.

This was not a first for me, as I'd certainly held in my hands that vast an amount before, dealing, playing, but by the way the rest of the group were all - excluding Benny of course - taking turns holding on to it, feeling it, and smelling it, I suspect that nary any of them had.

It didn't much matter to the group how

the money arrived; it had. A crony from the studio opened a Safe Deposit Box and would wrap, roll and throw this pile into it that very afternoon. Yeah, that's right. It was a pile. Standing it on end, it was a good eighteen inches high, even when we crushed it downward. It looked like a model sky scraper.

I could just imagine Sally that morning, digging the stash out of her mattress, or better yet, the coffee cans in the back yard. Sally had a Rottweiler whose domain was wherever it roamed, but it hung out in the back, in front of his dog house under a tree most of the time.

Ahhh – under the dog house.

Cash, that was what it was all about, and it didn't bother her one bit, so why should it bother us? Having Benny by our side lubed the deal. This was a dream come true for The Foolstars as much as it was for me personally, because she knew how much it meant to me and the group, the lovers circle be unbroken. The Foolstars have a new teammate in Sally.

Amazingly enough, out of all those bills in the box, only one turned out to be counterfeit. One fucking twenty dollar bill out of the whole damn batch was identified counterfeit. One might tend to reason, for good reason, that there should have been more than just one bogus bill in those boxes, considering the source. The authorities questioned me about the counterfeit bill, but neither the incident nor the bill amount to anything detrimental. We had been playing the horses a long time, came up a winner, then invested it all back into our business. Luckily, the group slid right through it, like a sled down a steep, snowy hill.

♩

Out of all the articles one can almost surely predict are in any given women's handbag, there were three things you will have always found in Sally's: Cash, Sniff and Ludes. Therefore, wherever the band happened to go, Sally joining in, or wherever Sally decided she wanted to take us somewhere, it always turned out to be an excellent adventure. She assumed the surrogate mother role over all of us, and we all play, or rather are, in whole and truth, the spoiled children just fine. We loved her. We did.

I developed a crush. Hell, we slept next to each other on Dominican Drive. I should have moved on it but did not want to be disrespectful. And my girlfriend was the closest girl ever that I held close and true to my heart. She deserved my best behavior. I heard later that Sally felt the same as I did.

Damn.

A typical night out to watch a performance, Sally would, just like any other woman, pack her bag. When the bartenders heard that Sally was coming, they would fight to tend her. It was no wonder, for it was Ms. Clarke's classy good habit to tip well. If she went to the bar, the least she would lay down would be a twenty, regardless of the tab.

She wasn't one to go to the bar and order just for herself, so each bill was often well over twenty dollars. She was making friends with all our friends, if she didn't know them already. If that was the case, down went another twenty, or maybe a fifty. Sally didn't believe in taking change from bartenders. The entire balance always went to the barkeep. And if that were not enough, down went another twenty. Sally knows what is going on with the help, so she purposely traverses from one bartender to the next, just to be fair and to share the wealth.

"*Sally.*"

She, in a word, is cool in that way - the way of the world - money, power and sex. She didn't flaunt it and didn't mean to in any case. It was like when someone wealthy, or famous, or both, is in a public place, everybody else there becomes, somehow, very aware of it.

On one occasion at Benny's, Sally took the crew grocery shopping. She had by then moved-in with us. It was to be merely a trip to the local Market Basket. She and her husband were divorcing, and she asked if she and her son could live there with the group. We imagined a man get mean. They never gave it a thought, and could never have refused, any hoot.

The band is rehearsing, but the crew, Sally and Benny all went in the band's Suburban to the shopping center. The band lost track of time and didn't realize how long the shoppers had been gone. We got to jamming, and as usual the magic carried us away and time became simply two hands across a face, four numerals on a monochrome screen, invisible measurement of pain, nothing more.

Having fun with Sgt. Pepper, we noticed the crew coming in with the ever-familiar brown bags with Market Basket maroon printing. The plastic ones were for frozen food. One after the other, then back out again, and back in with another, and back out again, and back in with another, and then back out for yet another, ad infinitum, the crew continued to tote. They should have known by then what to expect, but Sally surprised us yet again. It was more amazement than it was surprise.

"I envision the workers being not unlike the long trail of ants on a sidewalk in the summer," I said.

Whenever there is a sizable morsel, a steady trail, marching the goods to the colony, and then creeping back out for more, repeatedly.

"Ants they are, the teamwork, the steady rolling line, the little legs moving, the incredible show of strength," I interjected. "While ants can carry five times their own weight, our crew could carry about three quarters of theirs."

I remembered being amazed with the documentary "The Hellstrom Chronicles."

The groceries had arrived. Someone counted the bags in all; the ones in the kitchen, covering the counters, the floors, the butcher block; the ones in the laundry room, covering the washer, the dryer, the floor; the ones in the hallway, on the sofa table, and on the floor. All over the got-darned house were strewed one-hundred-twenty-three bags of groceries.

Our gal Sally; she'd done it again.

Granted, they had two over-size refrigerators and a freezer big enough to keep Haystacks Calhoun's family on ice; I really don't think the mighty shoppers were thinking about where they might store all that stuff once they got it home. It was just another day at the store with Sally. Many outings were unplanned, quite by whim. Sally was very casual about it all. As if implicitly to ask, who doesn't want, or need, to shop for whatnot occasionally? Mind over matter. If she doesn't care, it doesn't matter.

An especially enterprising trip with Sally had been one we made to our favorite music store in Miami. She went along on that outing and for the life of us all, we didn't know why she did, but in the end, damn glad she did.

What started as a typical little doodle down to the music store for some strings and picks, some sticks and heads, ended only when the group had all walked out of that store each with a special gift from Sally. Dollar for dollar, I didn't know what she spent that day, but it was, easily, a twelve-hundred-dollar item or items for each of the band and crew. Five band members at twelve hundred a piece is six large. Add the crew to that.

Sally bought Scott a vintage mandolin. Gene received a top of the line banjo. Allen got a midi something or other for his keyboard bank. Sally bought Dee the antique Fender Jazz bass that happened to be on display in the store window. In addition, I got a new cymbal set, new microphones and a few pieces of miscellaneous hardware for my drum kit. I wanted to rebuild my set, refurbish it. Add to that the sticks and heads I went for in the first place. Our lives had turned into Disney World by then, but yes, Sally took us on vacation to the real place in Orlando.

"Just for the pure joy of it!" She hollers like our town crier. If there's anything better than Disney World, it's Disney World with Sally Clarke. Because it's the land of dreams, she made sure dreams come true.

You may venture to say that Robin Leach could not have kept up with this group. We had to arrange for a Disney staffer with a golf cart to truck purchases out to the parking lot periodically throughout the day. Clothes, souvenirs, costumes, hats, plush goods, and masks.

Oh, the band loved the masks. Like other merry pranksters from our generation, we enjoyed goofing with the audience from time to time, and masks did sometimes just the right trick. We took after the Merry Pranksters. She knew that, clearly. She loved that in us.

Sally loved her gorgeous and handsome horses. She had an interest in breeding them, buying them, riding them, racing them, showing them, selling them and betting on them. She was determined to have the group join her on a trip there someday, and one day she follows through. Sally, being an equestrian, has a favorite western wear joint, as well. She took us to her stable stalls to show us her horses. They were nothing less than divine.

She had us drive her to the western shop, and although it wasn't like the day at the music store, it came, relatively speaking, close. The Executive Producer bequeaths to everyone that day, new boots, new hats, new vests and new spurs; Dress-up items. The money spent did not enter the mind, because by that time, we knew Sally, so Yee-fucking-Haw anyhow.

CHAPTER 28

Sean

If there's been painted an all too perfect picture of Ms. Sally, take heart in knowing that there was one aspect of the relationship with her that, even though just the one, was a major entity and terrifically negative force. It was the kind of slight and insignificant difference that flies under the radar, yet large enough to change history; like an assassination, or a flood, or a war.

Sean. The name alone evokes an image of the quintessential all-American boy. Red, curly hair, freckles speckled over a pug nose. He's just a wee bit shorter than the average, cap atop slightly askew. He wears torn dungarees with a red bandana hanging out of the left back pocket, comic books in hand, sporting perhaps, a black eye. He's the catcher on the Little League team, batting ordered somewhere right in the middle of the line-up. The Black High-Top All-Stars, right shoe untied, Sean will certainly not notice before his mom does.

The Sean about whom is written here may have once been reflected all over the preceding paragraph, but probably not, or at least no more.

If first impressions, however, too early to tell, do mean anything, his should have scared the hell right out of us. We had, by that time been involved long enough to know a jackass when we saw one. We might have been, one might suffice, at that point, too numb to notice. What we got out of the experience initially was a hell of a fright. Afterward, we had ourselves a good, long laugh and recognized it as the first of many reasons to hate Sean.

Like this one:

No matter where the band plays, one can always count on a routine. Our band plays a set, and the band takes a break; then we play the second of two long sets. Bands are under contract to do this for some predefined length of time, (or for however long they wish to, depending on who is watching).

The big shows and finer nightspots and show case venues provided break areas or dressing rooms, green rooms for the group, but there in South Miami the group spent most of their breaks outside in the parking lot. We hung out with the locals either outside, or in the RV, some usually getting high.

We were out in the parking lot for a break on a Friday night of that first impression of Sean. The break time excitement to date had been the episodic, almost weekly occurrence of the Barrow brothers going yet once again to fisticuffs, wrestling bare-chested all over the lot.

On that night, the twins had managed to slam each other right into our group's RV, breaking one of the side view mirrors right off the cab door and dented the passenger side door. Bloodied as usual, both boys were quite a sight. Typically, soon after the hell broke loose, they were hugging each other again - a mass of derelict wire and muscle, waist long, matted brown hair and tattoos - planning on their next big pit bull gig. The twins looked just like Anthony Keidis from the RHCP's when he had long hair. They bred, raised and fought pit bulls as a money-making endeavor.

No comment.

By the time the Barrow fight had ended, all would remain as calm as could be expected, considering the scene. Then, suddenly, around the corner came a loud, maniacally driven, speeding yellow jeep. The canvas was down on the Wrangler J5 and there were two men in the vehicle. The driver was blowing the horn, shrieking and cackling with lunatic laughter. The passenger was half standing, swaying wildly, and screaming insanely. He had one hand on the roll bar and the other on a gun.

Moonstruck chaos all at once filled the scene as the hot spur continued cracking off pistol shots. He fired shots into the air for fair warning, but then others hit the ground and ricocheted off the brick building all around the lot. Shots were fired everywhere in a barrage. The return sounded like a nine-millimeter, but the weapon could have been a three-eighty or perhaps something slightly bigger.

"Echo was a factor, and I am not any Joe Fucking Friday, mind you."

They went around the block and came back at us again.

Everyone out in the lot hit the deck and rolled under the nearest vehicle to them. Everyone except the band knew the identity of the shooter straight away. Although his reputation does precede him, the locals recognized Sean's jeep right away. It is Sally's crazy husband, Sean. The crowd also recognized that this was nothing more than a typical Sean incident.

"I have to admit," I looked to Scott. "I was a little impressed and taken aback at the same moment," I said to him in jest. Scott agreed, and said, "We should write a song about it."

"Yeah, Scott, I felt suddenly transported to some Good Fellas – slash – Zachariah (The Electric Western) dream world, come true."

We stayed right where we were, hugging the asphalt for a few minutes, then scurried back into the bar once the dust settled. The whole place caught wind of what had gone down and virtually everyone there got a big chuckle out of it. The Foolstars, upon re-entrance were given a standing ovation and applause, but it worried them to know their band was in danger. The murmurs revolved around this:

That ol' Sean. He's just crazy, man. He's done it again.

"We've just been shot at!" Dee nervously hollered.

"Nonetheless, the band plays on, ladies," I replied laughing. It was no social crises; it is just another tricky day for The Foolstars.

Sally had become a regular at the club, and usually traveled with the band wherever we went. As Executive Producer, she may have well been part of the band, if not an honorary member. In fact, in my view, she was and is -- forever. She was a welcome regular at whatever venue we happened to play, and always a welcome regular in the studio. So, she moved in with the group on Dominican Drive. That is what had Sean in a paroxysm. He let his imagination get the best of him, and on came the green streak.

Imagination inflation.

Go cúramach leis sin, ol' Seanie-boy.

The band had no idea her true marital status in the first place, and we had no reason to question her arrival. Moreover, when we did find out, we just took it in stride. She stated that her marriage had been failing for a very long time, and it didn't matter much to her anymore if it did collapse. Therefore, she surmised and directed, it shouldn't bother the band much either. We always tried to protect Sally, no matter the incident.

"Enough said." I told the others in the room. "We protect Sally. She is a lady, *our lady, our friend!*"

Sean had an entirely dissimilar view of the situation. Rumors and hallucinations were flying around that we had really pissed him off, hence, the shooting incident at Big Daddy's South Miami. He had this notion that the group had seduced his wife into being a rich, ultimate groupie for them, catering to our every whim; be it monetary, materially, emotionally, or yes, sexually.

The Foolstars may have stepped on a few toes to date, but never Sally's or even Sean's. We had no reason to use, or abuse anyone, period. Things turned convenient for us for a while, with Benny's generosity and Sally's support and friendship. It was a triangular love affair of sorts, but not the kind of affair under which Sean had mistakenly become obsessed.

Sally, at one point, did pine Scott to have her, but he had a girl from Atlanta with him at the time, and no one in the group ever saw Sally as a toy or an object. She was like a big sister, a fun loving and life living, rich, big sister. Still, I secretly wanted to be with her. And I knew she liked me. And like me, yes, she still does. We're pals. We chat socially.

I'm sure she could have appreciated that, yet especially on those horny, hot South Miami nights. She shared a bedroom on Dominican Drive with me and her son. Scott shared the other bed with her son, and the rest of the group and crewmembers shared other bedrooms. We all simply shared the house with nine more able-bodied rockers. We would together party nightly into the morn, but there was never any sexual connotation to be had, albeit, not with Sally, except for me. I froze. I didn't understand exactly why.

Yes, I caught a crush for Sally but did not want to chance insulting her. Doing it over again, I would have asked her to my bed. She slept on the floor between the two beds in our room. She insisted on it. She instantly took the floor, but just sometimes we shared it, and sometimes my bed. Simple affection from on high. And even all the way up to the current day we still talk and she knows now she was very well thought of by me. And I am glad of that.

♪

A second incident with Sean would come only two weeks later than the first and it confirmed the band's thought that they might be in more trouble with him than they had first imagined.

One afternoon, Dee and Allen went to run some errands with Benny. By then, Sean was watching us, or having us watched twenty-four hours a day. On that otherwise seasonally sunny day in home sweet Homestead, it was Sean doing the watching.

The boys weren't yet a mile away when suddenly, they heard thunderously close gunshots, deep, sporadic and crazy. Benny took a glance in his rear-view mirror, another in his side view, turned quickly around to see again, and then turned back to the road ahead. One more look in the rear view provided confirmation. Sure enough, there he was, riding right up their tails.

"S e a n!" Benny yelled, in almost perfect unison with Dee and Allen. A few more quick shots rang out. Two of them hit the car at about the same time Dee and Allen hit the floorboard, sweating, swearing in ululation. Poor Benny, slouched, head down, drove on as fast as he could go given the congested traffic.

Trying to lose someone following who knew the area as well as Benny did was not easy, but Benny did his best to shake him. Even though Benny would usually be the last person in the world to go for a visit to the Dade

County Sheriff's Office, that was exactly where he was heading, because if Benny had ten good reasons to stay away from the police, Sean had a hundred.

The sight had to be worth a million. Here we had a right-handed Irishman, driving his big, long green Lincoln Continental, clearly a phallic automobile using his good hand to steer, waving a forty-four magnum haphazardly, and firing randomly out the side window with the weaker left.

He could not have hit a standing target under those circumstances, let alone a moving, speeding, swerving one, unless by luck. Nevertheless, he did stand that chance; he did indeed had some luck of the Irish, after all.

Over medians, over lines and against the traffic, Benny, Dee and Allen finally arrived at the destination nouveau. They remained in the visitor's parking lot at the Sheriff's Office for an uncomfortable forty-five minutes. It took that long to regain the stamina for them to chance the ride back home. They didn't request a police escort, although the fantasy did cross their minds.

Living at Dominican Drive was entirely pleasant, productive and comfortable. We woke to coke and snoozed to Ludes. We used the back half of the great room as a rehearsal hall, and the front half as a sitting room or living room area. There are four bedrooms, one of which, the master, belonged to Benny. One of the other bedrooms had two sets of bunk beds, the second had two queen beds and the third and largest bedroom had four double beds. To fit any others, up to five would fit nicely in the third room, even if one occupant slept on the floor.

There were usually a few visiting stragglers,

sprawled out on the living room floor or couch somewhere. We put up a moderate overnight visitor in rotation of houseguests. Our live-ins depend on who the current girlfriends were, but we also made many friends who happened-in-and-out over time immemorial. We had many visitors and fast friends, but not all of them found themselves too incapacitated to drive away when the time came. Some did try, however.

Sally, for The Foolstars, often planned an activity for days off, but we were enjoying this afternoon at home. The band, crew, the girls and a few guests were sitting around, listening to music, watching a silent television and bullshitting about with flake.

A knock on the door sent TL, one of our biggest and strongest crew members out through the kitchen and then through the mudroom-laundry entry way to answer. The last person any one of them expected to have paying a friendly visit was Sean, but low and behold and lord give mercy, there he was, standing in the rainy door yard; Slowly soaking.

He is dressed neatly with his hair held down in a wet look like he OD'd on Dippity Doo. The wet look didn't help, and he is holding a colorfully wrapped present in his arms. Because the entire group was in such a pit of disbelief, they each took a comical turn peeking around the corner of the kitchen, through that entryway, to verify that TL's vision was indeed the reality. That one measly, little gift wasn't even going to gain any forgiveness from us.

Sean begged to let him in, everyone he saw looking around the corner at him. It was quite strange. He seemed to be groveling.

"My first plan of action is no action. Like

maybe if we ignore it, it will just go away." I suggested.

That didn't happen. He kept knocking on the door, pleading for someone to come let him in. He was calling out for Sally and their son.

"Jimmy?" Scott asks, "Please go see what he wants."

That's what I get for being the diplomat of the group.

While I was out speaking with Sean, Sally reminded the others that the following day would be her son's birthday. She offered that Sean probably just wanted to give the boy a gift. Our second POA was to convince Sean to leave the package on the doorstep. They would guarantee delivery for him. He pleaded with me that he wanted only to sit and spend some time with his son for his birthday. Just for a little while.

"I promise I mean no harm to any of you." He said. "Please. Just a few minutes with my boy."

Was he crying? Holy Hell.

Sally endorsed the idea, stating she thought he sounded sincere, but she would not send her son outside, and so the group did what it didn't want to do: We let him in.

It wasn't that casual or relaxed, however. He was practically made to strip search himself out there in the entryway. TL and Hogweed, the extra-large part of the crew, went out and patted him down. They disarmed Sean of a .38 Special and accepted a promise from him that he would behave or be hurt real bad. Then they escorted him through the door and into the house.

Sean's presence brought naturally with it, tension. It had become thicker than elephant shite when he entered the living room. Nevertheless, things were going along all right. He sat with his son and his estranged wife for twenty minutes. Everyone else cleared the room for a few minutes to give the dysfunctional family some time to themselves.

Given experiences, the crew and I were reluctant to leave Sally and the child alone with him for too long. We kept watch on the living room. Some of the guests left the house when we left the room, but after twenty-minutes, the rest of us returned to the living room in short order and found seats all around.

Sean had many questions for the band. He wanted to know where we'd been and where we thought they were going, and our plans for the future. He hinted at wanting to know the details of any deal we might have made with his wife. He wanted to know the sleeping arrangements in the house. I told him that he mind his business and leave us alone. I made it clear that we held Sally in the highest regard, and we would protect her under any circumstances that may rise. I added, "And so far, you are the biggest danger we currently see."

Suddenly, there he was as we had come to know him. I apparently hit the wrong button. Sean rose up and ran wildly through the living room, going berserk slashing at everything and everybody in his way. He had somehow managed to pack his buck knife in -- right past security!

"Follow me!" I screamed to Sally and her son. I grabbed them. "Now!"

I grabbed Sally and her boy and got them quickly into our bedroom. Dee and Allen followed, it being, besides Kenny's, the closest bedroom off the living room. Once inside, I locked the door and they all helped me jam it with a divan we had in there. That little couch was heavy.

Meanwhile, the others scurried into and locked themselves behind the closed doors of the remaining empty rooms. Sean was going nuts, and if he smuggled his knife in here with him, there was no telling whether he might have sneaked a pistol or even a fucking hand grenade!

There was a love seat in the hallway outside of mine and Sally's room. Sean put himself behind it, and easily on its castors positioned it so the end opposite him pointed directly at our door. He then began ramming the door behind which Sally, her son, Dee and Allen and I were sheltered. Sean screamed maddeningly at Sally to come out, threatening her *and* me repeatedly. Sally and her son cowered into the back corner of the room, as I instructed, but Dee, Allen and I held the door steady.

"Visiting hours are over asshole." I yelled back at Sean.

"Get the fuck out of this house, or I'm coming straight out of here with a big gun in hand motherf*cker!"

♪

I hadn't touched either of our rifles since an incident at Level III Orlando. Scott was being held at gun point. He had been flirting with the gun-man's girlfriend. I see him nervously twitching the revolver as he yelled at Scott and the girl.

I yelled over to him that I saw him, but he couldn't see me. I yelled, "If that handgun even moves a dite more, I'll put a 30.6 right into the side of your head. And I mean it, motherf*cker. You're in my sights. You've got one chance; don't blow it. You get away from the scene right now, and you'll live. If not, you're taking on a hell of a big chance." Everyone hears the police pulling in, lights, sirens. They took care of the threat.

♪

With that, I shot a twelve-gauge slug out about waist high from only four feet away. The explosion of the twelve-gauge round was deafening. Sally and son Mark were sobbing in the corner, ears covered. I shot the second barrel. The slugs blew a hole through the door, almost the size of a tether ball, and both hit Sean squarely in the belly. He was bleeding bad and crying. He ran away from my door.

Unfortunately, Scott didn't take a place to hide. He was just a little bit too slow.

He remained on the floor behind the couch in the living room that separated the front from the rear. He peeked over the back of the couch, and once Sean caught sight of him, another episode unfolded.

Sean chased Scott all over the house and finally tackled him roughly. Sean fell directly on top of him. The knife Sean was reeling came down hard just to the right of Scott's head, taking a small slice off the bottom of his ear. The wound was dangerously close to the jugular vein, however, and Scott knew it. After a wicked, slow-motioned second or two, while Sean seemed to have lost a bit of his drive, Scott was able push him off and roll away.

Once the couch ramming had ceased in the hallway upstairs, TL and Hogweed slipped from their room. They watched fearfully and apprehensively as Sean chased Scott around the living room, and when they saw Scott roll away from that extremely close call, Hog and TL took advantage of the moment and overtook Sean easily there on the floor. They punched him out but good.

Sean, with wobbly legs, struggled hard to regain his feet and his weapon. My boys were big and strong. Sean is just a wee little shitter. I tossed the rifle to TL. There will be no more from Sean today. He was screaming as though he were a gypsy possessed as he was bodily and roughly thrown out, literally, into the street. It was like a sack of big Maine baking potatoes. With a smack and a thud, they had no reason to be the least bit careful with him. They swayed him gaining momentum and let him fly. Watching cautiously from the window, he sat pressing on his gunshot wound. He was bleeding badly. They saw him get into his car, relieved that the incident had finally ended.

Sean sat in the street for a few moments, and then painfully climbed into his Lincoln. He appeared to be quiet and contemplated. He was quiet alright, but he was actually deliberating.

Fucking contemplating.

"Everyone to the back of the house." I ordered.

Sean started revving the engine in the Lincoln as if he was waiting for the tree to fall through to green on an NHRA strip. Suddenly, he threw it into reverse, hit the street and without coming to a stop, ground it into drive-1. But he wasn't heading down the street; he was heading toward the front lawn. He in the vehicle jumped the curb and ran over a dogwood tree in the yard, before ramming the first car he came to.

The Foolstars had to park some of the

vehicles on the front lawn because there simply wasn't enough room for them in the car port or parking curbside. Different parking arrangements would not have made a difference in this case. Sean rammed the hell out of Phyllis' brand-new Toyota.

She *just* bought it.

Phyllis was Scott's latest girlfriend. She was from Atlanta.

This added another ugly layer to the way Scott's day had thus far developed. The sound of the cars crashing together was utterly vexatious. It sounded like a complex sonic equation of a ram, plus a boom, plus a crunch, multiplied by a small explosion. Again, and again, Sean kept on backing, and ramming.

Phyllis, bless her heart, was completely losing her mind. In a true textbook scenario, which included pulling her own hair out, running rampant throughout the house and back, she was truly a woman run mad. She was moaning, sobbing and screaming as though she were witnessing her only daughter being dragged off to an all-girl prison. Scott did his best to calm Phyllis down. Not much there just yet.

There was one more hellacious ramming. That last one was the one that knocked Phyllis' car into and completely over the garden wall in front of the house, and into the house itself. There was now a front-end half a car in Benny's bedroom. The rear-end of the car stuck out of the house, lodged in between Benny's bedroom wall and the crawl space, and resting on the rock garden space beneath.

It was an ugly and atrocious sight, a mess, but one that had apparently satisfied the wild committer out there. Hogweed ran out and got a couple shots off the rifle I tossed him. TL followed. But Sean drove away laughing and screaming unintelligibly into the dusk.

The local police precinct received several calls from Dominican Drive besides ours that afternoon, so the dispatcher sent the units over quickly. The police arrested Sean shortly thereafter.

♪

After the car-ramming incident, Floyd paid the band a visit: One of his boys was in jail. Floyd was the only one standing between Sean and Grizelda Blanko in Miami, so he was concerned over the situation on Dominican Drive. He decided to visit us after he heard that Sean was losing his mind over matters... again. He thought his visit might help us better understand Sean, or at least explain Sean's erratic behavior.

I knew Floyd had come on a mission of peace, because I recognized Roy following him, as he often does, carrying with him up the driveway a large glass pipe and a torch. They never came into the house beyond the entryway, the laundry room just off the kitchen. No one else cared to question why, but based on my own shrewdness, it made perfect sense to camp there: Escape plan. Floyd or not.

That first visit was a monumental one; because it was the first time anyone in the group, besides me, ever tried smoking coke. Most of the others took one hit each and took no more. A couple of them took two and stopped. It felt so nice, so good, so warm and scalp-peeling that it absolutely scared the shit out of them. It was that good.

And the heart it go, boom, ba-boom, ba-boom.

Smoking coke is very close to lining it, but in addition to the warmth, there is a kind of hypercritical excitement. The results were immediate. The heart pounds, the head peels and one can feel the blood racing through the body. The ears buzz. Warmth surrounds you. And even though they say that cocaine is an upper, and it is for most, freebasing it relaxed me wrapped up in all those other feelings.

Dee was just two hits into it before implicitly getting Floyd's point. He had at least the wherewithal to have come forth with, "Man! No wonder Sean is so fucking crazy." Dee, of course, was right, and that was exactly what Floyd said to me, and wanted all of us to understand. Floyd promised he'd replace Phyllis's car within two weeks.

"Jesus, Jimmy, how do you do it?" Scott asked.

"I've had six hits and I just maintain, like I haven't done a goddamn thing: Relax and enjoy." I answered.

That was not the first time I heard that. I've always thrived on extremity. Subtlety and comfort depress me. I have found that nervous tension causes a heightened awareness inside. I discovered that at a very early age, first dabbling with astral projection.

I found that on those occasions where I felt very nervous, the inner self tended to rise easier, with far less conscious pseudo-concentration than usual. Therefore, while the others let the tension of an eight ball up their noses and another two or three grams in their lungs nibble away at their sanity, I just sat there, satisfied, thinking, wondering and feeling thoroughly entertained.

Poor Scott looked so wired after just two pulls that I warned him, "Don't go picking your nose, for fear you may poke your eye out!"

Everyone laughed like mad at that warning from me.

The band indulged in many recreational drugs along the way to South Miami, and there. With rock and roll came accessibility. Since moving in with Benny, however, we had taken to snorting coke and, in my case, also smoking it, usually with Floyd, smoking pot and chewing Ludes exclusively. All day and all night.

Up until I started smoking coke with Floyd, the most dangerous activity I had partaken was when the Hog and I would steal away for a night or two at a time to shoot some Dilladin he got from a friend in Lynn Haven. But there was never a habit. No one else knew about any of that, and if the rest of the group ever found out that he and I were using works, it would have shocked them seamless, and scared them to death.

A few years before, I bought the recipe for quick brew crystalline speed from a Tampa fan aptly nicknamed Mad Dog. Mad Dog lived daily on that speed and on M.D. 20-20 by the case, hence the Mad Dog moniker. Red bandana around his head, and all. The band never knew that the brown speed we bought was meant to be intravenously administered.

Luscious as the brown speed was, it burnt hell right into your nose, but it was as warm as mother's milk going into your vein. Either way, the high was immeasurably like meth. Soon, we all injected it. But the habit didn't last long. They were all curiously taken, you see. Then left it alone, certainly for the best. I did too.

The FDA finally wised-up, but for the

longest time we bought from the local drug marts a certain brand of inhaler, boiling them down, mixing the derivative with a crystalline agent and creating some of the most inexpensive and best meth-like speed ever done. I was an ex-mad scientist.

The stuff was a mystery to all, including law enforcement. The Tampa police stopped my girlfriend Donna as she was driving home from Jump River, where the band was playing. They found less than a half a gram of the brown powdery stuff after searching her purse. They had to let her go because they couldn't figure out what it was from the bottom of her Marlboro box spilled out at the bottom of her bag.

That was just as well, because she was carrying what was mine, not hers; luckily, it had spilled. Besides weed, Donna had been clean since we got together. I admired her. We were in love.

Isn't the music world glamorous?

Still think it's all about glamour?

Floyd was somewhat impressed with me, because I was the only one who kept up with him on the pipe.

After that first visit, he began stopping by to pick me up, and take me out to get high, leaving the others behind. I got the impression that, in all his massive glory and importance, he was secretly thrilled to hang out with 'a guy in the band; the drummer.' My tracks were laid at Studio Center and that's when the real bonding started.

Although our unofficial home was the house on Dominican Boulevard, The Foolstars had to get a temporary place up in North Miami, closer to the studio we had secured. So, with our sixty-five-thousand-dollar boxes of money, we bid a tentative "So long for now" to Dominican Drive and moved up to Biscayne Bay. That put us just seven miles south of Studio Center.

It made perfect sense, since we leased the studio for twelve full weeks, with an option to extend. The lease came with an engineer, assistant and 24-hour access. As well rehearsed as the band was, recording an album surely could take much more than that. The play room was like a laboratory. They also had to build time into the plan for the mix-downs and producing the master.

On the first night in North Miami, we decide to go to Tony Roma's. This is a first for the band. We were all eager to go because it was, at that time, world renowned for their baby-back ribs and oddly enough, onion ring loaves. We would partake in both, along of course with some adult beverages.

We passed a telephone booth on the way there with a poster ad on the bottom half of the enclosure. "Look who it is." I whispered to Scott, who took a glance at it. And, there she was. She was looking as good as she had ever, in a spaghetti-strap short, black petite gown and heels, champagne in hand. Everyone looked, noticing what me and Scott were looking at; our reaction, and instinctively next, everyone looked over at Lloyd. Halfheartedly trying to behave sincerely, the group was also openly excited at recognizing someone they knew in the business that appeared to be getting somewhere… anywhere. Cleaner than a Hustler spread, anyway.

"It doesn't look like a billboard to me," Lloyd said, blowing it off seeing his ex-fiancé on the side of a telephone booth. It was an off-hand and defensive remark, but just as he spat it out, and just as Gene turned the corner to get to the restaurant, there she was again. This time she is forty-two feet high and fifty-six feet wide. This time, she lay there seductively, again as sexy as legal, selling Miami Beach the spirit and cheer of the season.

"Whatever she has, I'll take it." Allen said, which led us into a laughing fit.

"I fully admit she makes *me* want to buy the store." I remark, smiling. More laughing broke out.

And that's when he lost it.

The floodgates opened, and Lloyd cried aloud; openly sobbing. However, he wasn't just sad. He was mad, jealous, humiliated and embarrassed all at once. Everybody had to sit in the rib joint parking lot for over twenty fucking minutes, waiting, while he gathered his wits and wrapped his head back together before they could all go in.

Truth not need be told that Lloyd drank quite a bit more than usual that evening, even though as much as usual was usually more than enough regardless. Delivered home, he spent the rest of the evening laying in his motor coach in the Studio Center parking lot, crying, nodding, puking and thinking.

♪

The Foolstars were in Augusta, Georgia, when I, beyond any doubt, figured out what kept that goddess covering Lloyd as long as she did. The band was playing a showcase venue called "The Whippin' Post." It is our last road date before the scheduled production would begin at Studio Center. The showcase and the money made the trip worthwhile. During the weekend engagement at the theater-size hall, the crew befriended a small bevy of young, negligent, along with two or three genuinely nice girls and had of course partied them rightly.

"Listen," I explained to everyone. "Lloyd has not yet fully recovered from the blow to his empire, and I have an idea that I thought might help bring him back around."

"Go ahead. More..." TL said.

Following through with it, TL asked the two lovelies that were with him in the shower to do a big favor for the band on the following night, when they expected Lloyd to arrive. I just wanted them to baby Lloyd through the night, show him a little affection and try to keep a smile on his face {wink}. My exact words were "Just be nice to him, really: He's been hurt. Show him a good time to help ease the pain and lift his spirits."

Nobody notices the three of them, Lloyd and our fair young girls, exit stage left toward the green room. The band played on, our final series of tunes for the night ending in crescendo, walking off on a high note. We waited just a few minutes for the ladies worshipping what a pants-down Lloyd had out in the corner.

CHAPTER 29

In Studio Center

Stereotypical categorization of music was yet to come out much beyond jazz, blues, Rock and Roll, bluegrass, folk, country and classical. There was no "alternative." There was no industrial Rock, electronica, arena Rock, techno-pop or EMO. Competing with punk, new wave, disco and hair-band-metal was humiliating enough, let alone having to go up against rap, hip-hop, pseudo-country, and the myriad of little niches carved out of the listening world today.

The door today is much wider ajar for young musicians than it was yesterday, yet trend remains paramount to commercial radio success, it seems. Finally, it settles into a category named by the decade from which it came; 60s music, 70s music, 80s music, 90's -- Alternative and so on. Pity? Or just ease? I preferred "Alternative Rock" and "Grunge" when they came about.

In those days, even back in the mid-eighties, early nineties, when we suddenly found ourselves in an anything goes era, all we could ever be to a record label is a "Southern Rock" band. That's just the way it was. We always felt we could break the mold, by our music alone, but never had there been management present to push it. The Foolstars got a bad rap because of looks and location. And we were, unfortunately, labeled. We received compliments however, on our music and performances. And I noticed bands like Blackberry Smoke getting a lift-off. That makes me feel good. A long-haired hippy band from the south. Just like us.

Our many influences shown through our music sometimes, and so did our "Live-Your-Life" attitude. We felt free and wanted everyone to feel free, too. It was not because the moniker we couldn't shake was the infamous "Southern Rock," we were always proud of where we were from, and the music we made.

Who's listening? Ask *them* what it is. It was everyone else in the plastic world of music, the business, adds to the complication. Unlike the practices of today, marketing a band from the south that didn't play Southern Rock was a marketing nightmare twenty-five years ago. Southern Rockers must carry with them a sub-cult of followers, and the band has got to be good. Very good.

Lloyd stumbled his way through the

responsibilities given him in the studio. It wasn't long before the band figured out why he went to the bathroom every twenty minutes or so.

You must have an ear to produce a record. You can't listen to someone else's work hoping to design and craft a uniquely different song. You must relax, and listen to the song at hand, and reach into your mind and your soul to hear the potential in the sound that's there, in the forefront that needs to be there, and needs to come out; hence *production*. Invent something new, damn-it. Listen to the band! Hear the demos. Get excited. Be enthused!

Sometimes, all it takes is a listen-to, everything else just flows, from the count on, but you have to have that ear to be able to notice and capture those great moments that come along. And make note of those not present, but you can "hear." You would add those into the mix. Lay it on a track, or at the least, write it down in case you want to use it.

You must have an ear to capture the moments that interrupt the flow as well. One must also display a bit of intuition, if not shrewdness and practical understanding to pick out what might or might not be fit, as there is hardly a formula. If there was, we'd all be rich. If you discover it, let me know.

Moreover, a producer must have guts. Lloyd did not have guts or imagination. Our engineer had guts, but little experience with Rock music. Lloyd was a trend follower, and Gary was just getting the hang of Rock and Roll, and he was excited by it. And, he was quickly becoming very good with it.

I remember after a good take on the song "Blood on the Tracks," Gary comes on in the headphones, "There's gonna be blood on the tracks by the time we finish *this* one."

I loved that guy.

Because "New Wave" was the latest flash out of the pan that was the music biz, we were compelled by Lloyd consistently to push the keyboards into the top of the mix. Not piano. Not organ. He wanted silly synthesizer samples. It was a constant struggle to keep Lloyd in the control room sane, and above the fads and beyond history. Here was the decisive factor for me. Lloyd, much more so than Gary, was seemingly deathly afraid to turn up the drums. Afraid to make a difference from what was on Lloyd's radio. That made me sick.

I argued with Lloyd daily that virtually no one had yet discovered the power of a pumped bass drum and toms, cymbals and no one was tripling the snare, but I wanted to.

I could hear it. And it was on its way – it's coming. Not merely because I was the drummer, but because I could hear what was missing in every song we ever mixed with him. It had been missing in every other song heard to that point. Our Audio Tech, TL, had it down. He knew exactly what need be done for the drummer's mix. We partnered Gary with TL for the drum mix.

Maybe I should have replaced Lloyd with TL.

"Jimmy," Scott said. "Did you just replace Lloyd with TL?"

"Yes, I did." I replied. "Lloyd doesn't know what the fuck he's doing in there. So yeah. I told him to grab a comfortable seat in the back."

"You never cease to amaze me," Scott said.

Very few bands had a decent drum sound. Without deep drums *with* high-end cut, it's enough to make the band, well, suck. Nowadays, fat drums are the standard. You don't have a record unless the percussion is better than real, but I knew it back then. I could *feel* it. I could hear it coming and I knew what I wanted to sound like on record, but Lloyd, overriding Gary wouldn't give it to me.

Gary, having engineered and produced several gold records in the disco era, knew how to tune and knob-turn the bass drum, so he's not far away from what I'd explained to or discussed with him; concepts of equalizing drums.

Nowadays, there many ways to capture all kinds of drum sounds. Everything from throwing a towel over your snare to purchasing a set of Rowlands. I've done both.

I couldn't blame Gary, because the gold records on his wall were from popular Miami disco bands who broke through. He did know his shit – the power behind all his recording equipment and outboard gear. Besides, he had the energy, the motivation, and shared the excitement.

Gary would have to do what Lloyd told him to do in that control room. But I'd had enough. I marched in there and I forcibly nudged Lloyd off the board and told him the band would be working with Gary and TL directly and exclusively, and that he should pick out a comfortable spot in the back of the control room and just listen. Try to think of something worthwhile. Jot it down. Otherwise to think things over.

The old cliché rings true and harsh. You get what you pay for. I did blame Lloyd, damn it, for he should have backed his drummer up, the band up, along with the engineer, no less. Eventually he might never again during our sessions. I called him to the mat, to be sure of that during mix-downs and mastering. Scott and I would do the mix-downs and mastering with Gary.

"That's why I said that Lloyd was a poser when we met him," I growled to the band, and Gary overheard.

Gary invited me to work with him on the drum tracks. I suggested that over and above the great things he had come-up with for our tonal, deep drum sound, to punch the highest frequencies on the EQ on the entire set. Usually that included all the cymbals, too.

He asked "Why, Jimmy?"

I said, "We need to capture the attack; the stick attack on the drums, hi-hat and cymbals. The tones are nice, the balance is good, and the stereophonics are wonderful. We got those down quickly on the first day there. But we need the sound that makes the drums cut. Cut like a mother. Especially the snare. That's also why I had you triple mic the snare: To capture the snares on the bottom head, the blow out by the vent, and the mic on the top – to capture the attack, besides the tone."

"Oh, I get it now, Jimmy." Gary said to me with enthusiasm. "Tomorrow you and I go through each piece until you are satisfied. That is a really good idea about capturing the attack of stick to head. Wow."

"Yup. Wait till you hear the difference."

♪

Lloyd enjoyed the regional success The Foolstars achieved by this time, and he knew he was on to something good. He figured he could use that success to fuel his nearly defunct, old booking agency a bit. Mistakenly, he allowed himself the luxury of thinking that he was responsible for the success my band was enjoying, but he was merely riding our coattails, and added nothing to our project. He had his chance but failed miserably.

He was a poser when we met and how he reacted in other night spots, like Dino's. He was a trend follower and he hadn't anything close to a true breakthrough Rock producer. It's our fault we didn't vet him more thoroughly. He took on a few additional bands from the Miami area, and called down a couple of his old acts from Orlando. He collected twenty percent from all the happy Rock acts he took on for Big Daddy's Miami, and that kept him happy. Our return trip into South Miami was coming soon.

"As far as we are concerned," I said. "Lloyd's business is growing in the wrong direction, as it applies to us.

"I thought this would piss me off when it

came, even though I knew it would. But it is more evidence that he'd rather book bands, like the agent he used to be. He belongs in a used car lot in a plaid jacket. He has no business being in a recording studio. He is not doing what we hired him to do. He is squandering the resources.

"That's my view and he has fallen back into his comfortable booking agent role. His true comfort zone. I vote we lose him now. That is why I dismissed him in the control room. He is no longer titled Producer. Period.

"We didn't rent him the office space in Studio Center so that he could build up his booking agency. Booking on the side may have been cool, if he had only performed his job for us. That's all we ever asked from anyone, right?

"Do what you say you will do."

Lloyd would maintain that he had indeed started to manage and book a few of his other bands in his spare time. They can pay for his office space. Good luck.

"Yeah, but you haven't completed your job for us yet; therefore, we would maintain that you had no spare time of which to spend. From this point on, things will not be the same between you and my band. No additional monies will be exchanged from The Foolstars with you Mr. Lloyd. I'm sorry, but you're out. Find a partner to help you successfully book your bar bands." I thought I caught it up and relayed it well.

Lloyd missed many good opportunities to shop the group with influential labels because he didn't keep his eye on the ball. He also, upon working with more and more bar bands, started in again with that trend-following, bullshit mentality that The Foolstars had tried so hard to break him out of; he suggested perms for our hair, wearing beach clothes on stage, and even mentioned once that they should enter the stage to "Good Vibrations", the Beach Boys masterpiece.

"Good lord, help us all."

Is that what he did all day long in that office we found for him? Were those his big ideas for The Foolstars? When we played on stage, we played for the long haul, forever, for fun, for each other, and everyone interested in listening. The Foolstars didn't just play the music; we *made* music. No need for gimmicks. A surprise, occasionally was alright, I suppose. But not corny at the cost of the band. Our Production is exceptional and I won't do anything to compromise it.

We were extremely serious about our sound, performance and production. No interest in gimmicks; they were merciless upon themselves.

It was Lloyd's good fortune to have been right there with The Foolstars when we fell into the good stuff, the hit records, the money, and his misfortune, and ours, to have blown it all away.

He fell into the pit of ignorance usually reserved for those who the outfit could only call, with no disrespect to the musical times, a licker. The Studio Center album came out well overall, fine indeed, plus, we took with us a few extra outtakes of the record. The group got a lot of mileage out of the production, but we could have gotten more. Lloyd especially could have done more. I still question that. We had a super-good Media Kit, thanks to a close friend in Birmingham, Alabama. When the band let Lloyd go, he stayed on at Studio Center for a short while. He had plans.

Moving to Key Biscayne raised the bar of

standard but did little to raise awareness. The glamorous island life, bluntly stated, was a bit too nice, in our opinions, for the likes of Lloyd Hart.

The last time we came to North Miami we stayed several miles up Ocean Beach Boulevard at the Voyager Inn, historically noted both famous and infamous. The Voyager is famous for the claim that Barbara Streisand was, many years ago, first discovered there, in the hotel lounge. It is infamously known as the hotel where the XXX movie classic "Deep Throat" was filmed. This trip to Miami was bound to be much different, because they had the money to make it so.

A celebrity acupuncture specialist owned the house rented by the band. She was a globetrotter, who traveled more than dwelled, presumably mixing house calls with vacationing. Renting her home on Key Biscayne during her absences brought her an extra twenty-five hundred a week. She certainly didn't need the money, she was rich already. She had her acupuncture practice, but several years prior, her dead husband left her a bundle. She was a multi-millionaire.

Although the home was handsome, expansive and exotic, it was relatively modest compared with others in the neighborhood. The Bee Gees' Gibb family lived several miles down on the left, and Eric Clapton had a cape on Ocean Beach Boulevard, just north of the bay. The Eagles were in town for a session with Bill Szcymzic, a few miles away in Coconut Grove, and they were staying right down the street from The Foolstars on Key Biscayne.

Our place was the first home on the left after crossing the bridge to the key from the Miami Mall exit off Ocean Boulevard. Ours is a sprawling and spectacular one-story home with a built-in pool in the back. Beyond the pool stood a seawall, which was all that lay between the beautiful bay and the inhabitants. A few of us climbed the wall and swam over to the small island fifty yards right behind our house. We had to watch out for boat traffic.

A wealthy Colombian family lived in the home right next door to us. Of all the neighbors on Key Biscayne, the eccentric and only son of rich Columbian parents next door was the friendliest and most fun. He is like a character right out of an old Gatsby movie, forty years old going on fourteen. He dressed daily in a silk smoking jacket, shimmering slacks, hair slicked, and kept a flask of vodka forever strapped onto his calf, and an elegant pipe between his teeth or in his jacket pocket. He constantly sang as he walked aimlessly through the neighborhood and around the adjacent gardens and lawns. I liked to call him Heff.

Lou Hefner.

Christ. I guess I'd have been whistling and singing the days away too, if I had his life of ease and leisure.

"But a man must break his back to earn his day of leisure."

--John Lennon

When he learned it was a band that moved in next door, he came running over to the house right away. He had his accordion strapped to his chest and was eager to play. He played and played on for over an hour, and the band agreed he was an excellent accordion player.

He knew all the traditional and well-known show tunes, as well as many cultural and popular classics. Impressed by his virtuosity, we twice invited him to the studio to lay down tracks for a couple songs we were working on.

His accordion tracks made the pivotal difference on the record's song "Who Will I Live For" and also for the medley "Ahh-Sunshine." We brought in a quartet of violin and cellists to play a crescendo for an interlude between two songs "Ahh+Sunshine" with us. A loud, hard, long climb to climax from one, leading into a key change to the final song on the album. It was intense. It was amazing.

The group always made plans for nights off: a movie, maybe a show, and a drive down through the Keys, or checking out the competition in town. A diversion with Sally was always fun. Shortly before moving up to Key Biscayne, I had been walking around South Miami completely numb, because of all the smokable coke and Ludes I had for months been ingesting.

Literally numb, I could no longer feel myself. I had also become somewhat delusive. For example, I refused to drink Evian water because it spelled 'naive' backwards. That was significant, because back then Evian was the only bottled water nationally distributed.

Stupid.

Sad.

On a band outing to the movies to see Apocalypse Now, I passed out shortly after settling down into my seat. I never even saw the beginning of the movie. Allen woke me up, with popcorn and beer spilled all over his lap, just in time to hear Dennis Hopper tell me that "'If'" was the middle word in "Life." That was something he picked-up from Colonel Kurtz (Marlon Brando).

My eyes stayed glued to the screen from that point forward. Me, Brando as Kurtz, Dennis Hopper and the movie itself had a queer, moving effect on me, as I went for days thereafter repeating the Brando line Hopper delivered in Mantra, thinking hard about nothing, thinking hardly of some things and *not* getting high.

I knew I was sick, but I was determined to last long enough to regain feeling of myself once again. The numbness had begun to hurt my instrumental performances. I, quite literally, could not feel the sticks in my hands, and had no idea whether the tempos were close, let alone correct.

Three weeks of sobriety brought me calm and cheer. The first two weeks were painful. I was getting really tired of Gene in rehearsals turning around mid-song and yelling at me that I was a fucking pussy. And to, "Speed it the fuck up, you c*nt." He'd always been a prick. A big old fuckin' redneck prick. Sorry, but he was, with not much of a musical leg to stand on.

By the time the group moved to Key Biscayne, and began working on the album, I was once again in top form. Although I was not able to lay off the white completely, I did lay off the Ludes considerably, and that made a lot of difference. Using the rests; just like in music.

♪

Rob and Deb were a fine couple, good people and devout fans of the band. They are both slender and strong. He has a nice, custom Sportster with a slight rake and a little extension on a Springer front end, and always that fine Deb holding up the rear end. The Foolstars met a large sum of folks at their wedding the year before, but they were the big stars on that day.

The group, by now, recognized most everyone from Big Daddy's, Dino's or the After Hours in South Miami. Rob had a good, lucrative black-market fencing business. The previous year, we purchased several electronics pieces from him to redesign the sound systems in our vehicles. He always had quality merchandise for incredibly short bucks. He specialized in electronics, such as name brand stereo components, televisions, car stereos and the like. Not surprisingly, Rob and Deb also had a little thing going on with the white stuff. In South Miami, after all, who didn't?

♪

Sally moved to Key Biscayne right along with the group, and certainly had the run of the place. She regularly accompanied us to the studio, and after a time, felt comfortable enough with the help there to befriend a couple of them. About eight days into the project, she fell for one of the studio hacks.

That was good for her, because she had been waiting for some loving for a long, long time. Admittedly, I wished it had been me. But I had the best girlfriend I could ever hope to have: Donna. I truly loved that girl. She was aware how much.

Donna and I shared the master bedroom, California King-size bed and all. Dee and his Asian girlfriend shared the bed as well. It was sometimes awkward, me and Donna laying there pretending not to hear or notice the Oriental girl's cooing through some Eastern language no one understood, as I did my best to perform the best I could under those circumstances. One week into it, Dee and his significant other were moved to a spare bedroom.

I had already completed recording my own basic tracks, and it would be weeks before being called back into the studio for the sweeteners, mix-downs and mastering. But, I checked-in often.

CHAPTER 30

Rob, Deb and Vaughn

Floyd parked in the driveway and came around to the back entryway. Having just come out of my room, panting, I heard the knock at the door.

Floyd announced imperatively that he wanted to see me, see me now, and added that it was private. I went out to the lanai; Floyd grabbed me by the bicep and hustled me off and into his van. After speeding along for several minutes, Floyd said there was something he wanted me to see. He was driving toward South Miami. Floyd was extremely upset over our mutual friend's frame-up and arrest. We both loved Benny Benito. I offered that I was also still reeling from the news about Benny.

Christ. I was also still reeling from my master Bedroom activities.

"Hey, we were talking," I told Floyd. "And the group's first thought was that Sean somehow framed Benny. But then, that seems so… obvious."

"No. I *know* who set Benny up." Floyd said deadpan, gruff voice louder.

My stomach turned as I began to put the pieces together.

"I want you to see what I do to informers, traitors and rats." He added in a low, slow, growling hoarse voice.

Shit, he is taking me there!

I could not stop farting.

♪

From the corner of the soup-house room, Roy watches as the volunteer tries waking the old woman. He senses something odd, something peculiarly funny about the scene. The elderly woman's nails were painted, but the hands looked younger, and, they looked rather manly. If one looks closely at the person, as he is this morning, the woman had the ruddy face of a younger man, a tough man, even through the worn foundational make-up. Is that a five o'clock shadow?

The volunteer's gentle vocal coaxing triggers Vaughn suddenly to awaken with a start. He opens both eyes not without a problem, and felt he had a little more control over his movements and senses.

He had wet his pants, he realizes, but

doesn't realize he is in drag. There was something on his head, a hat perhaps. His polished fingertips felt heavy. He felt bundled up and he felt very, very hot. He was sweating profusely, it was cold up there in New England, and worst, he could smell himself.

As the young woman attending to him repeated calls to remain calm, he realized something was dripping down his cheeks. He swiped at it with his left hand, making a smear across his cheek, and looked down at the substance on his fingers. It looked like powdery mocha ice cream. Yes, astronaut ice-cream. He was looking at a mixture of mascara, eye liner, outweighed by foundation and base powder. He started to freak-out. He shrieked. He still had not the strength or capacity to move from out of his seated position just yet. Oh, but in his mind, he was trying.

Roy jumped from his corner, along with two male attendants that were behind the kitchen counter. Roy was just a little person, an ex-jockey, but he was quite husky and muscular. The other two guys were huge black men. Between them, they were able to hold Vaughn right where he sat. Vaughn wanted to go wild but the two kitchen men holding him down did not permit it. They each outweighed him by an easy seventy-five percent. Roy patiently and unassumingly looked on, and offered comfort by repeating to Vaughn, "It's cool. It's cool. Calm down here, brother."

At that, all those around looked at Roy somewhat dismayed.

Brother?

For he just called the old lady brother. Roy picked-up on this right away and responded smartly by picking the wig off from atop Vaughn's head. Everyone there jumped and gasped at once, as though it was alive, and Vaughn himself almost got up and started to run, to where he couldn't have known, even if he were able.

Finally, Vaughn looked at Roy.

"Okay, Okay, I'll calm down," he said. "I'm having a hard time remembering exactly how I got here, but I think it's coming back to me little by little."

♪

Roy had been hand-picked by Floyd after meeting at the track on a winning day. By that time, Roy stood washed-up as a jockey and the owners demoted him to a groom, otherwise known as a stable boy. Roy works full-time for Floyd now, and his job was pure and simple. He did anything and everything that Floyd asked or told him to do, period, point blank; to have his back.

With the job came insurance - the kind of insurance only Floyd could provide, plus, a fair amount of cash and an endless cache of dope. What a peculiar couple they made. Floyd, a colossal, hairy, mammoth of a man, and Roy, a balding, stout rather dwarfish little fellow wire muscled. Nevertheless, Roy's eyes were as cold as Floyd's, and that was the attraction. That was how Floyd pegged him, by that look in the eyes between them.

The attendants let-up on Vaughn just a bit, but he could do little more than look down at himself in disgust, picking at the women's clothes in which he had been attired.

"I'm not a woman," he announced. What had become apparent when Roy removed the wig, became unmistakably confirmed the first time Vaughn opened his mouth. What a grotesque sight he was, sitting there, wet, make-up running, de-wigged, wretched and wrecked.

"Let's see what's in your bag," Roy suggests. "Uh… mind?"

"I didn't know I had a fucking bag," Vaughn replies. "Go ahead."

"Ain't nothin' but a change of women's clothes and a box of makeup, dude." Roy tells him, then asks, "Who are you?"

"My name is Dickey Vaughn, and I am from New England," Vaughn says. "Where am I?"

"Miami," the woman volunteer replies. "You're at the St. Henrietta's Shelter for the Wayward and Homeless." She seemed so meek, and she was dark skinned and very pretty.

"Shsh, now, got that?" Roy impatiently asked.

The group explained how Vaughn had shown up on a flight from up north and showed him the "Bent" sign he had been holding in his lap. They explained that the airport staff

On Me // On Music

brought him to the shelter when they found there was no car to pick him up, and they had no additional contact information, thus, nowhere else to send him.

He slept for thirty-six hours.

This sickens Dickey down to the bowels.

"Where's the head?" he asks Roy, the urgency resounding in the tone and timber. He looks like a tired B-movie actor rushing his way to the rear dressing room, as Roy leads him to the bathroom. Once there, Roy suggests Vaughn shower, and in the meantime, he would fetch some clothes from the thrift store across the street.

"What size are you, Dickie Vaughn?"

♪

Floyd and I arrived in South Miami heading into the neighborhood where Rob and Deb live.

Typically, Roy drove Floyd wherever he went in the big, black van. Absurdly, just then did I take notice that Roy was not among them. As we approached the house, I saw its drapes were drawn. There were no vehicles in the drive. Floyd pulled in.

I almost fainted when we walked into the home. The smell was like urine, feces, acidic and blood of some kind. Is this what death smells like? Floyd walked me through the kitchen and into the living room. There stood Roy and another fellow, completely bald, bearded, whom I hadn't seen before. There was something familiar looking about him, though - something in his eyes. I paid no attention, as the uglier scene was Rob and Deb.

They looked like they had been worked over in torture, executed and quite literally probed for answers. They had each been poked, not all stabbed deep, just deep enough, but had been poked, more like punctured a many number of times, no, many, no, maybe over fifty times. Each poke maybe an inch or two in deep from an icepick, with a prick-prick here, a prick-prick there, everywhere a prick-prick, punctured repeatedly. That being along with knife stab wounds that were leaking the most blood.

Blood was exuding, sprouting, dripping and running from many of the wounds, depending on the depth and location. The first administered were already clotting, the latest, running still. Presumably, they would be left there until they finally did bleed to death. Neither one was conscious once Roy sliced through their carotid arteries and veins and finally bled them out; what little blood they had left.

"More mercy was shown to that old goat we feasted on at their wedding." I said.

They were unconscious, barely but gravelly gasping for breath, and slowly but surely dying fast. Floyd, me, Roy and the other guy all stood there, staring down at the pale, impaled couple. Their dying lungs were rattling. We listened as Floyd spoke of the dying having been suspected then proven of turning informants.

"It has been confirmed," Floyd learned and shared, "Sadly late as it was that Rob and Deb were the ones that fucked Benny B."

"For sure?"

"Yeah, Jimmy," Floyd replies flatly. "For sure."

"I told you I was up for this, now get me the fuck out of those stables." The stranger said with a wink.

"Shut up!" Floyd yelled.

Both Roy and the other man had 44-caliber pistols tucked into the front of their pants. God please don't let either one of them shoot themselves in the genitals.

They all went to the kitchen and sat down. One night, Rob and Deb were right there with The Foolstars, as usual, partying, along with everyone else. Three days later, they were dead. Rob and Deb were found dead in their three-bedroom South Miami cape, each tied-up in a kitchen chair, sitting back-to-back in the middle of their living room. The first of those three days, Benny got busted. After years of dealing big time, undetected, he was caught doing a small-time side deal as a favor -- a favor for Rob.

"Roy, pipe." Floyd commands, "I think I need a hit." He erupts with laughter.

Roy went out, and then returned with a torch and a glass pipe. I kept my head down and remained silent. Finally, Floyd said, "I can't believe Robbie and Deb would do such a thing to Benny – of all people. Everybody loved Rob and Deb. Fuckin-A right, they did though," he said, frustrated. "I been watchin' them for weeks. I was just a little too late to rescue young Benny Benito. *Fuck!*"

As I would come to understand, this represented a discomposure for me. This was my turn-around. The following day came with it a noisy, busy head and confusion. This is the incident that opened the door to clinical and situational depression. I felt like I was becoming compartmentalized. With another hit from the pipe, I hid it. Masked it. That worked for me.

Ahhh, Oh god, okay. I'm good.

Floyd and I sat there for twenty minutes

passing the pipe back and forth, Roy providing the heat, and we were toasted. Looking up, I saw the stranger staring at me. Our eyes met.

"Jimmy," Vaughn hollered. "You barstid!"

Then, as he tried to stand to come over to me, Floyd raised his thigh-sized arm, knocked Vaughn on his ass and ordered him to stay put.

"You know him?" Floyd asked me.

"I think so Floyd," I replied with a sigh. "Or, at least I used to know him." I looked back at the man on the floor, and asked him, "Dickey Vaughn, is that you?"

"You damn well know it is, Jimmy!" Vaughn said arrogantly from the floor. Floyd motions for Vaughn to shut up and get back in his chair.

"He's one of the assholes that sent me

down here." Vaughn said to Roy as he climbed back into his chair.

"Don't speak to me Vaughn," I said in a loud strong voice. "I don't like you. I never have, asshole that you are!"

With that, Floyd and Roy busted out a hearty laugh, hysterically and laughed more until I thought they would burst. I could not stop smiling either.

In the darkness.

"Bravo, Mister Jim!" Floyd said finally, after coughing, then catching his breath. "Nicely done indeed, partner." He still cannot stop laughing.

Vaughn told them the whole story, or at least the parts he was able to remember and put together, about being dosed down and shipped out. Roy filled in the blanks once Vaughn hit Miami. I admitted that I was in on the design and original plan, but my posse carried out the winning operation in my absence. I took credit for the idea.

They all got back in the van and first took Vaughn to the stables, where Floyd had him switch license plates. Then we brought Roy to his apartment. Along the way, I knew better than to strike up a conversation about Vaughn and didn't want to anyway. Vaughn had kept his mouth shut, too. All the while, I was thinking how ironic it was that Vaughn ended-up working for Floyd. It was perfect. And Roy, the partner. Excellence! Two misfit stooges.

The people that were home never missed me. I told them I was just riding around with Floyd. They couldn't tell I was cooked. They probably assumed I was. I didn't mention right away to Droid and Hogweed that I saw Vaughn that afternoon.

♪

Twelve weeks of luxury ended, and The Foolstars moved, once again, back into the Voyager Hotel. We moved there instead of back to Dominican Drive in South Miami for three reasons. One; our next leg of gigs were booked at near-by North Miami Big Daddy's, two; we want to stay well away from Sean, who lives in South Miami, and three; we needed to remain close to the studio because they were still putting the finishing touches on the album. Each could be called upon at any moment. Some of us returned to Dominican Drive on the weekends.

Some of us also moved back to Dominican Drive when the North Miami gigs and studio work were done. I was on-call as the mix-downs began and would remain in that role until we were sure we had the perfect master. The hotel I was in was right around the corner from the studio, and a short drive to the North Miami Big Daddy's. But it was only twenty-five minutes driving to the studio from Homestead.

Our management did not want to believe it was happening, but they were, in the end, forced to cope with threats received from Sean. Sean's flair was tempered for a while by my growing friendship with Floyd, and by the consequences he paid for his rampage on Dominican Drive.

Nevertheless, he was back with a vengeance as soon as the group moved away from Key Biscayne. The latest rumor was that he planned to kill us all at the studio. He sent word to us that we had better beware, because he knew where Studio Center was, and he knew we were in there.

Although we always carried a rifle and a shotgun with us, we wanted to be ready for war, and we knew just who to go to for that. Little Rat (just because he was shorter than the other Rat -- Big Rat) was a good friend from South Miami, and he was an arms dealer. We met him at the Big Daddy's in Homestead, partied with him at Rob and Debs wedding and had been to his home for dinner and parties a few times since. Rat was happy to provide on loan a couple 9 mm semi-autos, a couple AK 45 submachine guns, and a couple thousand rounds of ammo. He threw in a few grenades; pun intended. He asked if we wanted a launcher. We declined for the time being.

The band and crew took turns sniping from outside the studio. The watch would sit hidden in the brush just outside the private entranceway and stake out any vehicle that came into range of Studio Center. Still coked to the max, they thought it just another day at the office. I was getting close to the point of asking Floyd to step in but was reluctant to do so because I did not want to put him on the spot.

Sean continued to be, after all, one of Floyd's under bosses. With Floyd in a difficult position, I wanted to be able to work it out with Sean the best way we could on our own. Of course, Floyd also knew that, as did The Foolstars, that Sean was losing his mind, and if Sean were to get too out of hand, Floyd himself would indeed step in on his own behalf, let alone for his favorite band and drummer.

♪

Kamani Kenyata was the manager of Big Daddy's North. He was an exciting young entrepreneur, as well. He was a tall, muscular island man who, through his mastery of martial arts, had a tendency toward keeping, by Miami standards, a tight club. His was nothing like the South Miami Big Daddy's. Kamani didn't quite know how to handle the bikers from the South that followed The Foolstars into his club, but he somehow did. Money was made, all got along. He felt so strongly about The Foolstars that he produced our John Lennon tribute record "Just like You."

He had a deep, low voice and had nicknames for us, like "Popcorn," for example the bearded members, "Womb Broom," "Flavor Saver" and the like. Good sense of humor – a nice guy.

The Foolstars went to the studio within one week of John Lennon's assassination and laid down a song that Scott and I co-wrote overnight after the news broke. We finished it in the studio. It was a dedication to John Lennon, his legacy and his memory, our loss. Once completed and 3,000 pressed, we gave the records away as gifts to all, including radio stations, until we ran out. I sent one to Yoko and Sean, at The Dakota, NYC in care of Elliot Mintz in their absence.

Christmastime was near, and the band heard a rumor that Kamani was pushing for Big Daddy to invite the band to his annual party. Big Daddy had never, ever invited a Rock band to his favorite annual gathering.

This was the office party of all office parties. Kamani pushed back for it, and by the end talked Big Daddy into inviting us. When we were confronted with the idea, we all had to promise to behave. With that, we accepted the invitation graciously. Neither Kamani Kenyata nor Big Daddy could have known then how the party would end. The group still wasn't completely clean, but no one was clean in Miami.

The party was always held in the Central Miami Big Daddy's. The place was elegantly decorated and had a sunken dance floor that lit up with the beat of the music, bi-leveled service areas, chandeliers and classic looking bars of mahogany, brass and copper. The patina was gorgeous.

The group sat at the upper level bar, in the dim, far corner. Although we moved freely about the room, that was camp. Had we been directed to sit anywhere in that room, that night, it would have been exactly where we had decided to seat ourselves, well and far away from all the distinguished guests and VIP's. Big Daddy took notice the Rock group took the back corner. That comforted him some.

The group snorted off the bar, I cooked the coke - I had recently picked-up the recipe for latest rage; crack, and it was too easy. The buzz exactly like basing. I cooked right there at the bar. And we all sat there sipping Kamikazes all night long.

Occasionally, someone would pop a Lude. We were the only ones there without suits and ties, leisure suits and the like. We dressed for the occasion, but suits and ties were not part of our wardrobe.

Neither were socks and shoes for that matter, but we wore them.

Hard times we've experienced probably have a lot more to do with who we are today than the easy times did, don't you think?

CHAPTER 31

Floyd and Julie

xxx

Floyd and Roy first eyed the fair beauty at Big Daddy's South Miami. The little wench was hanging all over one of the band's crewmembers – the spotlight guy. There is an unwritten rule among men that says you don't mess with another man's c*nt, and Floyd would not break it. He was a man. He could wait. And wait he did. Floyd waited a long, long time before carrying out his actions. Time gave him opportunity to devise.

Floyd is planning a party — a Snow White party, the party was in Floyd's pants, though, and nowhere else. He had so much time to think. The band already left South Miami, in fact Floyd saw them off with several hundred others. Julie, who fell in love with Droid, and with South Miami, stayed behind. She promised to wait for him, but now the young girl is free, and so is Floyd. Without knowing it, with only the mere thought crossing big Floyd's mind months before, Droid's girlfriend was already in trouble.

Droid met Julie in Daytona Beach. She had come from the upper-Midwest on Spring Break but extended her stay beyond the week by rooming with Droid through the next. Apparently disgusted with life in her cold and northern hometown, hungry to see the world, Julie latched onto Droid like a deer tick in the spring. What could be more attractive to a young girl than life on the road with a traveling Rock and Roll show?

Droid was a man all alone again, on the road, and he rejoiced in the infatuated, passionate relationship the two conjured up together. They grew serious enough, or so he believed, for them to arrange her moving in with, and traveling further with him and the group.

Droid had one hang up that nobody could ever get him to break. He remained too relaxed. He's the kind of guy who thinks everything is cool if he felt it cool. Instead of poking his head up occasionally to see what the rest of the world is feeling, like a meercat, he's liable to bask alone in the spotlight if it remains warm over him and him alone.

It's always been difficult to define virginity. Does it mean one is non-orgasmic-active, or does it mean one has not participated in intercourse? Although Julie was technically a virgin in either sense of the word, when she met Droid, she was merely a curious, violated kid who had yet to achieve a simple orgasm or reach any climax at all, ever, through her few previous low-down encounters, even by her own hand.

She didn't know how. That is a virgin - one who has yet to come. She experienced her first orgasm with Droid, and shortly learned the power and the beauty of oral sex, the clitoris and multiples: The spot. Oh… The experiences had Julie in a way worshipping Droid and his hydraulics. It was nice to see him finally behave as though he had gained some control of himself, and his life, for a change. Droid and Julie were inseparable. For months, they romped together with the band, from town to town, and state to state.

However, it wouldn't be long until Julie discovered as well, the power of sex with drugs. The more she hung with us, the more and more people she met and got to know. Everyone who ever met her adored her. She was indeed sweet, young, shapely, Wisconsin poontang.

She never met a man who didn't want simply to have her upon meeting, at first sight. Droid was aware but felt safe - he had a lot of friends in South Miami to watch out for her - but he missed it when she crossed her fingers and gave him the wink.

Now, that's a bitch.

She began to act upon her whims and urges while we were still in South Miami. There were just too many cool people, with lots of money and lots of coke. It wasn't long before Julie was out in the back lot mid-set giving out a blowjob for a nose full of blow and a couple of bucks. However, it wasn't all about the coke, for the group always had plenty of that. It was the attention. The excitement. Once the band left, she dick-teased her way from one short-term arrangement to another.

Droid found out about Julie just three weeks before Christmas, in South Miami. He wanted to be devastated, but he couldn't be. He already suspected she had been messing around on him, and he was too numb to take any dangerous notice. When the band fled Miami that December, Droid left without her.

> *Our Wisconsin dairy maiden pure,*
>
> *Is now a Homestead cocaine whore.*
>
> -- J.A. Landry

Floyd kept some sophisticated implements in his belonging. He had a full-size 50

Caliber Gatling gun mounted in the rear of his commercially industrialized van. He could literally back into any situation, let the doors fly open, and just start cranking. He kept a moderately large arsenal under the benches in the van too, and inside his house as well, including explosives, grenades, automatic and semi-automatic weapons, and, a swell knife collection.

He had a Dante-like basement room, and an Elvis-like bedroom. The man was eccentric. He was way up the ladder, living way out there on the fringe. Living the dream and knowing full well, he remained just one-step away from the Columbian number two woman stationed in downtown Miami, and their boss from Colombia.

Vaughn worked hard to seduce the girl through the horrid promise of the white stuff. If choice made, between Floyd, Roy and Vaughn, then Vaughn would be the likely candidate. Vaughn, however, was not exactly appealing to Julie. Nevertheless, as soon as she heard that there'd be other beautiful people there, and plenty of cocaine at Floyd's, she caved.

Grasping and spilling her fifth kamikaze of the night, she followed Vaughn out to the parking lot. He escorted her to the van, belted her into the seat, and drove north up Route 1. He had her now. All he had to do was deliver her back to Floyd's place, untouched and ready to party.

She was a goner the moment she set foot in the door. Had she fled, Vaughn would have pounced and forcibly brought her down, but she didn't, so that wasn't necessary. Nevertheless, they were ready. She felt it particularly odd that this was a party, yet she could see several other visitors there, some seated at the bar and others in the living room. All of them were quiet, for a party. Roy came out from the kitchen to greet the girl. Both Vaughn and Roy were being extremely polite, so as not to scare the poor darling. Julie ate it all up, and it made them feel good to be so nice, even though being that way came by way of direct orders from their boss.

Roy set up a couple lines on the coffee table and assured her that more guests would show up soon. Roy and Vaughn had arranged for the few that were there purely for show, and to not stay late. Only Floyd's boys knew how short-lived and temporary the part would play out for the extras. They happily did as told.

Pass the mirror this way, please.

Oh, how about that big glass pipe?

Talk brought another three rounds of sniff to the party attendees. Roy had been mixing Rum Runners in the kitchen - a Keys favorite - and Julie enjoyed more of those as served, too. The next go round brought with it sharing the pipe. Roy and Vaughn each took a tug. They had no trouble talking Julie into sucking the pipe with them. She took to it well and begged for more with each heart-wrenching toke.

That's just how it was. Once you get it the first time, you chase it forever more. All it takes is one. After basing twenty minutes, they gave her a couple well-deserved Quaaludes. The Ludes took affect within moments, really softening her down. Soon, they knew they would have her where they needed her -- where Floyd wanted her. Part of the plan never rang so despicably true. The extras left.

Floyd laid patiently, waiting in his room. He masturbated twice at the thought. He read Easy Rider and Motorcycle magazines. He kindled up his own torch and cooler pipe. That evening, by ten thirty, Julie, on top of ingesting line after line of cocaine and ingesting several Rum Runners, had done eleven hits off the pipe and had eaten six Quaaludes. It was time. She was nodding. Now it was Vaughn's and Roy's turn to wait, and wait they did, for all of ten short minutes. Then, she was out.

They carefully carried her to the basement. It had been pre-set with all the implements; hood, rope, cuffs, branding irons and alligator clips. They undressed her, cuffed her to the stockade and tilted it back so that she'd be in more of a moderately reclining position.

It was all Vaughn could do not to violate her himself, but he had been warned by Roy not to try it. How he wanted to tweak those little nipples and finger that slit. Their job was done, for now. She belonged to Floyd, and he couldn't wait to tell her how he felt about her -- to show her.

Floyd kept the poor girl enslaved with him for sixteen long days and nights. He kept her strapped 'round the clock in the basement room and shackled when it was time for sleep. With all the freebasing going on, there wasn't a lot of sleep indulgence. She kept right on doing the Ludes and sucking the pipe, because it seemed to her the only choice. And let's face it: It felt so damn good. It was one way she remained distant from the reality of the situation, and the thought of the potential danger it imposed.

Floyd liked to watch her when she peed and had her pee into his cupped hands just below her crotch, but he allowed her to use his master bath for number two. Oh, but he did keep her clean. He enjoyed wiping up after her, and especially enjoyed sponge bathing her every couple of days. He sodomized her repeatedly and fucked her dry every day. He had her give him head, but only twice. His favorite thing was anal sex. He called it butt-fucking. He loved violating her with his big-ass fingers, but he absolutely gorged himself pumping away at her rear end. The girl's rectum was literally growing with every assault. As you may have guessed, Floyd's penis sized well and well in proportion with the rest of his gigantic stature.

At first, she bled. She bled from both places, but after a few days, it stopped. She wouldn't discover until months later, and Floyd didn't even know he did this at the time, for he showed no visible signs or symptoms, but he inadvertently gave her perianal and genital warts, HEP-C, chlamydia, syphilis and herpes simplex-2. She was afraid of having an HIV test done.

Thankfully, Julie thought after a week had passed, he appeared to like her enough not to want to hurt her any more than he would by virtue of his own humongous flesh nunchaku. He refrained, after the first couple of days, from using the rubber-tipped alligator clips on her nipples, and when she cried at the sight of the branding iron, he put it away unused this time. He liked her that much. She was silently thankful.

Julie had dreamt in the past, as most women will, about the big dick -- of having it, even if just once. Or maybe deciding needed it always. In her fanciest imagination, she never dreamt of anything the size of Floyd's. She was thankful he didn't demand head from her anymore after her first two attempts. Coincidently, mutual oral was her favorite thing to, in normal circumstances. Little did she know he didn't because there had never been a girl able to administer enjoyable fellatio to him. He was just too damn big, and he knew it. By the time her stay with Floyd ended, all fantasies involving the big one she happily sent to the back mind, and eventually out.

They were incompatible and did not have chemistry, Julie thought through the fog.

Floyd liked his privacy. Roy would check-in every morning and get a list of errands from his boss. Floyd, during times he entertained company, would not leave the house. The two hands had more time off than usual during Julie's near three-week stay with Floyd, but they kept busy running the daily dope, numbers, shakedowns and dollars for their employer. They happily stayed clear of the office for the time being.

Floyd loved the bathing, but he also enjoyed the feeding. He planned the menus for the following day in the evening prior and left an order sheet for his boys to address in the morning. Roy and Vaughn would shop in the morning each day, and then prepare the meals for Floyd and the guest. They wrapped each portion up for easy reheating later.

Floyd enjoyed spoon feeding Julie and wiping up the little messes she made around the corners of her mouth, chin and down her chest. Aside from the sexual assaults, he took care of her as though she were his little baby girl.

Indeed, whenever he felt the ironic sorrow called up by the cross-wired emotion of the situation, he felt compelled to cover her head with the hood. Sometimes, he would just cover her eyes with a blindfold, for he just had to see that exquisite face as he felt the tightness of the young lovely one enveloping his big thing. She was so tight she actually squeaked as he worked her.

Julie was one of few long-timers. Floyd usually kept his girls no more than a week. Some, he tired of within days. Nevertheless, Julie was different. He knew she would be, and certainly, she was. But, it was getting to the point where he could no longer avoid his everyday responsibilities.

He had been putting off meetings and such for over two week now, indulging himself with his basement mistress. Into the third unscheduled week, he was losing money. He couldn't put it off any longer. He never kept his little friends locked up without his company. He was very sensitive about that. He thought they deserved better, more.

Therefore, when he could no longer afford to look in on, and care for Julie daily, he reluctantly decided to let her go. It was a sad day for Floyd, as he really did like that one.

Aww, Floyd.

He called Roy and Vaughn back in on a Thursday night and told them to take the girl and bring her wherever she wanted to go. Anywhere. Floyd had told her that there would be no trouble if she kept quiet. His boys were warned not to touch.

She took from him the token half-ounce bag, a roll of money and the ride, and, she did keep her mouth shut. She knew Floyd and his reputation. Roy and Vaughn knew better than to try anything funny with the girl. She was still Floyd's, even though he had, for now, finished himself with her and turned her loose.

Roy and Vaughn dropped Julie off at Dino's

bar and grill. They sped away quickly as she slowly scuffled to and through the entrance. Her head hurt, her stomach hurt, her tits were sore, her crotch hurt, and her butt hurt. She had a pocket full of Floyd's money, the sniff in her handbag, and she was finally free again, but she still felt like crap; limping into the bar and every trip to the Lady's Room. He had given her five-thousand dollars.

She sat at the bar munching on beer nuts and drinking cold "California Dry" wine. Every thirty minutes, or so, she'd go to the restroom to pee and snort a little flake. Julie sat in Dino's all night long, ignoring everyone but herself, and thought about how living with Droid was not that bad, after all.

CHAPTER 32

The band and crew met back in Panama City with the unscheduled Christmas hiatus behind us. Our first order of business was to decide where we were going to get work, and keep working, without the lost gigs in Miami.

Even though the arrangement with Big Daddy's had been convenient, it felt kind of good to be out from under the green scrutiny. The bigger problem was that The Foolstars' master tapes are shelved in the vault in Studio Center in North Miami, and the band wanted them back in their possession.

I've never had a hard time managing to

get work and play dates, but decent studios outside Miami, or anywhere were few and far between. We wanted to get back down there to retrieve the master reels, then split fast, but going back to North Miami for any reason seemed and felt out of the question for the time being.

Dangerous.

I arranged a comeback of sorts between The Foolstars and JAM. So, I began subcontracting the band with them, still out of Raleigh. The circuit through the Carolinas wasn't near as grueling as it had been the last time the band performed there. The itineraries were better planned, tighter and the venues booked were usually appropriate. Additionally, the Carolinas were no longer intermittent stops along a much longer route. They constituted the core route and seldom did the group have to travel outside of that core during the ten months we worked with JAM.

While on the road in the Carolinas, we met many bands and reconnected with fans, but we recognized fast two fellow-JAM groups: "Doc Holiday" and "Nantucket." JAM had scored a major label deal for Nantucket, so that band bounced for a while back and forth between regional and national concert tours and appearances. Eventually, Nantucket would disappear, presumably off and out of the limelight, but they reappeared home soon enough, too soon, which told us that the "Nan" had not fared all that well away from their mid-Atlantic base.

Nantucket's A/R SNAFU by releasing that first single, indirectly competing with AC/DC did have an impact. Blame the record company, JAM but not the "Nan." The label fucked-up royally. They should have picked another single! Simple!

Doc Holiday was also hoping for more attention and fair treatment from JAM. Unlike Nantucket, Doc Holiday was not in competition with any Rock and Roll trend. They were more interested in continuing to blaze and carry on the southern style and country Rock tradition they do so well. And they are still active!

So, they were not in the least disillusioned by the poor management behind Nantucket's untimely release, and their soon coming demise. Doc's enthusiasm behind JAM had us thinking of giving the management company an official try, so we signed a short-term contract with the company and spent another eight months under JAM management.

JAM was excited to have The Foolstars back on their roster, but the band soon realized

JAM did not have the resources to support them on top or equal of "Nan" and "Doc," mostly out of seniority. One thing they did do, and do well, was keeping the band booked busy on a short road. The Foolstars saw more of the Carolina territories than General Lee!

JAM was another team that had corny ideas about marketing the group. They had already signed "Doc Holiday" and "Nantucket," who were their 'Big Stars,' so from the beginning, The Foolstars really didn't stand a chance at much more than sucking the hind nipple. JAM was too small and unprofitable an outfit to be able to professionally commit to and invest in more than the two bands they already had, plus their sideline booking agency.

One thing that surprised us was that JAM did fund a road trip for themselves to North Miami, with hopes of retrieving our masters. They were told, after a search through the vault left them unfound, that they must have been stolen.

Montalvo and Gary admitted that Lloyd had come in unnoticed and then lifted and left with all the tapes. With a story that security bought, Lloyd walked into the vault one afternoon, and left with a quarter of a million dollars' worth of music on a series of tins containing three-inch reels just fifteen minutes later. The security cameras caught it all. It hurt, but it was unsurprising to me that Lloyd ran off with The Foolstars' masters. He took a heck of a chance.

The ideas from JAM weren't much bigger than anyone else's The Foolstars had seen thus far. Understandably, they failed to come up with any means to retrieve our Miami masters, but at least they tried. They looked. They failed to procure any additional studio work for the band. By the end of the eight months, my group returned to Lynn Haven, once again discouraged and upset. I was, personally and lividly, pissed-off about losing the masters. We did come away with one-hundred boxes of 100 of the finished LP cassettes (which were the latest medium in retain sales, stuck right there between 8-Track and soon to come – CDs). The comeback pull for vinyl had not come out yet, but was slowly becoming the hipster runaway favorite. Everybody pretending to understand the differences when the music is played using tube amps and the output was an analog flow, not digital. What a comeback. We had the license to distribute as many as we needed to go anywhere. We had ten-thousand copies to work with. And we could add to that supply in short order when or if that time came.

CHAPTER 33

We returned to and were welcomed home by a wanting crowd at JJ's. JJ's used to be called Cowboy's, renamed under new management. People in Lynn Haven were eager to welcome us back, as they always treated the group like royalty, big, whenever we returned home. We then went to the beach and played a series of dates at Tombstone Saloon in Tombstone Territory.

There is nothing like playing to the birthplace of the band. Everyone in the group was from Lynn Haven, which is right outside of Panama City, except for me, and although

I'd been called a damned Yankee more than once, I was always treated like a native there. For that, I remain ever grateful. The people in Panama City Beach were plenteous, noble and grand in every way – proud to the rebel, just like those from Lynn Haven. Good people.

The radio stations at home played the entire new album of our songs, and people came out regularly to see us perform. We had always had a good home base settled there in Lynn Haven. JJ's, Tombstone and a few other occasional local gigs, like "Breakers" took care of an income for a while, but the band was still working on trying to figure out a long-term plan to continue to be productive and to reach our recording goals.

In the meantime, we released another single; an old, but previously unreleased song, which went into the Top Ten on the

Regional Billboard Charts. That had helped get lots of work. Everyone loves a record on the air. A Rock song.

♪

The Foolstars' circuit was huge. During the prior seven years we had played throughout the Southeast. After playing two-hundred and forty cities, in fourteen states, and logging well over a quarter-million-miles on the odometers, we decided to try a different approach.

Although I wanted to relocate to an established business center, like New York City, Los Angeles, Austin or Nashville, I was outvoted. I never relented, but every time I brought it up, Gene turned all pissy-pants. And as usual, the followers in the group stayed on the fence.

The group decided to concentrate on finding

a "House Gig," and at most, a circuit tight enough where we could commute home each night from each show we played. The rest of the band was turning lazy. I agreed to give that plan a try and did what I had to do to make it happen.

The plan had worked well in Miami, so why not try it again elsewhere? Panama City Beach was not the Mecca that it is today; I knew we had to set sights elsewhere. Unfortunately, and much to my chagrin, the other boys were never keen on relocating out of state, so for the time being, we looked only at the cities in state that might be lucrative. Besides Miami, we had spent a lot of time in Orlando, Naples, Daytona Beach, Jacksonville and Tampa, and more, considering all those possible candidates for a base.

We had burned out Orlando in the younger days. It was a regular stop for us usually two weeks at a time, two or three times a year. It was a very commercial town, with not much room to showcase original music anymore. It was a town full mostly of commercial dance clubs. We considered the fan base there, but in the end decided against moving there. Fans drive to see us. With hope that we could work together, Otis Blackwell came to see us there! That's what I thought of when I thought about Orlando.

Daytona Beach was an excellent gig, but too seasonal to call home. The clubs there were quirky, somewhat trendy and faddish, and for the most part, commercial. There was no studio action in Daytona Beach either. Besides all that, we didn't want to live east; The Foolstars preferred the majestic Gulf Coast.

Between the five cities we considered, there was more year-round work in and around

Tampa, St. Pete, Clearwater Beach and all the Gulf beach clubs than ever. There were at least a dozen clubs to choose from, and lots of Rock rooms where bands were urged to play original music. Gene's wife and her family were from Tampa, so they thought that she, her family, and others the group knew in the area, might help us set some new roots down.

In the end, Tampa it was. I began once again to book the group, self-managing and essentially starting over. Glamour Rock was huge in central Tampa at the time, so The Foolstars stuck out like a big ol' callused birdie finger. Being less pretty-boy than the rest, or simply once again being, in jest, the ugliest band in town, was a little tough on us at times, but we did *not* do perms, make-up, hellish masks, spandex or glitter. Most others did. But our sound and lights were expertly done, we resurrected our special effects and the band was playing extraordinarily well. Nowadays, long-haired country-Rock bands are thriving.

We played Skip's in Clearwater Beach. The weekend went over big. Packed with loud, hard-drinking fans and friends. That was the only club we hadn't played in the earlier days when we played in Clearwater. It had something to do with an exclusive agent clause.

Late Saturday night brought with it payday. I went to the office with Skip. Three out of four walls were shelved with bottle after bottle of some kind of precious nectar, I guessed. After counting me the money, Skip got up and grabbed a bottle off one of the shelves. The label read "Skip's Swill" with a date.

I asked what it was, and he explained to me that anytime a bottle behind the bar or in the rack got low, the bar tenders saved it in a special bottle: Day in and day out.

"The collection grew awfully fast." I said.

"Well, Jimmy, consider it an honor that I present this one to you and your band. Only the *best* bands ever get a bottle of my Swill. If you are afraid of it, just think of it as a Skip's Clearwater Ice Tea."

Despite the aversion of managerial arguments, we stayed busy and were appreciated everywhere. People liked to see a genuine act up there for a change, for what was then, an occasion. We were still, without a doubt, the best sounding and looking band around. We fit nicely the venues we played. We remained a band tighter than a clam with lockjaw.

The band made the move to Tampa and rented a suite of apartments. We, for the first time in our collective professional lives, set stakes down, and we were on our own. I managed and booked the band, and made sure Gene kept the books current. We added Bradenton and Sarasota to our circuit.

He skimmed for years his first daughter's tuition for a private school, because his new wife did not want to raise her. I have no anger or guilt, but why not discuss this with the group? And it did not surprise me. I merely forced him to admit it to the group. And I asked what else he'd been taking. He and Scott were the only ones with health insurance. I caught double pneumonia and spent eighteen-days in the hospital. No insurance for me; the band had a $20,000 bill to pay – out of pocket. I requested Gene to deliver monthly P&L Sheets and the few other standard financial artifacts that keep us all current and in the know. Scott agreed with me.

Gene blew-up and absolutely loathed me for doing that.

Fucking bum.

We bought a twenty-four track Fostex tape machine, used our own mixer as a console and set up a studio in Scott's and my apartment. The Fostex and mixer, along with an old four track Teac was all we needed to produce professional mixed-down recordings. We also rehearsed in my apartment. That's where it all came together; I'm not lying: Those sessions produced some of the best output-CDs we had ever heard of ourselves.

The rooming at our newly settled homes was exactly as it had been on the road. Scott and I shared an apartment, and Dee and Allen shared one too. Gene and his wife, and the children they would soon breed, had their own place.

Then, there was the crew. They had the largest apartment, but the most roommates. They also received the most company. The property manager smartly placed them out in the furthest back corner of the property. They got the one finely tucked away. Good idea.

The most painful part of self-management was at the brokerage end. Often and with the pain, I had to work through agents that held exclusive control over a venue. All that, and more made more paid, so we had to pay them a percentage. Within a short time, however, I managed to book The Foolstars into the rooms direct, through the owners – all of them. Like I said, I can be quite persuasive. Besides that, *no one* likes agents. They're pretty greezy. Moreover, the owners liked me.

Although that infuriated a lot of agents, it meant twenty percent more for The Foolstars on pay day, as well as more direct contacts for the future. After all, even the club owners recognized that they'd much rather work with the good ol' boys in the band over the sappy agencies that screw them but well on nearly weekly a basis.

For several months, the band worked a circuit that covered Tampa, St. Pete, Deepwater, Clearwater, New Port Richey, Sarasota and Bradenton. During that time, there were good nights and good times, happy and productive all. Settling down off the road, all in all, felt good for everyone.

For then.

I hired a music attorney and gave him a six thousand dollars to go to New York, Austin, Nashville and Los Angeles to shop our Media Kits and demos in hand. The Foolstars Media Kits and Demos were left with the A/R guys he spoke to. But he came back only hung-over and empty handed.

Epic Records and Arista called me to let

me know what happened. They both offered a deal that did not include a point for the attorney, so he simply walked. He didn't even stick around to hear what his flat-rate purse *would* have been. I wanted to shoot that motherf*cker. And in this business, there are no second chances.

That was a huge disappointment for us - and from that point on, we decided the business would be ours and ours only. No more representative outsourcing at all. Willingness without willfulness could do it. I would handle it from then on.

We experimented with the studios in town, but always returned to my own apartment. At one semi-famous studio in Tampa, we made a deal to back up Dennis Yost, the lead singer from "The Classics IV" - famous mostly for his recordings of "Sonny" and "Stormy."

This work with us constituted a solo

come-back attempt by Dennis. We got to record two of our own songs at this studio as part of the deal, but just like a trip to Atlanta to record a song named "Room 28" in Axis Studio a couple years before, the tape went to my locker, and *not* in the vault.

We recorded a great version of "You Blow Me Away." What the fuck were we, the black-market secret, or what? I found out that the brothers told them they weren't happy, and the studio could have them. They decided "Blow Me Away" was good enough, but not the other cut. I retained the master, just like I did "Room 28."

Idiot winds.

The latest strategy was to record our own demos and send them out ourselves with someone we could trust. I said that being the band managing owner, that I should be the one to go shopping. And I did. The recordings were better than good, but back then, studio heads and A/R people no longer talked directly to bands on initial contact.

They wanted "appropriate legal representation," such as an agent, attorney or professional management. We did that. I *was* the Band Management. I *was* the business Owner. The executives wanted face-to-face meetings over big, wet lunches, where the agent would show up like a wise man bearing gifts. From then on, I would be the representative 'face' on our side and making the shopping trips. I trimmed my hair and went clean-shaven from then on.

A reference would have helped, but the group knew no one that high up in the business. I was great at acting the role. There would be no favors for us. I had already called everyone I knew, plus, a few old friends of my Dad's, who had died back in 1970.

The best offer I got, but the band turned down, was a contract to write and perform new "7-Up" commercial jingles and theme music. It would have been a three-year contract! The Foolstars would have also starred in the television commercials and get lots of endorsements, and tour and session support. I was voted down: the band turned it down. Dimwits they were sometimes.

"That's just not what we do."--Them.

"You people are dumbasses!"--Me.

Another California family friend, Bob Parkinson, called to announce he'd lost years ago all his contacts in the music business. He and my father had been friends and partners. Together, until my Dad died, they owned the Miss Universe franchise. He was sorry he couldn't help at the time.

The Foolstars eventually played a

made-for-Rock room and pub called The Port Hole. We had known of the room and were eager to get into it because it was so close to home. The owner had contracted a house band several months prior, so the place was locked down until that contract ran out. The fact that they were open to auditioning The Foolstars, as well as the possibility of another house band option, made the group more eager to play it. They heard of us and so took us in quickly.

I booked it and we played a two-week engagement, and by the time it was over, the management there offered us the house gig. The Port Hole in Tampa: It couldn't be better, except that it was truly another nudge towards the end.

CHAPTER 34

The number of famous Rock stars on Florida's 'dead-celeb' circuit was amazing, and it grew by the year. The Foolstars met and opened for many artists past and current - from John Cafferty, Vassar Clements, Savoy Brown, Black Oak Arkansas, Rick Derringer, Fog Hat, Grinderswitch, Star Castle, The Outlaws, The Producers, Henry Paul Band, to Mother's Finest, to Tommy Talton and Cowboy and more. Many musicians, eager to retire to the land of stink-weed, move to the state as well. We befriended many stars in their Tampa-St. Pete and Bradenton days, but were inspired most with Robbie Steinhardt, from the band "Kansas."

He was a funny man and a happy drinker, and always had nice things to say about the group. He is a gentleman and a talent beyond. Everybody loved him. He never missed a show or an After Party. Of course, all the girls were star-struck. He's a Rock Star.

A career highlight was playing with Gregg Allman at PJ's House of Rock in Daytona Beach. He was *far* from a dead celeb. His mother lived down that way, and he frequented Daytona Beach often. I was lucky enough to catch-up with him just a year before he passed.

One night, he happened to be in the crowd at PJ's, and asked if he could jam with the band. The Foolstars had been duped once by a fake Jimmy Hall. He had made his way onstage with us only to blow it totally once there. He looked exactly like the star he claimed to be, and had a belt full of harmonicas on him, as well, which added to the credentials. It was only when he hit the stage attempting to play and sing the notes that we realized we had been taken. Maybe he was just…drunk?

Randy Bachman also made his way into PJ's one night. He bought the group rounds and rounds of drinks and invited me and Scott to sit with him and his date at their table. He refused to play onstage with the band, queerly we thought, but he did let Scott play his black, gold-plated Les Paul Deluxe.

Randy continued to party with us all week long. He had a limousine and driver, an assistant, and a beautiful blonde with him. I spent the days driving up and down Daytona Beach in the limo, and hanging out with him in his room, all the time doing coke, smoking, drinking and partying. During his week in Daytona, he kept the group supplied with drinks, pot and cocaine at night as well. He even *gave* Scott the Les Paul Deluxe half way through the week.

He made phone calls transferring "funds" from his bank in Hawaii' to his girlfriend's bank in Tampa. He made other calls to Burton Cummings, who Randy said was also in town for a video shoot they would do together for VH1. Burton has a cream-color limo. Except for refusing to jam, Randy seemed the real thing.

We arrived at the club to practice late Saturday morning, just in time to see tables and chairs flying, with Randy being wrestled finally to the ground and arrested by the FBI and Florida State Troopers. We learned he was an escaped convict from Michigan State Penitentiary, and he knew he looked exactly like Randy Bachman. The man was on the FBI's Ten Most Wanted list. He was a convicted felon -- grand theft, forgery and murder. A fake Randy Bachman? What the fuck?

He escaped from the facility at lunch hour, walked into a Detroit music store that evening, claiming to be Randy Bachman, and walked out with the guitar -- no money down. He had talked his way onto a plane to Orlando, also in the name of Randy Bachman, and then, once there, swept the rent-a-car girl off her fuck-a-star feet -- no money down. Walking into a limo agency, Randy, and girl now in tow, left within the hour in a limo, and full-time driver -- no money down.

He had borrowed five-thousand dollars from the girl he duped, and then made one of his phony phone calls to transfer funds. She had far less left in her account. They turned up in Daytona Beach, at the club we were playing. He lived the lost life of Randy Bachman, having his way with everyone he met, and got everything he wanted by merely playing the part and asking for it. In his right, he almost commanded it. And he never laid down a dime for any of it. He was bad, but he was good at it.

Everyone was questioned, and Scott was forced to return the guitar. It was worth at least twenty-five-hundred dollars. The poor girl the felon had picked-up in Orlando was completely blown away, distressed and emotionally devastated. She could hardly function, and she needed comforting.

Naturally, she stayed with the band a while, choosing to sleep with me. I was always the least scary of the bunch, despite my waist length hair. I was the nice guy. The band and crew took good care of her. The limo driver had a big laugh over the whole thing, and simply drove the large automobile back to Orlando as soon as the police gave him the go ahead to do so. He gave the girl a ride home. We all had to visit the Volusia county courthouse to answer questions many times over the next two weeks.

So, reluctantly, at the demand of Gene – our one resident doubting band member, I embarrassedly asked Gregg Allman for his ID before allowing him onstage. Allman understood the incident and did indeed show me his Florida driver's license to me. He said, "There you go; Gregory Lenoir Allman. Right there. Now, come on, Jimmy. You don't wait for me, I don't wait for you."

I said loud and clear, "Let's go!"

After a short talk upstairs in the band dwelling, he joined us onstage for a quick boogie jam, and I've never heard the B3 played any louder or sound any better than that. "Have You Ever Loved a Woman" came next. He said he knew the song from when his late brother, Duane, played with Clapton on the Derek and the Dominoes "Layla" Album.

The entire Allman Brothers Band had been invited to the studio for those sessions, and Gregg knew the song well. It was a good warm up tune. Then we jammed on "Statesboro Blues" and played, with Gregg's beautiful voice drawing tears from many, "Stormy Monday." We could have done "Whippin' Post" and "Southbound," too, but we ran out of time. It was an interlude I've remembered all my life.

On his way by me, Gregg whispered, "Jimmy, thanks man, but you gotta get rid of that big guy."

Yeah, I know. Jesus, don't I know it.

I remained friends with Gregg and saw him every so often either with The Brothers or The Gregg Allman Band. We were friends till death, God rest his soul. I have a framed photo of him and me from one of the last visits we shared on May 5, 2016 -- The last I would see him before he passed away. I reminded him of the "ID Incident" and he broke out in that wonderful laughter of his.

CHAPTER 35

The house gig at The Port Hole was a blessing for the group. The venue was a mere three miles from the apartments, and the crowd there was hippie-cowboy Rock and Roll. They requested original tunes as well as the selection of covers that we did. The gig afforded the band the comfort level to record regularly in our home spun studio, rehearse literally at will, in house or out, and the chance to try to meld with mainstream society for the first time in our adult lives.

For all the good things about The Port Hole, one of the downfalls of that job was that it made the band drunkenly fat and quite lazy. Free drinks will do that to ya. We still rehearsed a couple days a week, and still managed to record, but the musicians individually did not practice, and performances began to suffer. Even though their chemical intake had all but disappeared, Scott, Gene and Dee were drinking more than ever. If anything will hurt a performance, it's alcohol. Under the influence of alcohol, one simply cannot hit the notes.

Dee and Allen were smoking more pot than ever, on a daily and nightly basis: Allen drank much less than the others. I was straight - more sober than I had ever been in my adult life, and so the sight of my fellow musicians, sloppy and haphazard, night after night was sickening. I was not the only one who noticed the changes in the band. Close friends did, and the band's girls did, too.

People kept asking me, "Where's the band tonight?"

You see? People talked to me.

It's a hidden blessing that The Foolstars had a lot of practice playing drunk. But that was still not enough.

"I feel like they are each caught in their own little vertical conduit." I explained to the close knowing curious. "They're oblivious to what goes on around them."

Scott worked solo early in his career, performing in what he always considered disgusting playing situations: fronting agency-built bands. He was always the undisputed, up-front star of the show, but deep inside he always wanted a real Rock band, more a brotherhood.

Scott was an extremely talented singer, songwriter and guitarist. He eventually taught himself keyboards, as well. Everyone that saw him recognized his mountainous talent right away. If he had just one fault, it may be that he tended to stretch some of his solos a bit too long - sometimes missing the sweet ending or return spot, like missing his exit. And another, the worst, listening to his big brother.

He would set out to form that real Rock band by recruiting his two best friends and his brother. One friend, Dee, knew a little guitar, but Scott taught him how to play the bass. Allen blew a little trumpet and knew a bitty bit of keys. And Scott taught him how to better play keyboards. Gene always wanted to play guitar, like his younger brother, but never had the time. Sure. He started out playing drums, and you know I liked that; a comrade. …Never happened. Scott trained his older brother how to hold a guitar. Music didn't excite Gene. It was a chore to him, like swabbing the deck. And thought and hoped it would be easy money.

That was our existence for almost three years. Scott would learn each part, instrumental and vocal, and then teach the parts to each respective player, note-by-note, and chord-by-chord. They would eventually memorize it, then play it all together several times, and voila! They had a new tune on the repertoire. I said it before, they sounded just right as a unit.

Eventually, by force of habit and progressive nature, each player learned enough to be able to pick up most song parts on their own, but Scott was never really off the hook, especially over his brother's dependencies.

Gene never seemed to catch fully on, nor did he seem to care to. He could never get up with another band to jam, because he had no idea what to do - he hadn't 'learned' it.

He had zero stage presence. He looked awful just standing up there, especially as big as he was. The problem was that he fixed his care for being an entertainer on crowd size. At least Dee and Allen had learned their crafts well enough to be able to jam a little bit, but not Gene.

Without Scott, they were a lost soul's cause in the music world. Mind you, the rest of the world never would have guessed, because the band sounded great. Part of the reason why might probably be that they were all so married to their parts. God forbid we make any changes! Spontaneity was gone, but they played their parts so well. Remember: Tight and in-the-pocket.

As long as they were sober.

As the band developed and grew, and traveled more and more, Scott was in his glory, so happy. When I joined the band, it made it all complete. He was overjoyed to have a real, honest-to-goodness fellow professional musician, a real musician, along with him for the ride, and to help support the others, who learned instrumental performance from him and me, and stage animation and performance from me.

I had been playing professionally two or three years longer than Scott, but we had full and unconditional respect for each other and our respective backgrounds, and for the rest of the group he put together as they developed. We would room together on the road, and once there, in Tampa, cumulatively for over ten years.

Existence in Tampa did us well for a while but offered no genuine exposure. After repeated failures, I tried repeatedly to push the band into relocation. I thought, concurred and conveyed they could do much better for themselves in a major music outlet. Tampa had no outlet for music. Once it was a fountain of great talent, but now that was gone. It wasn't uncommon back then for bands to get signed right out of a bar or club, but I thought it would be a lot easier to do any kind of business in a busier music city. I thought they were ready for that then. They were perfectly rehearsed. I knew it, Scott knew it, yet we had to swallow it.

By then, a couple of the band members had married and established roots in Tampa and they simply refused to leave. They became breeders, too. I viewed this as a major flaw in the design of things, and admittedly, took it quite personally that the group would no longer follow my direction anymore. The group, mostly Gene, grew too comfortable in the house gig situation. If not for Gene, I think Scott would have packed it all in for a found Mecca of musical choices. We still had that energy.

All things considered, they upset me by shunning my ideas, everyone's own growth and experimentation, including my own, and even began to shun. They were throwing The Foolstars in the garbage – out with the trash. Totally trashing our plans made together not that long ago. It boiled down to Gene. The man that does not move, in any sense of the word.

The girls loved me and easily understood my quandary and reasoning. They were not subservient enough to keep it to themselves, and that drove the boys mad. It made me feel good. I really did love them all, even though no one particularly liked my girlfriend at the time. No one gave her a chance. Stage presence plummeted for everyone except Allen and me. Scott still had his moments.

On Me // On Music

Almost everything the band did, individually and as a group, began to upset me. I felt I was choking. Ever since moving to Tampa and settling into the house gig at The Port Hole, I was the only one who had managed to remain sober. Since recognizing, realizing and facing the truth before me, I started smoking coke again and staying high for some After Parties. Now, I was looking at another wasted one in my own mirror. I was sad.

Staying slightly high was good for me. But I had to practice self-control. That was all that calmed the noises I constantly heard in my head. Masking, self-medication, kept me arrested and comfortably happy and mellow and soothed. Without it, I not only heard voices, I heard noises. My head was so busy; I heard sounds and noise forever, clattering and clunky through my brain.

Never was there a quiet, somber moment in

time, except when I played and when I masked afterward. Even when the voices were silent, I heard pops and chirps, and pink and white noise, and snippets of rhythms and beats looping endlessly on. It was enough to drive a man insane. I partially blame witnessing Rob and Deb switched something wrong in me: Simple care.

If I had not already arrived.

I faced a self-inducted ultimatum: I clean-up, or I go. I cleaned-up. No question. I had a problem, however. The straighter I got, the more depressed I got. Clinically, situationally...if not for the crew and friends by my side, I never would have been able to stand the tension and anxiety the band members served me.

Thanks for all your support to my crew: Droid and Hogweed, TL and Stump. May you all RIP.

Depression finally fully surfaced the realities in a clearly defined way for me, and I made the gargantuan decision to leave the group. I thought I would split for New York myself if the band decided not to come. The band refused to move, so I decided I could. I would. And I did.

The end came slow. I did not share my decision with the group for over ten months. I did maintain to all that I thought a move to the city was the best idea for the group. Those months provided a buffer period, just in case things turned around between the band and me. It gave me time to make in advance the necessary arrangements for the move, which unfortunately, did seem eventual, inevitable.

After a while, I knew I'd never get the group out of Tampa. It had become undeniable. The times thereafter became tense and dark, because I ended up bullshitting the group along, virtually all the time. It was hard: the photo shoots, videos, recording and playing, living behind the fronted schemer. Meanwhile, the voices were loud and clear, depression set-in darker and deeper, and everyone else in the group played The Port Hole drunken and high almost every night. They were just fine.

Yuh.

CHAPTER 36

Breaking the news to the band that I was leaving was obviously a hard thing for me to do. Thoughts reeled of having been through so much together in the decade plus we had lived, traveled and played together. We had history and investment. As much as it hurt me to leave, it hurt them more to lose me. I was their drummer, agent, manager and councilor, glue and their business owner. But they never offered an alternative either.

Fuggum.

The boys were atrociously pissed off, in fact Dee tried to bodily attack me the day

I signed a delayed action Partnership solely over to Scott, effective in two years. He let it lapse two years later and without a thought, let it pass by. There's been no Foolstars since mid-1986, no matter what the signs may say.

There was bitterness, revulsion, ignorance and attacks between them after the announcement until the day I left. By then, it had become so intense and insane and unreasonable that I was happy to leave. Every reason I had for leaving had been multiplied and replicated during that intermittent time between telling them and my driving away in a U-Haul truck. They had no idea what would become, for now, finding a decent drummer. I don't mind admitting that I set the bar high for whoever followed.

Shortly before leaving north, the fact that the band was against it made me want to do it even more. The band-mates displayed defiance and proven no support for me or for one another even though we were all going through a difficult time.

And that, toward the guy who taught them well, and worked triple hard to make them better musicians, among all the other things I sacrificed to that band. I gave them over ten years of my professional talents all, I did it for everyone, not just me. Everyone grew exponentially, except the egocentric Gene. He would never had been there if not for little brother Scott.

Show after show, I watched with a weird mix of fading disposition and sadness, as they auditioned and played with a series of shitty drummers. How do they ever decide on a replacement? Because they, nor I ever heard a one they would have hired. They'd have to pick the best of the worse. But alas, the band was forced by desperation of time to settle on one, considering they had work I had pre-booked for them for months to come. His name was Rich, the best of the bunch and a friend of mine from New Port Richey.

Before leaving the band, I was stripped of everything except what I had left home with eleven years earlier in the first place; my clothes, my records and my drums. Several years earlier, Scott had given me an early model Fender White Jazz master electric guitar, but he decided to take it back from me because I was leaving the group.

Pricks.

I bought some audio outboard gear, and they tried to keep it, saying it was band property. I disagreed, we argued, and I, by god, got those back. I owned more than what I took. I was just so fucking tired of arguing with them.

On Me // On Music

There were many incidents of the same caliber with everyone except Allen, and of course, the girls and the crew; I would almost have paid them to let me leave in peace at that point. I felt like a tired bride whore.

"Ooh, but you know there was one other thing I left with, something that no one knew I had."

Even on the cusp of my departure, I took the time to continue to teach Allen everything I did to keep the band afloat. He was thankful and told me he was very sorry the band ditched me and my ideas. Allen was always the nicest guy and most sensible in the group. And he treated the crew with respect. Me and him. The rest of the band crawled constantly up the crew's ass and left something to die there.

Very early on, as has much been the case from day to day since birth, we can imagine, so I listened and learned. I may have chosen not to see, some may say, in defense I'll plead I did not demand to be heard. It was I, who formed the legal partnership ten years ago. It was I who was licensed and able to sign and seal legally on behalf of the group and myself. I could have done more damage to them than they were shoveling over me. Sometimes, I regret not doing more in defense of myself and the Foolstars Brand and on the offense toward them.

Gene merely thought I was giving him, or rather, them, a way out of paying individual and band business taxes. It really was quite easy. All I needed was one day with an attorney, and a signature.

The CPA came in on behalf of Gene and Scott's mother, no less, so touché again, boys, and true-ché too, motherf*ckers. I'm sorry to have to tell you this, but feel the time is right you know that I made money off every mile the group ever drove. Call it brokerage and management fees.

Forced straight face.

I loaded up the U-Haul myself with the crew and made a three-day trip to New York. I slept in the truck at rest stops, along the way. I kept the Certified Check from the band's bank in the underside of my pillowcase. The $250,000 - which coincidentally comedic - works out closely to one dollar per mile, the agreement I signed, kept the trip exciting, but as trips go, it was uneventful.

CHAPTER 37

Good Bye Everybody

It became dreadfully obvious that I had been the glue holding that band together for the decade plus that band existed. Within just a few months of my leaving the group, Dee the bass player quit. He had been one of the most irrational upon my leaving and had been one of them to physically altercate, charge and attack over the incident.

As it turned out, I had committed to a move that Dee wanted to make for years, but he never had the guts to go through with it himself. Now, because someone did it ahead of him, he did. Following came easier than leading for Dee, and that had simply always been his way.

Poor Dee had always followed whatever the brothers said and did, mostly for lack of confidence in his own ideas, but also over fear of the ugly faces and rude behavior that consequence will most times bring from them. There was a certain maturation that had yet to take hold, but leaving the band was Dee's first step on that positive movement.

Soon after Dee departed, Allen digressed, as well. He, quite clearly, could not see the potential anymore. He was tired, as they all became, of the brothers' bigoted, irrational, self-centered and one-sided ideas, as well as his absence. When I left, I gave Allen a crash course in promotion, booking and management. My old job was then his. With his leaving, now what are they going to do? Just hand it to Gene, the character would come up with it somehow, anyway.

Sneering smile.

Scott and Gene, in a sort of crude underground duo-dictatorship, barely survived the cavalcade of mutiny. The brothers had been running with the innards of the show too much of the time, too much their own way. Gene had been skimming off the top. Allen's announcement came with a certain amount of twisted glee, as he had a little bit of a bone to brew with the group.

A few years prior, Allen announced that he was thinking of leaving the band. The band would have you believe that they were the ones that asked Allen to go, but it was Allen who broke it through. And through complicated negotiations, Allen changed his mind, or was reprieved to remain in the group after all, depending on who you talk to, but he had been weary for ever after. It was a good thing he had become a brilliant on-stage performer, and learned how to manage and book a band. The underlying sentiment that revolved around his teetering position within the group came to a stop.

The band came very close to firing big brother Gene at one point, but, needless to say, that never rolled.

Besides all that, without his roommate and his best friend, Dee, and without me there to carry the torch with Scott, and feed everyone confidence, Allen found it easy and attractive to leave once he decided it would be so. He went home to Panama City Beach and formed a blues band, bounced around and recorded records solo and with his band. If there ever was any doubt, let there be no more. Allen had guts. And now, he had primo chops.

By the time I left, we already lost TL, our audio-tech, and the best knob-turner in the country. He left immediately after a big fight with Gene. I promoted lighting technician Droid to the open position. Everyone in the crew moved up a notch, and they hired another fellow to take the slack at the bottom. Merely weeks after Allen's departure, as if disbanding wasn't enough, the road crew dismembered next.

Droid, the audio technician, and Hogweed, the lighting technician, and both my assistants, decided to relocate back to our hometown in New England. They wanted to find me, with hopes for something brighter there. They too lost their desire to work with the band, for the band as they had once known it, ceased to exist. Stump agreed.

There was virtually nothing left.

♪

I was hated for years, and to this day, there is still friction there between a couple of them and me. I couldn't care less. I once wrote a book about a band, and had a character representing Gene, so telling the truth here and now, does not affect me at all.

Once thinking early on in my deliberations, that I will have flushed over ten years and two-hundred-fifty-thousand miles right down the pipe was surprisingly unregretful. Non-regretful, all that time had been, however what a waste, and what a waste it was not, both. The end of a promising run could have been avoided entirely, if the brothers would have lightened up and played fair with the rest of the crew, not to mention with the guys in the band, and especially *me*. But they turned into dick heads. Well, it had been brewing in Gene for ever.

All they needed was to grow up together, in mutual respect and fairness, but those brothers couldn't make that graduating step past their arrogance and ego. Scott mistreated the crew. Gene disregarded and dismissed me, and much worse, which I will leave out here, except that I spent hours with him in private, trying to talk some sense into him regarding the band's future and considering different plans for the band. He rejected everything. He couldn't even look me in the eyes.

I cried. I said, "I know my girl is a little wild and acts perhaps a bit less mature then some of the others. But, so what. If you let her stay, I will stay and all this shit can be forgotten. Come-on, Gene. You and the others broke the sacred credo a long time ago, and I've had no one. You fuckers get away with everything, while the rest of us are forbidden. Now you refuse to let my girl live with me in my apartment, you unfair SOB. After all that will have passed, you will be sorry. You'll see. You have the chance to put this band back together right now. Right here. Come on, Gene. What are you thinking? Keep me here. Fuck my girlfriend. That is none of your business! Final answer? If it is, I guarantee you the entire band and crew will split, too. They can't stand you."

He didn't care one bit. He refused to look at me. I care not whatsoever for that man. So, that was it. They didn't like my girlfriend. Holy shit! I will never understand what they were doing, and did. Over a girlfriend? I was knocked into a loop of disbelief. The brothers pulled a coup based on my private life. It came back hitting them right in the face when they learned I didn't need them as much as they needed me. They would eventually find out though.

The brothers ended up forming a trio, with Gene, one of the original guitarists, taking up the bass. I wonder how long it took Scott to teach him that! Between the two of them, Scott and Gene would pick-up drummers, ad hoc. Pick-ups. It didn't take long to lose Chris. Another touring dead-celeb in the South was all they would become, but generally they were unaccepted.

They tried calling themselves "The Foolstars," but virtually no one recognized them as such. They could not draw a crowd by pulling that shit. And the real Foolstars members were insulted and said so – making it very clear. Fans felt slighted and insulted, as well. Can you blame them? False representation at its very least. It had come time for me to remind them that I owned the name and charter.

Eventually, they slowed down, and finally laid down and died. They clearly were not the same band, nor could they ever be by themselves, and certainly not resourceful enough to pull it off as a trio, but for their own pathetic reasons, continue to exploit the once revered name. Generally, they were not that smart or shrewd. They blew away their magic along with the band, the crew and following. In part of my legalities, I remained owner of the brand name "The Foolstars" an additional two years.

♪

Wrapped up in the excitement of living so near the big city, I wanted to shop myself every day and out every night. Day after day, and night after night, I continued to remain busy, but nothing came to me that I could get excited about or offer longevity. It wasn't long before the end of a three-year period that I simply ran out of money.

Fifth Set

The Gray Lions

An Incredible Studio Experience

With Mark Hudson

CHAPTER 38

Over the many years in the music business, from my first introductions from Platt, to my first bands in Cleveland, to my basement jams, the several bands I hatched or brought up, such as Dead Man's Bluff, Francis Kirk, along with the Teneriffe Mountain Band, The Foolstars and beyond, I truly thought I saw retirement coming. But music doesn't leave the blood.

Once back up north, I played in some capacity with several groups, including The Isley Brothers and Tokyo Rose, and some no-name commercial shite heads. I was up for the drum throne with "Journey" for their "Radio Free" tour. I had numerous talks with Bill Graham and Benny Collins, but the band had run out of audition time and had to hire out of desperation. I was sent tickets and All Access passes for one of their shows near me, in Philly. Backstage, Graham, Collins and the band recognized me from the Media Kit I sent them. As it turned out, my old photographer and videographer was manning stage right video position to cover the Journey keyboardist and stand-in bass player Randy Jackson. He is now a VP of CMT.

♪

I settled in the woods of Maine but kept my eye out for any opportunities in music. I worked on an LP demo album with the great Ray Hilton who was near south from my home. My house was the playroom and Ray's the control room, where the mix-downs were made. I left the mastering to Ray. When I left, there was only one song I would have liked to do over. But it would not be me to do it.

♪

I was contacted about joining a band called The Gray Lions, from a small town in Maine. Rollie Doron was a singer-songwriter and the owner and operator of his own, very popular Light Show. He had played The Fillmore East, The Capital Theater, when the Joshua moved on. He also toured with numerous groups with his light show.

He needed a drummer to lay tracks for his debut album, with the possibility of playing out on the table.

He learned of me by reading my BIO on the back flap of a book I published called "Fool Star." I accepted the offer but no signatures just yet. He brought on an old friend up from New York to play bass.

Rollie met the legendary Mark Hudson at one of the "Rock & Roll Fantasy Camps."

Mark Hudson is an American record producer, musician and songwriter based in both Los Angeles and New York City. After first rising to prominence as a performer, songwriter and TV personality in the 1970s and as a member of the Hudson Brothers trio, he achieved independent success as record producer and songwriter – working with a broad variety of artists including Cher, Ringo Starr, Aerosmith, Scorpions, Ozzy Osbourne, Hanson, Harry Nilsson, the Baha Men, and so many more. Look him up!

I had a lot of questions, and we had many discussions. Finally, I was satisfied to accept the gig in pencil. Only then did I learn that Mark Hudson would be the Producer. I took the job. In ink. We had two rehearsals three days beforehand; one with no drums and the second with.

I entered "The Studio," in Portland, Maine early on the first day of the sessions. I was floored when I saw the in-house drums in the studio play room. It was an antique 1932, four-piece set of Slingerlands, including a Hi-hat and three cymbals; a ride and two crashes. I tuned them to my liking and made all the necessary adjustments to suit my comfort. The engineer and I finished sound-checking the drums quickly. It usually takes all day. But he was a drummer, too. It came easy to him and me.

We then began recording my basic tracks. It is typical to lay down the drums first of the basic tracks that had also to be done over mine. Mark urged me on and cheered for me. After the first take on the first song, through my headphones I hear, "That's a take! I love it! Let's move on."

I laid down track two in one take, as I ended up doing song for song. By the end of the day I got eleven out of twelve tracks done in one take each. I went into the control room, and the drummer-engineer, said "Those tempos were perfect."

In a session with our producer, Mark Hudson, I brought up Rollie Duran insisting on using the verb "swoon" referring to a grieving man. Rollie argued with me, but once I showed it to Mark, he patted me on the back and said softly that we will change that very *not-Rock* lyric. Rollie was extremely protective of his songs, but he learned a lot working with Hudson because with him, there would be no arguments. Marc was humbled and in check and learned more than one lesson during our session. Frankly, he needed that.

Mark Hudson is also a drummer, and can hold his own expertly on string instruments, keyboards and still had his big-time vocals. He loved my intro to the one slow blues song I played – it is half-way through the album. He helped me out on some of the percussion sweeteners and liked my use of my guiro on "Smaug's Revenge," which is my favorite song off the record.

The song is about the dragon from "The Hobbit." Mark said the guiro made it sound like the dragon was scratching his way in and out of his cavern.

I said, "Well, that was my intention, so I'm glad you caught-on." I smiled at him.

On another song, I played the snare on the 1 and 3 beats, typically played on bass. Mark hollers with glee, "Ginger Baker!" And then I added, "And Jimmy Gordon!"

I went outside for a breather and noticed a race car parked along the curb. I went in and asked who was driving the tricked-out black Mustang out front with skull decals and Massachusetts plates. Mark said, "I borrowed it from Steven."

Mark penned the Grammy winning hit song "Livin' on the Edge" for Aerosmith, a favorite band and friends of his. He was Steven's best friend, and was staying with him, helping with music, and Steven's upcoming book. So, he borrowed one of Steven Tyler's cars to drive from Massachusetts to Maine.

I remember seeing Aerosmith in Rye, NH before they were signed, in a place called "Pinegrove Pavilion." I met them for the first time at the pavilion. I remember their drummer, Joey Kramer, taking off his shirt *during* his solo. As a kid, I thought it was pretty cool. It wasn't long after those gigs, that they hit it big with "Dream On."

We finished-up the week-long session, then Rollie and I did mix-downs and masters with the engineer. I went home, and soon I received a box-full of CDs. It was our album, called "The Gray Lions – Run Wild." I give them away for free. I still have plenty from the second box I received. I still give them away.

EPILOGUE

My last performance was with a trio of pick-up players from Panama City for the Infidels MC Annual in 2012. That puts a cap on the years between 1966 and 2012 inclusively that I remained active to some significant degree, in music, and the music business.

I am retired now, a published author, and freelance writer.

♪

John holds a job, but continues to play every chance he gets.

Bean-town Bobby hangs out in Portsmouth,

just wandering away the time. He'll sit-in with a local act occasionally. He moves from job-to-job. Just like when we first met. It was like no time had passed.

Mac and Trisha run their own foster care agency. They are rich. Wealth in the name of children. They never replied to my texts, so I gave up on them.

Sonny and his wife are still warmly close to me. I am not close to any other Teneriffe Mountain Band members, except John.

Benny Benito, last I heard, sat alone in jail, a pitiful, toothless, fallen man. I don't even know if he's still alive or not: No one does. I wish I did.

Sally is still alive and well, settled once more in Homestead, South Miami. We stay in-touch to this very day. I still love her.

Sean served his time, for what he did to

us, but also for the kidnapping of the band's biggest fans. In prison, it seemed he had picked-up enough Christian-like wherewithal to find The Foolstars in Tampa one Friday. He wanted to apologize for all the harm he had ever done to us, and our friends. We shared a smoke for peace.

Floyd died of a heart attack two weeks before he was due to appear for the last time before the 9th Circuit of Appeals Court. He would have died in prison regardless, so he got off easy in the end. Floyd won the game.

Apparently, Roy went back to the stables and kept his eyes wide open. He had nowhere else to go to work last I knew.

Vaughn disappeared. Myth has it that he may have gone to The Keys and became a male prostitute. It was easy money. He kept his eyes closed.

Chuck remained in Nashville, finally having found his calling. A full-time radio talent and personality, he peddles his songs street to street in the music capital, and occasionally hobnobs with real talent.

Lloyd disappeared without a trace, until eighteen months after stealing our masters, when his naked, shredded body washed up on a beach in Key Largo, a trio of three-inch nondescript canister tins twisted around his neck and bent about his head. They were hammered-on tight. The label from each tin said THE FOOLSTARS – 1 – 2 and – 3.

Scott is a long-haul truck driver but is still a songwriter and guitar collector and craftsman. His ReverbNation subscriptions continue to grow. He does well with them.

Gene teaches agriculture at a local elementary school. How's this for Karma: He used the "N" word constantly; it was built in to his every day vocabulary. So was his extreme prejudice during our time together. He would say and do very awfully prejudicial things to black people. On a visit to The World Fair in Knoxville, TN, he yelled at the workers in the Korean display house, saying things like, "If it wasn't for us, you would never be here!" It was so disgusting, I once threatened to leave if I heard anything like it again. I said, "Do not make the mistake by thinking that I won't."

And now? Well, all his daughters married dark boys, and now Grandpa has his own little African-American family with more beautiful black grands.

BOO!

Allen is an airline attendant, but still plays the blues big time with his band or for solo gigs whenever he has a layover at home in Panama City Beach.

Dee is a nurse in Panama City for a Plastic-Surgeon. I hear he plays out occasionally. He and his brother-in-law, done me wrong. I was done with them in 2012. We've gleefully lost touch.

Is there anyone left about whom I once knew? Of course! Is there anyone left about me who cares? Yes, there are too many to write about, but I've rounded things out concerning those most in this book. So out of this work, I'll repeat the name: Donna, the girl I was to marry. I made a big mistake, one huge mistake, and lost her forever. I couldn't find her, and we lost each other. We are back in touch, and we both agree now that if I had tried just a little harder to find her, back then, she would have said "Yes," in a heartbeat, and we'd have a beautiful life and family. She is married and has a son and lives in Tennessee now, but we still share a friendly, chat or conversation now and then.

It makes me happy that so many people are still alive and well. We have our ailments, caused by all the heavy travelling and lifting, and of course, A.G.E. Too many of my friends have passed away.

♪

Immediately after arriving in NYC after leaving The Foolstars, I stood there looking, without seeing; hearing without listening; slowly sinking on my back. Woven through it all - the chirps, the pops, the buzzing, the waves, the laughter, coughing and cries, the noise and the clatter - with those fucking voices railroading through my busy head like cold, sharp, blue steel blades.

The Clash thundered on in a loud long loop:

"Should I Stay, or Should I Go?"

I went.

And I got help. Finally.

The End